A Garland Series

THE ENGLISH BOOK TRADE
1660-1853

156 Titles relating to the early history of
English Publishing, Bookselling,
the Struggle for Copyright
and the Freedom of the Press
Reprinted in photo-facsimile in 42 volumes

edited, with bibliographical notes,
by
Stephen Parks
Curator, Osborn Collection
Beinecke Library, Yale University

George Lyttelton's Political Tracts
1735-1748

Garland Publishing, Inc., New York & London

1974

Robert Manning Strozier Library

AUG 1 1975

Tallahassee, Florida

Copyright © 1974

by Garland Publishing, Inc.

All Rights Reserved

Library of Congress Cataloging in Publication Data

Lyttelton, George Lyttelton, Baron, 1709-1773.
   George Lyttelton's political tracts, 1735-1748.

  (The English book trade, 1660-1853)
  Reprint of Letters from a Persian in England to his friend at Ispahan, printed for J. Millan, London, 1735; Considerations upon the present state of our affairs, printed for T. Cooper, London, 1739; A letter to the Tories, printed for E. Say, London, 1747; and A modest apology for my own conduct, printed for M. Cooper, London, 1748.
  1. Great Britain--Politics and government--1727-1760--Collected works. 2. Liberty of the press--Great Britain--Collected works. I. Title. II. Series.
DA500.L93   320.9'42'072   74-16018
ISBN 0-8240-0960-6

Printed in the United States of America

Contents

A. Lyttelton, George (1st Baron Lyttelton): *Letters from a Persian in England to his Friend at Ispahan.*

B. Lyttelton, George, 1st Baron Lyttelton: *Considerations upon the Present State of our Affairs...*

C. Lyttelton, George, 1st Baron Lyttelton: *A Letter to the Tories.*

D. Lyttelton, George, 1st Baron Lyttelton: *A Modest Apology for my own Conduct.*

Preface

George Lyttelton's *Persian Letters,* his first important prose work, utilizes a device developed by Montesquieu, of presenting ideas on government and society through the guise of a foreign observer. The *Letters* were well received, running to a fifth edition in 1744. Lyttelton's views on press censorship, in Letter 48, are related to the other pamphlets in this volume and in *Horace Walpole's Political Tracts, 1747-1748, with Two by William Warburton on Literary Property, 1747 and 1762.* Horace Walpole's replies to Lyttelton will be found in that volume.

    A.   Brit. Mus. 712.d.14
    B.   Brit. Mus. E.2030.(1.)
    C.   Yale NZ.747h
    D.   Brit. Mus. 1414.h.23.(1.)

April, 1974   S.R.P.

LETTERS
FROM A
PERSIAN in ENGLAND,
TO HIS
Friend at ISPAHAN.

Non ita Certandi cupidus, quam propter Amorem.
Quod te imitari Aveo —

The SECOND EDITION.

LONDON:
Printed for J. MILLAN, *Buckingham-Court*,
near the *Admiralty-Office*.

MDCCXXXV.

[Price Three Shillings]

THE
PUBLISHER
TO THE
BOOKSELLER.

SIR,

*Need not acquaint you by what Accident these Letters were put into my Hands, and what Pains I have taken in translating them; I will only say, that having been*

A 2   *long*

long a Scholar to the late most learned Mr. Dadichy *Inerpreter of the Oriental Languages, I have acquired Skill enough in the* Persian *Tongue, to be able to give the Sense of them pretty justly; though I must acknowledge my Translation far inferior to the* Eastern Sublimity *of the Original, which no* English *Expression can come up to, and which no* English *Reader wou'd admire.*

I am aware that some People may suspect that the Character of a Persian *is fictitious, as many such Counterfeits have appear'd both in* France *and* England. *But whoever reads them with Attention will be convinc'd, that they are certainly the Work of a perfect Stranger. The Observations are so* Foreign *and* out of the Way

Way, *such* remote Hints *and* imperfect Notions *are taken up*, our present happy Condition *is in all Respects* so ill understood, *that it is hardly possible any* Englishman *shou'd be the Author.*

Yet as there is a Pleasure in knowing how Things Here *affect a Foreigner, though his Conceptions of them be ever so extravagant,* I think you may venture to expose them to the Eyes of the World, the rather because it is plain the Man who wrote them is a Lover of Liberty; *and must be suppos'd more impartial than our Countrymen when they speak of their own admir'd Customs,* and favourite Opinions.

I have nothing further to add but that it is a great Pity, *they are not recommended to the* Public

The Publisher *Publick by a Dedication to* some Great Man about the Court, *who wou'd have Patroniz'd them* for the Freedom of their Stile; *but the Publisher not having the Honour to be acquainted with any Body* There, *they must want that inestimable Advantage, and trust entirely to the Candour of the Reader. I am,*

S I R,

Your most humble

Servant.

LETTERS

LETTERS
FROM A
PERSIAN in ENGLAND,

LETTER I.
SELIM to MIRZA at *Ispahan*.

From *London*.

THOU knowest, my dearest *Mirza*, the Reasons that moved me to leave my Conntry, and visit *England*; thou wast thyself in a great measure the Cause of it. The Relations we received from our Friend *Usbec* of those Parts of *Europe* which he had seen, rais'd in us an ardent Desire to know the rest, and particularly *this famous Island*, of which, not having been there himself, he cou'd give us but imperfect Accounts.

By

By his Perſuaſion we determin'd to travel *thither*, but when we were juſt ready to ſet out, the ſublime Orders of the Sophi our Maſter detain'd thee at the Feet of his ſacred Throne.

Unwilling as I was to go alone, I yielded to thy Importunities, and was content to live ſingle among Strangers, and Enemies to the Faith, that I might be able to gratify thy Thirſt of Knowledge.

My Voyage was proſperous, and I find this Country well worthy our Curioſity. The Recommendations given me by *Uſbec* to ſome *Engliſh* he knew at *Paris*, are a great Advantage to me; and I have taken ſuch Pains to learn the Language, that I am already more capable of Converſation than a great many Foreigners I meet with here, who have reſided much longer in this Country.

I shall apply myſelf principally to ſtudy *the Engliſh Government*, ſo different from that of *Perſia*, and of which *Usbec* has conceiv'd at a Diſtance ſo great an Idea.

Whatever in the Manners of this People appears to me to be *ſingular* and *fantaſtical*, I will alſo give thee ſome Account of; and if I may judge by what I have ſeen already, this is a Subject which will not eaſily be exhauſted.

Communicate my Letters to *Uſbec*, and he will explain ſuch Difficulties to thee
as

as may happen to occur; but if any thing shou'd seem to you both to be *unaccountable*, do not therefore immediately conclude it *false*; for the *Habits* and *Reasonings* of Men are so very different, that what appears the Excess of *Folly* in one Country, may in another be esteemed the highest *Wisdom*.———

LETTER II.
Selim to Mirza at *Ispahan*.

From *London*.

THE first Objects of a Stranger's Curiosity are the Publick Spectacles. I was carried last Night to one they call an Opera, which is a Concert of Musick brought from *Italy*, and in every respect *foreign* to this Country. It was perform'd in a Chamber as magnificent as the resplendent Palace of our Emperor, and as full of handsome Women as his Seraglio: They had no Eunuchs among them, but there was *one who sung upon the Stage, and by the* luxurious Tenderness of his Airs seem'd fitter to make them wanton than keep them chaste.

Instead of the Habit proper to such Creatures he wore a Suit of Armour, and call'd himself *Julius Cæsar*.

I ask'd who *Julius Cæsar* was, and whether he had been famous for *Singing*.

They told me, he was a Warrior that had conquer'd all the World, and debauch'd half the Women in *Rome*.

I was going to express my Admiration at seeing him so properly represented, when I heard two Ladies who sate nigh me cry out as it were in an Ecstacy, O that dear Creature! Madam, a'n't you quite *in Love with him*?

Bless me, said I, why should the Women in this Country be so fond of Eunuchs? Methinks they have Men enough about them.

At the same time I heard a Gentleman say aloud, that both the Musick and Singers were detestable.

You must not mind him, said my Friend, he is of the *other Party*, and comes here only as *a Spy*.

How, said I, have you Parties in Musick? Yes, reply'd he, it is a Rule with us to judge of nothing by our Senses or Understanding, but to hear, and see, and think, only as we chance to be differently engaged.

I hope, said I, that a Stranger may be neutral in these Divisions; and to say the Truth

Truth, your Musick is very far from inflaming me to a Spirit of Faction; it is much more likely to lay me asleep. Ours in *Persia* sets us all a-dancing, but I am quite unmoved with this.

Do but *fancy it moving*, return'd my Friend, and you will soon be *mov'ed* as much as others: it is a Trick you may learn when you will with a little Pains; we have most of us *learnt* it in our Turns.

LETTER III.
Selim to Mirza at *Ispahan*.

From London.

BEING desirous to see the Form of an *English* Wedding, I was obliged to go into one of their *Mosques*, for Marriage here is esteemed *a Religious Ceremony*, and that I believe is one Reason among others why so little Regard is paid to it. There were two Couple to be married that Day; the first was an Old Man and a Young Girl, the next, an Old Woman and a Young Man.

I was surprized at the Extravagance of their Choice; but was told that the two Old People were very rich, and that the Young Ones married them for their Money
—— Out

—— Out of the *four*, said I to my Companion, I cou'd make one happy Match: I wou'd give the two Women to that Youth who wants the Fortune of one to maintain the other; and I wou'd make the Old Man guard them *by way of Eunuch*.

WHEN the Ceremony was performing I observ'd the poor young Maid; and saw, that though her Hand was in the Gripe of decrepit *Threescore*, her Eyes and Heart were fix'd on *five and Twenty*: The young Fellow too bent his Glances all that Way, and seem'd to tell her that he was entirely at her Service, notwithstanding any Obligation to the contrary: Nay, the Priest himself look'd as if he had much rather have perform'd the *Conclusion* of the Ceremony than the Beginning; and on my Conscience the Holy Man was as well qualified for *that* Office as for *this*.

I WAS ready to laugh to hear them vow that they wou'd love one another *all their Lives*, as if it was possible to answer for Inclination so long before-hand; though indeed they might safely promise to love *to Eternity* as *well* as they did *then*.

BUT I cou'd not help rejoicing that I was born in a reasonable Country, where Marriages are made for Pleasure not for Profit, and where they last no longer than *the Liking* which form'd them first.

SELIM

LETTER IV.
Selim to Mirza at *Ispahan*.

From *London*.

I WAS this Morning present at a Diversion extreamly different from the Opera, of which I have given thee a Description, and they tell me it is peculiar to this Country. The Spectators were placed in Galleries of an open Circus; below them was an Area filled not with Eunuchs and Musicians, but with Bulls and Bears, and Dogs and Fighting-Men. The Pleasure was to see the Animals worry and gore one another, and the Men give and receive many Wounds for so much Money. I had great Compassion for the poor Beasts which were forcibly incens'd against each other; but the *human Brutes,* who unexcited by any Rage or Sense of Injury could spill the Blood of others, and expose their own, seem'd to me to deserve no Pity. However I look'd upon it as a Proof of the martial Genius of this People, and imagin'd I could discover in that Ferocity a Spirit of Freedom. A *Frenchman* that sate near me was much offended at the Barbarity of the Sight, and reproach'd my Friend who
brought

brought me thither with the sanguinary Disposition of the *English*, in delighting in such Spectacles. My Friend agreed with him in general, and allow'd that it ought not to be encourag'd in a civiliz'd State: But a Gentleman who was placed just above them cast a very sour Look at both, and did not seem at all of their Opinion. He was drest in a short black Wig, had his Boots on, and held in his Hand a long Whip, which, when the Fellow Fought stoutly, he would crack very loud by way of Approbation. One wou'd have thought by his Aspect that he had fought some Prizes himself, or at least that he had receiv'd a good Part of his Education in this Place. His Discourse was as rough as his Figure, but did not appear to me to want Sense. I suppose, Sir, said he to my Friend, that you have been bred at Court, and therefore I am not surpriz'd that you do not relish the Bear-Garden: But let me tell you, that if more People came hither, and fewer loiter'd in the Drawing-Room it wou'd not be the worse for Old *England*: We are indeed a *civiliz'd* State, as you are pleas'd to call it, but I cou'd wish upon certain Occasions we were not quite so *Civil*. This Gentleness and Effeminacy in our Manners will soften us by Degrees into Slaves, and we shall grow to hate fighting in earnest when we don't love to see it in Jest. You fine Gentlemen are for the Taste of
modern

modern *Rome*, squeaking Eunuchs and a Pension, but I am for that of ancient *Rome*, Gladiators and Liberty. And as for the Barbarity which the Foreigner there upbraids us with, I can tell him of a *French* King whom their Nation is very proud of, that acted much more *barbarously*; for he shed the Blood of Millions of his Subjects out of downright Wantonness, and butcher'd his innocent Neighbours without any Cause of Quarrel, only to have the Glory of being esteem'd *the greatest Prize-Fighter* in *Europe*.

LETTER V.

To KOULI MOLLACK *one of the Ministers of the Tomb at* Medina.

ALAS! most venerable *Mollack*, I fear I am too bold in writing to thee: Thou wilt shudder at receiving a Letter infected with the Air of an impure and unhallowed Climate. Thy Sanctity is equal to the Angels who are joined with thee in guarding the holy Tomb. Thy Soul is continually with the Prophet far removed from the Dust and Corruption of this earthly Spot: *Thou* art *asham'd* of the *Glories of the World*; *Thou* seekest no *Precedency* but in *Goodness*: *Thou* art *humbler* than the Worm which thou
well

well knoweſt muſt one Day feed upon thee. If any Man ſhould offer thee his Gold thou wouldſt trample it under thy Feet: If the Sultan thy Maſter ſhould conſult thee on his temporal Affairs, thou woud'ſt tell him thy Knowledge is confin'd to the *Book of God*, and all thy Thoughts taken up with *that alone*.—What then ſhall I ſay to thee, O holy *Mollack*, that is worthy a Moment of thy Attention? Shall I tell thee of the Laws and Cuſtoms of the People with whom I dwell? No, thoſe Subjects are too prophane, and would diſturb thee from higher Meditations. I will therefore tell thee what I know will pleaſe thee better; that the true Religion is by Degrees introducing itſelf among theſe Infidels. A Beam of Light from the Temple of *Chaaba* has pierced the Darkneſs that encloſ'd them, and gives a comfortable Promiſe of a brighter Day. The moſt difficult Precept of our Law is already received in *Englaud*, there are Numbers who *abſtain from the Uſe of Wine*.

THAT Prohibition ſo often broke by *Muſſlemen*, is here religiouſly obſerv'd, and I am aſſured that the Sect of theſe *Water-Drinkers* encreaſes daily. The Prieſts indeed are alarmed at this new Practice, which they look upon as dangerous to them, and therefore do not encourage it by their Example; but, notwithſtanding their Obſtinacy the Truth prevails, and thou may'ſt ſoon expect a general Reformation.

MIRZA

LETTER VI.
SELIM to MIRZA at *Ispahan*.

From *London*.

IT is the Law of *England*, that when a Debtor is infolvent, his Creditors may fhut him up in Prifon, and keep him there if they pleafe for all his Life, unlefs he pays the whole of what he owes. My Curiofity led me the other Day to one of thofe Prifons: My Heart is ftill heavy with the Remembrance of the Objects I faw there. Among the various Caufes of their Undoing, fome are of fo extraordinary a Kind, that I can't help relating them to thee. One of the Prifoners who carried in his Looks the moft fettled Melancholy, told me he had been Mafter of an eafy Fortune, and liv'd very happily a good While, till he became acquainted with a Lawyer, who in looking over fome old Writings of his Family unluckily difcover'd certain Parchments that gave him a Right to an Eftate in the Poffeffion of one of his Neighbours; upon which he was perfuaded to go to Law; and after profecuting his Suit for twenty Years with a

Vexation

Vexation that had almoſt turn'd his Brain, he made the Lawyer's Fortune, reduc'd his Neighbour to Beggary, and had no ſooner gain'd his Cauſe, but his Creditors ſeiz'd on both Eſtates, and ſent him to enjoy his Victory in a Jail.

Next to him was a young Fellow of great Vivacity, and who ſeem'd nothing dejected with his Misfortune. He had run out a good Eſtate in a little Time by putting his Affairs in an Attorney's Hands, who involved him in ſuch a Laberynth of Mortgages, Annuities, and Bonds, that he was not able to extricate himſelf out of it. I found him very buſy among a Heap of Law Books which he told me was his Study, and that by the Help of them he did not doubt but he ſhou'd raiſe a better Fortune than he had loſt; for, added he, I know by my own Experience, whoſoever is ſkill'd in their Myſteries can never be poor. Lands and Tenements are tranſitory Things; but this is an inexhauſtible Fund, which the more you draw from it, will yield the more. At theſe Words he fell a reading again, and ſeemed not to care to be longer interrupted.

A third inform'd me that he was a Citizen, and born to a conſiderable Eſtate, but being covetous to improve it, had married a very rich Heireſs, who was ſo vaſtly genteel in her Expences, and found ſo many Ways of doing Credit to herſelf and her Husband,

Husband, that she quickly sent him from his new House near the Court, to the Lodgings in which I found him. Why did not you divorce her, said I to him, when you found that her Extravagance wou'd be your Ruin? Ah Sir, replied he, I shou'd have been a happy Man if I cou'd but have caught her with a Gallant, I might then have got rid of her by Law; but to my Sorrow she was virtuous as well as ugly; her only Passions were Equipage and Gaming. ―― I was infinitely surpriz'd that a Man should wish to find his Wife an Adulteress; or that he shou'd be obliged to keep her to his undoing only because she was not one.

ANOTHER said he was a Gentleman of a good Family, and having a Mind to rise in the State, spent so much Money to purchase a Seat in Parliament, that though he succeeded pretty well in his Views at Court, the Salary did not pay the Debt; and being unable to get himself chose again at the next Election, he lost his Place and his Liberty both together.

THE next that I spoke to was reputed the best Scholar in *Europe*; he understood the Oriental Languages, and talk'd to me in very good *Arabick*.

I ask'd how it was possible that so learned a Man shou'd be in Want, and whether all the Books he had read cou'd not keep him out of Jail? Sir, said he, those Books are

the

the very Things that brought me hither. Wou'd to God I had been bred a Cobler: I shou'd then have possess'd some useful Knowledge, and might have kept my Family from starving: But the World which I read of, and That I liv'd in were so very different, that I was undone by the Force of Speculation.

There was another who had been bred to Merchandize, but being of too lively an Imagination for the Dulness of Trade, he applied himself to Poetry, and neglecting his other Business, was soon reduced to the State I saw him in: But he assured me he shou'd not be long there; for his lucky Confinement having given him more Leisure for Study, he had quitted Poetry, and taken to the Mathematicks, by the means of which he had found out the Longitude, and expected to obtain a great Reward which the Government promis'd to the Discoverer. I perceived he was not in his perfect Senses, and pitied such an odd Sort of Frenzy; but my Compassion was infinitely greater for some unhappy People who were shut up in that miserable Place, by having lost their Fortunes in the publick Funds, or in private Projects, which the Wickedness of these Times has been very fertile of, that under the fallacious Notion of great Advantage, draw in the Unwary to their Destruction. Good Heaven, said I, can it be possible that in a Country govern'd by Laws, the Innocent who are cheated out of all fhou'd be put in Prifon, and the Villains who cheat them left at Liberty! With this Reflexion I ended my Enquiries, and wifh'd myfelf fafe out of a Land where fuch a Mockery of Juftice is carried on.

LETTER VII.
SELIM to MIRZA at *Ifpahan*.

From *London*.

I WAS the other Day in a Houfe where I faw a Sight very ftrange to a *Perfian*; there was a Number of Tables in the Room round which were placed feveral Setts of Men and Women: They feem'd wonderfully intent upon fome *Bits of painted Paper* which they held in their Hands: I imagin'd at firft that they were performing fome Magical Ceremony, and that the Figures I faw traced on the Bits of Paper were a Myftical Talifman or Charm: What more confirm'd me in this Belief was the Grimaces and Diftortions of their Countenances, much like thofe of our Magicians in the Act of Conjuring: But enquiring of the Gentleman that introduced me, I was told they were *at Play*,

and

and that *This* was the Favourite Diverſion of both Sexes.

We have quite *another* Way of *diverting* ourſelves with the Women in *Perſia*, anſwered I. But I ſee no Signs of Mirth among them: If they are merry, why don't they Laugh, or Sing, or Jump about? If I may judge of their Hearts by their Looks, half of theſe *Revellers* are ready to hang themſelves! That may be, ſaid my Friend, for very likely they are loſing more than they are worth.— How! ſaid I, Do you call that *Play?* —— Yes, replied he, they never are well pleas'd unleſs their whole Fortunes are at Stake: Thoſe *Cards* you ſee them hold are to decide whether he who is now *a Man of Quality* ſhall be a *Beggar*, or another who is now a *Beggar*, and has but juſt enough to furniſh out one Night's Play, ſhall be *a Man of Quality*.

The *laſt*, ſaid I, is in the Right; for he ventures nothing: But what Excuſe can be thought on for *the former?* Are the Nobility in *England* ſo indifferent to Wealth and Honour as to expoſe them without the leaſt Neceſſity? I muſt believe that they are generally *ſure of Winning*, and that thoſe *they* play with *have the Odds againſt 'em.*

If the Chance was only *equal*, anſwered he, it wou'd be tolerable; but their Adverſaries engage them *at great Advantage*,
and

and are too wife to leave any thing to Fortune.

This comes, said I, of your being allow'd the Use of Wine. If these Gentlemen and Ladies were not quite *intoxicated* with that cursed Liquor, they cou'd not possibly act so absurdly. —— But why does not the Government take Care of them when they are in that Condition? Methinks the Fellows that *rob* them in this manner should be brought to Justice.

Alas, answered he, these *Cheats* are an innocent Sort of People: They only prey upon the *Vices* and *Luxury* of *a few Particulars*; but there are *others* who raise Estates by the *Miseries* and *Ruin* of *their Country*; who *game* not with their *own* Money, but with the *Publick*, and securely *play away* the Substance of the *Orphan* and the *Widow*, of the *Husbandman* and the *Trader*. Till Justice is done upon these, the others have a Right to Impunity; and it is no Scandal to see *Gamesters live like Gentlemen*, where *Stock-jobbers live like Princes*.

SELIM

LETTER VIII.
Selim to Mirza at *Ispahan.*

From *London.*

THOU woud'ſt be aſtoniſh'd to hear ſome Women in this Country talk of Love: Their Diſcourſes about it are as refin'd as their Notions of Paradiſe, and they exclude the Pleaſure of the Senſes out of both. But however ſatisfied they may be in the World to come with ſuch Viſionary Joys, it is my Opinion, that the niceſt of them all, if ſhe were to enjoy her Paradiſe here wou'd make it a *Mahometan* one. I had lately a Converſation on this Subject with one of theſe *Platonicks* (for that is the Title they affect.) in Anſwer to all her pretty Reaſonings; I told her the following Tale of a fair Lady who was a *Platonick* like herſelf.

The Loves of Ludovico *and* Honoria.

THE City of *Genoa* has been always famed above any Town in *Europe* for the Refinement of its Gallantry. It is common there for a Gentleman to profeſs himſelf

himself the humble Servant of a handsome Woman, and wait upon her to every publick Place for twenty Years together, without ever seeing her in private, or being entitled to any greater Favours than a kind Look or a Touch of her fair Hand. Of all this sighing Tribe the most enamour'd, the most constant, and the most respectful was Signor *Ludovico*.

His Mistress *Honoria Grimaldi* only Daughter to a Senator of that Name, was the greatest Beauty of the Age in which she lived, and at the same time the coyest and most reserv'd. So great was her Nicety in the Point of Love, that although she cou'd not be insensible to the Addresses of Signor *Ludovico*, yet she cou'd not bring herself to think of marrying her Lover, which, she said, was admitting him to Freedoms entirely inconsistent with the Respect that Character requires. In vain did he tell her of the Violence of his Passion for her; she answer'd, that her's for him was no less violent; but it was his Mind she loved, and cou'd enjoy that without going to Bed to him. *Ludovico* was ready to despair at these Discourses of his Mistress: He cou'd not but admire such fine Sentiments, yet he wish'd she had not been quite so perfect. He writ her a very melancholy Letter, and she return'd him one in Verse full of sublime Expressions about Love, but not a

Word that tended to satisfy the poor Man's Impatience. At last he applied himself to her Father, and to engage him to make use of his Authority, offer'd to take *Honoria* without a Portion. The Father, who was a plain Man, was mightily pleas'd with this Proposal, and made no Difficulty to promise him Success. Accordingly he very roundly told his Daughter, that she must be married the next Day or go to a Nunnery. This Dilemma startled her very much. In spite of all her Repugnance to the Marriage Bed, she found something about her still more averse to the Idea of a Cloister: An absolute Separation from *Ludovico* was what she cou'd not bear; it was even worse than an absolute Conjunction. In this Distress she did not know what to do, she turn'd over above a hundred Romances to search for Precedents; and after many Struggles with herself resolved to surrender upon Terms. She therefore told her Lover that she consented to be his Wife, provided she might be so by Degrees, and that after the Ceremony was over, he wou'd not pretend at once to all the Rights and Privileges of a Husband, but allow her Modesty leizure to make a gradual and decent Retreat. *Ludovico* did not like such a Capitulation, but rather than not have her, he was content to pay this last Compliment to her Caprice. They were married, and at the End of the

first

first Month he was very happy to find himself arrived at the full Enjoyment of her Lips.

While he was thus gaining Ground Inch by Inch, his Father died, and left him a great Estate in the Island of *Corsica*. His Presence was necessary there, but he cou'd not think of parting from *Honoria*. They embark'd together, and *Ludovico* had good hopes, that he shou'd not only take Possession of his Estate, but of his Wife too, at his Arrival. Whether it was, that *Venus*, who is said to be born out of the Sea, was more powerful there than at Land, or from the Freedom which is usual aboard a Ship, it is sure, that during the Voyage, he was indulged in greater Liberties than ever he had presumed to take before; nay, it is confidently asserted, that they were such Liberties, as have a natural and irresistable Tendency to overcome all Scruples whatsoever. But while he was sailing on with a fair Wind, and almost *in the Port*; Fortune, who took a Pleasure to persecute him, brought an *African* Corsair in their way, that quickly put an End to their Dalliance, by making them his Slaves.

Who can express the Affliction and Despair of this Couple, at so sudden and ill-timed a Captivity! *Ludovico* saw himself deprived of his Virgin Bride on the very Point of obtaining all his Wishes; and

Honoria had Reason to apprehend, that she was fallen into rougher Hands than his, and such as no Considerations cou'd restrain. But the Martyrdom she look'd for in that Instant was unexpectedly deferr'd till they came to *Tunis*. The *Corsair* seeing her so beautiful, thought her a Mistress worthy of his Prince, and to him he presented her at their landing, in spite of her own and her Husband's Tears.——O unfortunate End of all her pure and heroical Sentiments! Was it for this that her Favours were so long and so obstinately denied to the tender *Ludovico*, to have them ravish'd in a Moment by a rude *Barbarian*, who did not so much as thank her for them? But let us leave her in the Seraglio of the Dey, and see what became of *Ludovico* after this cruel Separtion. The *Corsair* finding him unfit for any Labour, made use of him to teach his Children Musick, in which he was perfectly well-skill'd. This Service wou'd not have been very painful, if it had not been for the Remembrance of *Honoria*, and the Thought of the Brutalities she was expos'd to: These were always in his Head Night and Day, and he imagin'd that she had by this time kill'd herself rather than to submit to so gross a Violation. But while he was thus tormenting himself for one Woman, he gave equal Uneasiness to another. His Master's Wife saw him often from her Window, and fell violently

violently in Love with him.——The *African* Ladies are utter Strangers to Delicacy and Refinement. She made no Scruple to acquaint him with her Desires, and sent her favourite Slave to introduce him by Night into her Chamber. *Ludovico* wou'd fain have been excus'd, being ashamed to commit such an Infidelity to his dear *Honoria*; but the Slave inform'd him that if he hoped to live an Hour, he must comply with her Lady's Inclinations; for that in *Africk* Refusals of that kind were always revenged with Sword or Poison. No Constancy cou'd be strong enough to resist so terrible a Menace: He therefore went to the Rendezvous at the Time appointed, where he found a Mistress infinitely more complying than his fantastical *Italian*. But in the midst of their Endearments they heard the *Corsair* at the Door of his Wife's Apartment: Upon the Alarm of his coming, the frighted Lover made the best of his way out of the Window, which not being very high, he had the good Fortune to get off unhurt. The *Corsair* did not see him, but by the Confusion his Wife was in he suspected that somebody had been with her. His Jealousy directed him to *Ludovico*, and though he had no other Proof than bare Suspicion, he was determin'd to punish him severely, and at the same time secure himself for the future. He therefore gave Orders to his Eunuchs to put him in the same Condition with themselves, which inhuman Command was perform'd with a *Turkish* Rigour far more desperate and compleat than any such thing had been ever practis'd in *Italy*. But the Change this Operation wrought upon him so improv'd his Voice, that he became the finest Singer in all *Africk*. His Reputation was so great, that the Dey of *Tunis* sent to beg him of his Master, and preferr'd him to a Place in his own Seraglio. He had now a free Access to his *Honoria*, and an Opportunity of contriving her Escape: To that end he secretly hired a Ship, to be ready to carry them off, and did not doubt but he shou'd find her very willing to accompany his Flight. It was not long before he saw her, and you may imagine the excess of her Joy, at so strange and agreeable a Surprize.

CAN it be possible, cried she, can it be possible that I see you in this place! O my dear *Ludovico* I shall expire in the Pleasure of your Embraces. But by what Magick cou'd you get in, and deceive the Vigilance of my Tyrant and his Guards?

MY Habit will inform you, answered he, in a softer Tone of Voice than she had been us'd to. I am now happy in the Loss which I have sustain'd, since it furnishes me with the Means of your Delivery. Trust yourself to me, my dear *Honoria*, and I will take you out of the Power of this *Barbarian*, who
has

has so little regard to your Delicacy. You may now be happier with me than you was before, as I shall not trouble you with *those coarse Sollicitations* which gave you so much uneasiness. We will love with the Purity of Angels; and leave sensual Enjoyments to the Vulgar, who have not a Relish for higher Pleasures.

How, said *Honoria*, are you really no Man? No, replied he, but I have often heard you say, that your Love was only to My Mind, and that, I do assure you, is still the same. Alas, said she, I am sorry mine is alter'd: But since my being here, I am turn'd *Mahometan*, and my Religion will not suffer me to run away with an Unbeliever. My New Husband has taught me certain Doctrines unknown to me before, in the Practise of which I am resolved to live and die. Return to your own Country, good Signor Eunuch; but don't think of carrying me with you, for you have no need of a Wife in your present Circumstances. Adieu I tell thee; my Conscience won't permit me to have a longer Conversation with such an Infidel.

Thus ended the Loves of Ludovico *and* Honoria.

B 4   LETTER

LETTER IX.
SELIM *to* MIRZA *at* Iſpahan.

From *London.*

I HAVE receiv'd thy Anſwers to my Letters with a Pleaſure, which the Diſtance I am at from my Friends and Country, render'd greater than thou wouldſt believe: I find thee very impatient to be inform'd of the Government and Policy of this Country, which I promis'd to send thee ſome Account of; but though I have been diligent in my Enquiries, and loſt no Time ſince my Arrival here, I am unable to anſwer the Queſtions thou demandeſt of me, otherwiſe than by acknowledging my Ignorance.

THOU aſkeſt if the *Engliſh* are as free as heretofore: The Courtiers aſſure me confidently that they are; but the Men who have leaſt Relation to the Court are daily alarming themſelves and others, with the Apprehenſion of Danger to their Liberty.——I have been told that the Parliament is the Curb to the King's Authority; and yet I am well inform'd that the only way to Advancement in the Court is to gain a Seat in Parliament.

THE House of Commons is the Representative of the Nation, nevertheless there are many great *Towns* which send *no* Deputies thither, and many Hamlets almost uninhabited that have a Right of sending *Two*. Several Members have never seen their Electors, and several are elected by the *Parliament* who were rejected by the *People*. All the Electors swear not to *sell* their Voices, yet many of the Candidates are undone by the Expence of *buying them*. This whole Affair is involv'd in deep Mystery, and inexplicable Difficulties.

THOU askest if *Commerc* be as flourishing as formerly: Some whom I have consulted on that head say, it is now in its Meridian; and there is really an Appearance of its being so; for *Luxury* is prodigiously encreas'd, and it is hard to imagine how it can be supported without an inexhaustible Trade: But *others* pretend, that *this very Luxury* is a Proof of its Decline; and they add, that the *Frauds* and *Villanies* in all the *trading* Companies are so many inward Poisons, which, if not speedily expell'd, will destroy it entirely in a little time.

THOU wou'dst know if *Property* be so safely guarded as is generally believ'd: It is certain that the whole Power of a King of *England* cannot force an Acre of Land from the weakest of his Subjects; but a *knavish Attorney* will take away his whole Estate by those

those very *Laws* which were design'd for its Security: The *Judges* are uncorrupt, *Appeals* are free, and notwithstandng all these Advantages it is usually better for a Man to lose his Right than to sue for it.

THESE *Mirza*, are the *Contradictions* that perplex me. My Judgment is bewilder'd in Uncertainty; I doubt my own Observations, and distrust the Relations of others: More Time and better Information may, perhaps, clear them up to me; till then, Modesty forbids me to impose my Conjectures upon thee, after the manner of Christian *Travellers*, whose prompt Decisions are the Effect rather of Folly than Penetration.

LETTER X.

SELIM *to* MIRZA *at* Ispahan.

AS I now understand *English* pretty well, I went last Night with some Friends to see a Play: The principal Character was a young Fellow, who in the Space of three or four Hours that the Action lasted, cuckolds two or three Husbands, and debauches as many Virgins. I had heard that the *English* Theatre was famous for killing People upon the Stage, but

but this Author was more for *propagating than destroying*.

There were a great many Ladies at the Representation of this modest Performance, and though they sometimes hid their Faces with their Fans (I suppose for fear of shewing that they did *not* blush) yet in general they seem'd to be much delighted with the *fine Gentleman's* heroical Exploits. I must confess, said I, this Entertainment is far more *natural* than the Opera, and I don't wonder that the Ladies are pleas'd at it: But if in *Persia* we allow'd our Women to be present at such Spectacles as these, what would signify our Bolts, our Bars, our Eunuchs? Though we should double our Jealousy and Care, they would soon get the better of all Restraint, and put in practice those Lessons of the Stage which it is so much pleasanter to ACT than to BEHOLD.

LETTER XI.

Selim *to* Mirza *at* Ispahan

From *London*.

A Friend carried me lately to an Assembly of the *Beau Monde*, which is a Meeting of Men and Women of the first Fashion: The Crowd was so very great

great that the two Sexes promiscuously prest one another in a manner that seem'd very extraordinary to Oriental Eyes. I obferv'd a young Man and a beautiful young Woman fitting in a Window together, and whispering one another with so much earneftnefs, that neither the great Noife in the Room, nor Number of Paffengers who rubb'd by them continually, gave them the leaft Difturbance: They look'd at one another with the moft animated Tendernefs; the Lady efpecially, had in her Eyes fuch a Mixture of *Softnefs* and *Defire*, that I expected every Moment to see them *withdraw*, in order to fatisfy their mutual Impatience, in a manner, that even the *European Liberty* would not admit of in fo publick a Place. I made my Friend take Notice of them, and afk'd him *how long they had been married*. He fmil'd at my Miftake, and told me, they were *not* married; that the *Lady* indeed had been married about a Year and half, to a Man that ftood at a little diftance; but that the *Gentleman* was an unmarried Man of Quality who made it his Bufinefs to corrupt other Men's Wives. That he had begun the Winter with this Lady, and that this was her *firft Affair* of that fort; her Hufband and fhe having married *for Love*.

I ASK'D my Friend, if there was any *Seminary*, any *publick Foundation* for educating young

young Men of quality to this *Profeſſion*; and whether they could carry on the Buſineſs without frequent Interruptions from the reſpective Huſbands. I'll explain the whole Matter to you, ſays he. There is indeed no publick Foundation or Accademy for this Purpoſe; but it depends upon the private Care of their ſeveral Parents, who, if I may uſe the Expreſſion, *negatively* breed them up to this Buſineſs, by making them entirely unfit for *any other*: For leaſt their Sons ſhould be diverted from the Profeſſion of *Gallantry* by a dull application to *graver* Studies, they give them a very ſuperficial Tincture of Learning, but take care to inſtruct them thoroughly in the more ſhewiſh Parts of Education, ſuch as Muſick, Dreſſing, Dancing, &c. by which means, when they come to be Men, they naturally prefer the gay and eaſy Converſation of the Fair Sex, and are well received by them. As for the Huſbands, they are the People in the World who give them the leaſt Diſturbance, but on the contrary, generally live in the ſtricteſt Intimacy with thoſe who intend them the *Favour* of *Cuckoldom*. The Marriage Contract being here perpetual, though the Cauſes of it are of ſhort duration, the moſt ſenſible Men are deſirous of having ſome Aſſiſtance to ſupport the *burthenſome Perpetuity*. For Inſtance, Every Man marries either *for Money*, or *for Love* —— In the firſt

Caſe

Cafe the *Money* becomes his own as foon as the *Wife* does, fo that having *had* what *he wanted* from *her*, he is very willing fhe fhould *have* what *fhe wanted* from *any body* rather than from him. He is quiet at home, and fears no *Reproaches*.

In the latter Cafe, *the Beauty* he married foon grows familiar by uninterrupted Pof-feffion: His own Greedinefs furfeited him; he is afham'd of his Difguft, or at leaft of his Indifference, after all the Tranfports of his firft Defire; and gladly accepts Terms of domeftick Peace through the *mediation of a Lover*.

There are indeed fome Exceptions: Some Husbands, who preferring an old miftaken Point of Honour to real Peace and Quiet at home, difturb their Wives Pleafures: But they are very few, and are very ill look'd upon.

I thank'd my Friend for explaining to me fo extraordinary a Piece of *domeftick Oeconomy*; but could not help telling him, that in my Mind, *our* Perfian *Method* was more reafonable, of having *feveral Wives* under the *Care* of *one Eunuch*, rather than *one Wife* under the *Care* of *feveral Lovers*.

LETTER

LETTER XII.
SELIM to MIRZA at Ispahan.

From London.

WE have often read together and admired the little History of the *Troglodites*, related by our Countryman *Usbeck*,* with a Spirit peculiar to his Writings. Unequal as I am to the Imitation of so excellent an Author, I have a Mind, in a Continuation of that Story, to shew thee by what Steps, and through what Changes the original Good of Society is overturn'd, and Mankind become wickeder and more miserable in a State of Government, than they were when left in a State of Nature.

Continuation of the History of the TROGLODITES.

THE *Troglodites* were so affected with the Virtue of the good old Man who refused the Crown which they had offer'd, that they determined to remain without a King. The Love of the Publick was so strong in every Particular, that there was no need of Authority to enforce Obedience. The Law of Nature and uncorrupted Reason was engraven on their Hearts; by that alone they

* Vide Persian Letters from Paris Vol. I. Let. XI. to XIV.

they govern'd all their Actions, and on that alone they established all their Happiness. But the most perfect Felicity of mortal Men is subject to continual Disturbance. Those *Barbarians* whom they had defeated some time before, stirr'd up by a Desire of Revenge, invaded them again with greater Forces. They fell upon them unawares, carried off their Flocks and Herds, burnt their Houses, and led their Women Captive: Every thing was in Confusion, and the want of Order made them incapable of Defence. They soon found the necessity of uniting under a single Chief. As the Danger required Vigour and Alacrity, they pitch'd upon a young Man of distinguish'd Courage, and placed him at their Head. He led them on with so much Spirit and good Conduct that he soon forced the Enemy to to retire, and recovered all the Spoil.

The *Troglodites* strewed Flowers in his Way, and to reward the Service he had done them, presented him with the most beautiful of the Virgins he had delivered from Captivity. But animated by his Fortune, and unwilling to part with his Command, he advis'd them to make themselves amends for the Losses they had sustained, by carrying the War into the Enemy's Country, which, he said, would not be able to resist their victorious Arms. Desirous to punish those wicked Men, they

very

very gladly came into his Proposal. But an old *Troglodite* standing up in the Assembly, endeavour'd to perswade them to gentler Councils. 'The Gods, said he, O my
' Countrymen, have given us Strength to
' repulse our Enemies, and they have paid
' very dearly for molesting us. What more
' do you desire from your Victory, than
' Peace and Security to your selves, Repen-
' tance and Shame to your Invaders? It is
' propos'd to invade them in your Turn,
' and you are told it will be easy to subdue
' them. But to what End would you subdue
' them, when they are no longer in a
' Condition to hurt you? Do you desire to
' tyrannize over them? Have a Care that
' in learning to be Tyrants, you do not
' also learn to be Slaves. If you know
' how to value Liberty as you ought, you
' will not deprive others of it, who, tho'
' unjust, are Men like your selves, and should
' not be oppress'd.

This wise Remonstrance was not heeded in the temper the People was then in. The sight of the Desolations, that had been caus'd by the late Irruption, made them resolve on a violent Revenge. Besides, they were now grown fond of War, and the young Men especially, were eager of a new occasion to signalize their Valour. Greater Powers were therefore given to the General; and the Event was answerable to

his

his Promises, for in a short time he subdued all the Nations that had join'd in the League against the *Troglodites*. The merit of this Success, so endeared him to that grateful People, that in the heat and riot of their Joy, they unanimously chose him for their King, without prescribing any bounds to his Authority. They were too innocent to suspect any Abuse of so generous a Trust, and thought that when Virtue was on the Throne, the most absolute Government was the best.

LETTER XIII.

SELIM *to* MIRZA.

THE first act of the new King was to dispose of the conquered Lands. One share of them by general consent, he allotted to himself, and the rest he divided among those who were Companions of his Victory. Distinction of Rank and Inequality of Condition, were then first introduced among the *Troglodites*: Some grew rich, and immediately Comparison made others poor. From this single Root sprung up a thousand Mischiefs; Pride, Envy, Avarice, Discontent, and universal Depravation. Unheard of Violences were
com-

committed; every *Troglodite* encroached on his Neighbour's Property, and refused to submit to the Decisions of ancient Custom, or the Dictates of natural Justice. Particulars could no longer be allow'd to judge of Right; it became necessary to determine it by stated Laws. The whole Nation applied to the Prince to make those Laws, and take care of their Execution. But the Prince, too young and unexperienced for so difficult a Task, was obliged to have recourse to the oldest and wisest of his Subjects for Assistance. He had not yet so forgot himself, by being seated on a new erected Throne, as to imagine that he was become all-sufficient, or that he was seated there to Govern by Caprice. It was therefore his greatest Care, how to supply his own Defects, by the Counsels of those who were most famed for their Knowledge and Abilities.

Thus a Senate was formed, which, with the King, compos'd the Legislature; and thus the People freely bound themselves, by consenting to such Regulations, as the King and Senate should decree.

LETTER

LETTER XIV.
Selim *to* Mirza.

THE Inftitution of Laws among the *Troglodites*, was attended with this inevitable ill effect, that they begun to think every thing was right, which was not legally declared to be a Crime. It feemed, as if the natural Obligations to Virtue were deftroyed, by the foreign influence of human Authority, and Vice was not fhun'd as a real Evil, but grew to be thought a forbidden Good.

One *Troglodite* faid to himfelf, " I " have made Advantage of the fimplicity " of my Neighbour, to over-reach him " in a Bargain: He may reproach me " perhaps, but he cannot punifh me; for " the Law allows me to rob him with " his own Confent."

Another was ask'd by his Friend for a Sum of Money, which he had lent him fome Years before.

Have you any thing to *fhew* for it, anfwer'd he.

A third was implored to remit part of his Tenant's Rent, becaufe the Man, by unavoidable Misfortunes, was become very

very poor. Don't you see, replied he, that he has still enough to maintain his Family? by starving them he may find Money to pay me, and the Law requires him so to do.

Thus the Hearts of the *Troglodites* were harden'd, but a greater Mischief still ensued. The Laws in their first framing, were few, and Plain, so that any Man could easily understand them, and plead his own Cause without an Advocate.

Some Inconveniences were found to flow from this: The Rules were too general and loose; too much was left to the Equity of the Judge, and many particular Cases seem'd to remain undetermined and unprovded for. It was therefore proposed in the great Council of the Nation, to specify all those several Exceptions; to tie the Judges down to certain Forms; to explain, correct, add to, and reverse whatsoever might seem capable of any doubtful or different Interpretations. While the matter was yet in Deliberation, a wise old Senator spoke thus.

" You are endeavouring, O *Troglodites*,
" to amend what is defective in your Laws,
" but know that by multiplying Laws,
" you will certainly multiply Defects.
" Every new Explanation, will produce
" a new Objection, and at last the very
" Principles will be lost, on which they
" were

"were originally form'd. Mankind may
"be govern'd, and well govern'd under any
"Laws that are fix'd by ancient Use:
"Besides that they are known and
"understood, they have a Sanctity attending
"them, which commands obedience; but
"every variation, as it discovers a weak-
"ness in them, so it lessens the Respect,
"by which alone, they can be effectually
"maintain'd. If Subtleties and Distinctions
"are admitted to constitute Right, they
"will equally be made use of to evade
"it; and if Justice is turn'd into a
"Science, Injustice will soon be made a
"Trade.

LETTER XV.

SELIM to MIRZA.

AS the old Man foretold, it came to pass. The Laws were *explained* into *Contradictions*, and *digested* into *Confusion*. Men could no longer tell what was their Right, and what was not: A sett of *Troglodites*, undertook to find it out for all the rest: But they were far from doing it out of pure Benevolence; their Opinions were rated at so much Money, and how false soever they might prove,

the

the Payment was never to be returned. This Point being once well eſtabliſhed, Cauſes, that before were diſpatched in half an Hour, now laſted half a Century. There were three Courts placed one above another: On the Door of the loweſt was writ, Juſtice; on that of the ſecond, Equity; and on the higheſt, Common Senſe. Theſe Courts had no Connection with one another, and a quite different method of Proceeding: If a Man had occaſion for the laſt, it was neceſſary to paſs through the two firſt, and the Journey was ſo tedious, that very few could ſupport the Fatigue or the Expence. But there was one particular, more ſtrange than all the reſt. It was very ſeldom that a Man could read a Word of the Parchment, by which he held his Eſtate; and they made their Wills in a Language, which neither they, nor their Heirs could underſtand.

Such were the Refinements of the *Troglodites*, when they had quitted the Simplicity of Nature, and ſo bewildred were they in the Labyrinth of their own laying out.

LETTER

LETTER XVI.

Selim *to* Mirza.

THE Religion of the *Troglodites*, had been hitherto as simple as their Manners. They loved the Gods as the Authors of their Happiness; they feared them as the Avengers of Injustice; and they sought to please them by doing good. But their Morals being corrupted, their Religion could not long continue pure: Superstition found means to introduce itself, and compleated their Depravation. Their first King, who had been a Conqueror, and a Law-giver, died rever'd and regretted by his Subjects. His Son succeeded, not by any Claim of Hereditary Right, but the free Election of the People, who loved a Family that had done them so many Services. As he was sensible that he owed his Crown to their Veneration for the memory of his Father, he endeavoured to carry that Veneration as high as possible. He built a Tomb for him, which he planted round with Laurels, and caused Verses to be solemnly recited in praise of his Atchievements. When he perceived that these Honours were well received in the Opinion
of

of the Publick, he thought he might venture to go farther. He got it to be propoſed in the Senate, that the dead Monarch ſhould be deified, after the example of many Nations round about them, who had paid the ſame Compliment to their Kings. The Senators were become too good Courtiers, not to give into ſo agreeable a piece of Flattery, eſpecially as their own Honour was concern'd in raiſing the Character of their Founder, and the People, in the ſimplicity of their Hearts, thought thoſe Virtues, which had render'd him the Protector and Father of his Country, very juſtly entitled him to Divinity.

But that their Devotion might not abate by Length of Time, the prudent King thought it neceſſary to inſtitute an Order of Men, to be perpetually maintain'd at the Publick Coſt, whoſe only Buſineſs ſhou'd be to ſerve the Idol, and keep the Zeal of the Worſhippers always warm.

It is not to be conceiv'd what an Alteration this Eſtabliſhment produced.

Then firſt the *Troglodites* were made believe that the Gods were to be gain'd by rich Donations, or that their Glory was concern'd in the Worldly Pomp and Power of their Prieſts. A Temple, ſaid thoſe Prieſts, is like a Court; you muſt preſent your Petitions by the Miniſters, or they will not be receiv'd. As the People remember'd that their Deity had once been a King, this Doctrine seem'd plausible enough, and the Priests grew absolute on the Strength of it. That the Comparison between the Temple and the Court might hold the better, a great Number of Ceremonies were invented, and a Magnificence of Dress was added to them as essential to Holiness. The Women came warmly into this, and were far more zealous than the Men in their Attachment to the exterior Part of Piety. Thus the Devotion of the *Troglodites* was turn'd aside from Reality to Form, and it was no longer a Consequence, that a very religious was a very honest Man.

LETTER XVII.

SELIM *to* MIRZA.

BY the Artifice of the Priesthood their Superstition encreas'd every Day, and nothing was thought so indifferent to Religion as the Practice of Virtue. It was common for a *Troglodite* to say, "I will "plunder my Neighbour or the Publick; "for the Anger of our God may be appeas'd "by an Offering made out of the Spoil."

ANOTHER quieted his Conscience in this Manner; "I am indeed a very great Villain, "and

" and have injured my Benefactor; but I
" am a constant Attender on all Processions,
" and have crawl'd thrice round the Temple
" upon my Knees."

A THIRD confest to a Priest that he had defrauded his Pupil of an Estate; give half of it to our Order, said the Confessor, and we freely endow you with the rest.

BUT the Mischief did not stop even here: From sanctifying Trifles they proceeded to quarrel about them; and the Peace of the Society was disturb'd to know which Impertinence shou'd be preferr'd. This was the Work of the Priests who took upon them to declare what was most agreeable to their God, and declared it differently, as it happen'd that their Passions or Interests required. But how slight soever the Foundation was, a Dispute of this nature cou'd not fail to be warmly carried on. No-body concern'd himself about the Morals of another, but every Man's Opinions were enquir'd into with the utmost Rigour; and woe to those who held any that were dislik'd by the ruling Party; for though neither side cou'd tell the Reason why they differ'd, the Difference was never to be forgiven. An aged *Troglodite* endeavour'd to put a Stop to this pious Fury, by representing to them, " That their Ancestors who were better Men, had no Disputes about Religion; but served the Gods in the only Unity requir'd by them, a of Affection. All that the poor Man got by his Admonition was to be call'd an Atheist by all the contending Sects, and after suffering a thousand Persecutions compell'd to take Refuge in another Land.

LETTER XVIII.
Selim *to* Mirza.

THE Court had a deeper Interest in the Establishment of this Priesthood among the *Troglodites*, than was at first attended to or foreseen. The very Nature of their Office particularly attach'd them to the Crown: They were Servants of a deified King, and it was no very great Stretch of their Function to deify the living Monarch also. Accordingly they preach'd to all the People with an extraordinary Warmth of Zeal, that the Family then reigning was *divine*; that they held the Crown not by the Will of the Society, but by a Pre-eminence of Nature: That to resist their Pleasure was resisting God; and that every Man enjoy'd his Life and his Estate by their Grace and at their Disposal. In Consequence of these Doctrines his *sacred Majesty* did just what he thought fit. He was of a Martial Genius, and had a strong Ambition to enlarge his Territories. To this End he

rais'd

rais'd a mighty Army, and fell upon his Neighbours without a Quarrel.

THE *Troglodites* lost their Blood and spent their Substance, to make their Prince triumphant in a War which cou'd not possibly turn to their Advantage; for the Pride and Power of their Tyrant encreas'd with his Success. His Temper too became fiercer and more Severe by being accustom'd to Slaughter and Devastation; so that his Government grew odious to his Subjects. Yet the dazling Glory of his Victories, and the Divinity they were taught to find about him, kept them in Awe, and supported his Authority. But the Gods wou'd not suffer him any longer to vex Mankind. He perish'd with a great Part of his Army by the united Valour of many Nations who had allied themselves against his Encroachments. Content with having punish'd the Aggressor and Author of the War, they immediately offer'd Peace to the *Troglodites*, upon Condition that all shou'd be restor'd which had been taken from them in the former Wars. That Nation, humbled by their Defeat, very willingly parted with their Conquests, to purchase their Repose.

LETTER XIX.
Selim *to* Mirza *at* Ispahan.

UNDER their third King, who succeeded to his Father, upon a new Notion of Hereditary Right, the Spirit of the Government was wholly changed. He was young, and of a Temper much addicted to Ease and pleasure; yet bred up with high Conceits of Kingly Power, and a Royal Disregard to his People's Good. There was a Mixture of Bigotry in his Disposition, which gave the Priests a great Advantage over him; and as his Predecessor had govern'd by them they govern'd now by him.—— The People too, in Imitation of their Prince, soon contracted another Character, They begun to polish and soften all their Manners. The young *Troglodites* were sent to travel into *Persia:* They came back with new Dresses, new Refinements, new Follies, and new Vices. Like a Plague imported from a Foreign Country, Luxury spread itself from these Travellers over all the Nation. A thousand Wants were created every Day which Nature neither suggested nor cou'd supply. A thousand Uneasinesses were felt which were as unnatural

tural as the Pleasures that occasion'd them. When the Minds of the *Troglodites* were thus relaxed their Bodies became weak. They now complain'd that the Summer was too hot and the Winter too cold. They lost the Use of their Limbs, and were carried about on the Shoulders of their Slaves. The Women brought their Children with more Pain, and even thought themselves too delicate to nurse them: They lost their Beauty much sooner than before, and vainly strove to repair it by the Help of Art. Then first Physicians were call'd in from Foreign Lands to contend with a Variety of new Distempers which Intemperance produced: They came; and the only Advantage was, that those who had learn'd to live at a great Expence, now found the Secret of dying at a greater.

Such was the Condition of the *Troglodites*, when by the Benefit of a lasting Peace, they tasted the Sweets of Plenty and grew *polite*.

LETTER XX.
Selim *to* Mirza *at* Ispahan.

THE ancient *Troglodites* were too busy in the Duties and Cares of Society, to employ much of their Thoughts in Speculation. They were skilful in Mechanicks and Agriculture, the only Sciences for which they had any Use. At their Leisure they amus'd themselves with Poetry, and sung the Praises of the Gods, the Virtues of their Countrymen, and their own Loves. They shew'd a wonderful Force of Imagination in a great Number of Fables which they invented, under most of which was concealed some Moral Sentiment; but for History, they contented themselves with consulting the oldest Men among them, thinking it impossible to know the Truth of any Fact beyond the Memory of the Age in which they lived.—— The Alteration of their Government and Manners produced a Change also in this respect. A great many People withdrew themselves entirely from the Offices of Life, and became a Burthen to their Family and Country, under a Notion of Study and Meditation. One Set of them very modestly undertook, to explain all the Secrets of Nature, and account for her Operations. Another left Nature quite behind, and fell to reason about immaterial Substances and the Properties of Spirits. A third profest to teach Reason by a Rule; and invented Arguments to confute common Sense. These Philosophers (for so they stil'd themselves) were to be known from all Mankind by a certain Air between bashfulness and Presumption. To distinguish themselves from the Vulgar, they forgot how

how to say or do one common Thing like other Men. They were perfectly well acquainted with the Annual, and Diurnal Motion of the Sun; but never in their lives cou'd tell you what o'Clock it was.

This render'd their Behaviour very awkward, and they were conscious of it; for which Reason they came little into Company: Yet in Private their Pride swell'd to such a Pitch, that they imagin'd they were arrived at the very Top of human Merit, and look'd down with Contempt on the greatest Generals and best Servants of the State. By setting such a Value upon themselves they imposed upon others to that degree, that all their Fellow Citizens sent their Sons to be educated under their Instructions. It was even propos'd in the Council of the King to establish an Academy of Philosophers, and endow it with great Revenues, for the Support and Encouragement of Learning. One of the Counsellors who was a Man of a very plain, but strong Understanding, singly expres'd his Dislike of this Design. ' If, said he, it had been propos'd to us to ' build an Hospital for Decrepit Husband- ' men or decay'd Manufacturers, I wou'd ' willingly have come into it for the Support ' and Encouragement of Industry. But it ' seems to me that what you are now about ' will ruin Industry; and that you will take ' the Bread from the most useful of your Subjects

'Subjects to pamper the moſt Uſeleſs.
'deſire to be inform'd what Service theſe
'Men have done to recommend them to
'the Publick? Has this Learning, of
'which we are grown ſo fond, made us
'wiſer or better than we were? Shew me the
'Effects of it in our Councils or in our
'Morals.——If it be nothing but an idle
'Curioſity to pry into Things that don't
'concern us, it is my Opinion that we buy
'it much too dear. I have been told indeed,
'that they have diſcover'd an Art of Reaſon-
'ing without which no Propoſition can be
'maintain'd, and by which *any* may. Our
'Anceſtors, O *Troglodites*, were wiſe, and
'reaſon'd well: Yet they never heard of
'Syllogiſms, Modes, or Forms, or any
'Part of this Science, by which their Sons
'can ſo nicely diſtinguiſh and define ſo juſtly.
  'Our Children are bred up to all this
'Learning; and what are the Fruits of it?
'They come into the World extremely
'knowing in the Courſe of the Planets, and
'the nature of the Soul; but the Manners
'of the World, and the Heart of Man they
'know nothing of. If we offer to inſtruct
'them they receive our Admonitions with
'Contempt, and confound us by ſome
'Subtilty of the Schools. Inſtead of a quiet
'Temper, and a Love of Truth they have
'acquir'd a Fondneſs for Diſpute, and a
'Habit of Evaſion. I ſuſpect too that
            there

'there is something slavish in the Obedience
'which these Dogmatical Preceptors require
'of them, and that a Narrowness of Mind
'must be the Consequence of so implicit a
'Belief.

'Trust me, Countrymen, you wou'd
'better serve the State, by setting all these
'idle Fellows to the Plough, than by
'publickly authorizing their Follies, and
'pensioning their Laziness."

LETTER XXI.
Selim *to* Mirza *at* Ispahan.

AMONG the various Speculations that this modern Fashion of Philosophizing produced, there were two more pernicious than the rest, and which greatly contributed to the Corruption and Ruin of the People. One was, that Vice and Virtue were in themselves indifferent Things, and depended only on the Laws of every Country; the other, That there was neither Reward nor Punishment after this Life. —— It has already been observ'd how many Defects the *Troglodites* found in their Laws, and how many Quibbles were invented to elude them. But still there was some Restraint upon their Actions, while a Sense of Guilt was attended with Remorse, and the Apprehension of
suffering

suffering in another State. But by these two Doctrines Men were left at perfect Liberty to Sin out of the Reach of the Law; and Virtue was deprived of Glory here, or the Hopes of Recompense hereafter. There was a third Notion, less impious indeed, but of very ill Consequences to Society, which placed all Goodness and Religion in a *Recluse and contemplative Way of Life.*

THE Effect of this was, to draw off many of the best and worthiest Men from the Service of the Publick, and Administration of the Commonwealth, at a Time when their Labours were most wanted to put a Stop to the general Corruption.——It is hard to say which was most destructive, an Opinion that like the former embolden'd Vice, or such a one as render'd Virtue impotent and useless to Mankind.——

LETTER XXII.

SELIM to MIRZA at *Ispahan.*

WHILE the Principles of the People were thus depraved, and their Understandings taken off from their proper Objects, the Court became the Center of Immorality and every kind of Folly. Though

Though Flattery had been always busy there, yet the former Kings who were frequently at War had been us'd to a certain military Freedom, and there were not wanting Men about them who had Courage to tell them Truth; but the Effeminacy of the present Set of Courtiers took from them all Spirit as well as Virtue, and they were as ready to suffer the basest Things, as to act the most Unjust. The King wholly devoted to his Pleasures, and seldom seen out of the Walls of his Seraglio, thought it sufficient for him to wear the Crown, without troubling himself with any of the Cares and Duties belonging to it: The whole Exercise and Power of the Government was lodged in the Hands of a Grand Vizir, the first of that Title which the *Troglodites* had ever known. It seem'd very strange to them at the Beginning, to see the Royalty transfer'd to their Fellow Subject, and many thought it was debasing it too much. The Priests themselves were at a Loss how to make out that this Sort of Monarchy was divine; however, they found at last that the Grand Vizir was a God by Office though not by Birth. If this Distinction did not satisfy the People, the Court nor the Priests were not much concern'd about it. —— But a Prime Minister was not the only Novelty these Times produced.

THE *Troglodites* had always been remarkable for the Manner in which they used their Women: They had a greater Esteem for them than any other of the Eastern Nations. They admitted them to a constant Share in their Conversation, and even trusted them with their private Affairs: But they never suspected that they had a Genius for publick Business, and that not only their own Families, but the State itself, might be govern'd by their Direction. They were now convinc'd of their Mistake. Several Ladies appear'd together at the Helm: The King's Mistress, the Mistress of the Vizir, two or three Mistresses of the Vizir's Favourite Officers, join'd in a political Confederacy, and manag'd all Matters as they pleas'd. Their Lovers gave nothing, and acted nothing but by their Recommendation and Advice. Sometimes indeed they differ'd among themselves, which occasion'd great Confusions in the State; but by the pacifick Labours of good Subjects such unhappy Divisions were compos'd, and every thing went quietly on again. If there was any Defect in the Politicks of these Female Rulers, it was, that they cou'd never comprehend any other Point or Purpose in the Art of Government but so much *Profit to themselves*. The History of the *Troglodites* has recorded some of their wise and witty Sayings.

ONE

One of them was told, that by the great Decay of Trade, the principal Bank of the City wou'd be broke. What care I, said she, I have laid my Money out in Land.

Another was warn'd, that if better Measures were not taken, the *Troglodites* threaten'd to revolt; I am glad to hear it, replied she, for if we beat them, there will some rich Confiscations fall to me.

LETTER XXIII.
Selim *to* Mirza.

Painful Experience had by this Time taught the *Troglodites* what their Fathers were too happy to suspect, that human Nature was not perfect enough to be trusted with excessive Power: They saw an evident Necessity of restraining that which had been given to their Kings, as well for the Dignity of the Crown itself as for the good of the Commonwealth.

The whole Nation unanimously concur'd in this Resolution, and that Unanimity cou'd not be resisted: They therefore consider'd by what Means to reform their Government, and did it with equal Vigour and Moderation. It was decreed that the Crown shou'd be preserv'd to the Prince then reigning,

reigning, out of Respect to the Family he was of; but that he shou'd wear it under certain Limitations which divided his Authority with the Senate.

To prevent the Mischiefs that might arise from evil Ministers, and the too great Power of any Favourite, they declared, that the Ministers of the King were the Servants of the People, and cou'd not be protected by the Court, if they were found disloyal to the Nation.

Under these wise Regulations the shatter'd State recover'd itself again: Their Affairs were managed with more Discretion, and many publick Grievances were redrest. They thought that in limiting their Monarchy they had cut the Root of all their Evils, and flatter'd themselves with a permanent Felicity. But they quickly discover'd that this new System was not without its Inconveniencies. Very favourable Opportunities were sometimes lost by the unavoidable Slowness of their Councils, and it was often necessary to trust more People with the Secret of publick Business than cou'd be relied on with Security. There were many Evils which the Nature of their Government obliged them to connive at, and which grew as it were out of the very Root of it. The Abuse of Liberty was inseparable in many Points from Liberty itself, and degenerated into a shameless Licentiousness. But the

the principal Mischief attending on this Change, was the Division of the Senate into Parties. Different Judgments, different Interests, and Passions, were perpetually clashing with one another, and by the unequal Motion of its Wheels the whole Machine went but heavily along.

YET one Advantage arose from this Disorder, that the People were kept alert, and upon their Guard. The Animosities and Emulation of Particulars secur'd the Commonwealth, as in a Seraglio; the Honour of the Husband is preserv'd the Malice of the Eunuchs and mutual Jealousies of the Women.

UPON the whole, the *Troglodites* might have been happy in the Liberty they had gain'd, if the same publick Spirit which establish'd, cou'd have continu'd to maintain it.

LETTER XXIV.
SELIM *to* MIRZA.

THERE was in the Senate a certain Man of great natural Cunning, and Penetration, Factious, Enterprizing, vers'd in Business, and above all, very knowing in the Disposition of the Times in which he lived. This Man came secretly to the King, and

and entertain'd him with the following Discourse.

'I perceive, Sir, you are very much cast down with the Bounds that have been set to your Authority: But perhaps you have not lost so much as you imagine. —— The People are very proud of their own Work, and look with great Satisfaction on the Outside of their new-erected Government; but those who can see the Inside too, find every thing too rotten and superficial to last very long.

'The two Things in Nature the most repugnant and inconsistent with each other, are the Love of Liberty, and the Love of Money: The last is so strong among your Subjects, that it is impossible the former can subsist. I say, Sir, they are not HONEST enough to be FREE —— Look round the Nation, and see whether their Manners agree with their Constitution. Is there a Virtue which Want does not disgrace, or a Vice which Riches cannot dignify? Has not Luxury infected all Degrees of Men amongst them? Which way is that Luxury to be supported? It must necessarily create a Dependance which will soon put an End to this Dream of Liberty. Have you a Mind to fix your Power on a sure and lasting Basis? Fix it on the Vices of Mankind: Set up private Interest against publick; apply to the Wants and Vanities

'of

'of Particulars; shew those who lead the
'People, that they may better find their
'Account in betraying than defending them:
'This, Sir, is a short Plan of such a Con-
'duct as wou'd make you really superior to
'all Restraint, without breaking in upon
'those *nominal Securities*, which the *Troglo-*
'*dites* are more attach'd to a great deal than
'they are to the Things themselves. If you
'please to trust the Management to me,
'I shall not be afraid of being obnoxious to
'the *Spirit of Liberty*; for in a little while
'I will extinguish every Spark of it; nor
'of being liable to the *Justice* of the Nation,
'for my *Crime* itself shall be my *Protection*.

LETTER XXV.
Selim to Mirza at *Ispahan*.

From London.

THERE is a very pretty, fair-complexion'd Girl, who lodges in a House just over-against me. She was always staring at me from her Window, and seem'd to follicit my Regards by a thousand little Airs that I can't describe, but which touch'd me still more than all her Beauty: At last I became so enamour'd of her, that I resolv'd to demand her in Marriage. Accordingly I
went

went to visit her in Form, and was receiv'd by her Mother, a Widow Gentlewoman, who desir'd very civilly to know my Business.

MADAM, said I, I have a Garden at *Ispahan* adorn'd with the finest Flowers in the East: I have the *Perrian* Jasmin, the *Indian* Rose, the Violet of *Media*, and the Tulip of *Candahar* : But I have lately beheld an *English* Lilly more fair than all these and far more sweet, which I desire to transplant into my Garden. This Lilly, Madam, is now in your Possession, and I come a Suppliant to you that I may obtain it. The old Lady not conceiving what I meant, begun to assure me very faithfully that I was mistaken, for she had neither Lilly nor Rose belonging to her.

THE Lilly, return'd I, is your lovely Daughter, whom I come to ask of you for my Wife.

WHAT do you propose to settle on her replied she? That is the first Point to be consider'd.———

I WILL do by her very handsomely, answer'd I; I will settle upon her ——— *Two Black Eunuchs*, an old Midwife, and a Chambermaid.

Two *Blacks*, answered she, are well enough, but I shou'd think *Two* French *Footmen* wou'd be *genteeler.*

How-

However, Sir, we won't quarrel about *her Equipage*: The Question is, what *Provision* you think of making.——

Don't trouble yourself about that, return'd I,——she shall have *Meat* enough I warrant you; Plenty of *Rice*, and the best *Sherbet* in all *Persia*.

Don't tell me of *Rice* and *Sherbet*, said the old Woman; I ask what *Jointure* you will give her?

This Word stopt me short, for I did not know what a *Jointure* signified: At last she explain'd herself by demanding of me, how her Daughter was to live if I shou'd die?

I have an I*ndian Wife*, answer'd I, that intends to *burn herself* as soon as I expire, but I wou'd not recommend that Method to your Daughter.

How! said she,—— you are married then already! Yes, said I, in *Persia* we are allow'd to *take* as many Women as we can *keep*, and it seems to me that the Men in *England* do the same only leaving out *the Ceremony*.

It is a very wicked Practice, answer'd she,——but since it is your Religion so to do, and that my Daughter's *Fortune* is too small to get a Husband among *Christians* I am not much averse to give her to you upon reasonable Terms, because I am told you are very *rich*.

She

SHE had scarce spoke these Words, when my little Mistress, who had been list'ning to our Discourse behind a Screen, came out from her Concealment, and told her Mother, 'That if so many Women were to live 'together she was sure there wou'd be no Peace in the Family, and therefore she desir'd her to insist on a good *separate Maintenance*, in case her Husband and she shou'd *disagree*.

WHAT, said I, young Lady, do you think already of *separating your* Interests from *mine*? And must I be obliged to pay my Wife *for living ill with me*, as much as I shou'd *for living well*?

No — by *Hali* — I will never wed a Woman who is so determin'd to *rebel* against her Husband, that she *articles* for it in the very Contract of her Marriage.——

✽✽✽?✽✽✽✽✽✽✽✽✽✽✽:✽✽✽✽✽✽✽✽✽✽✽

LETTER XXVI.
SELIM to MIRZA at *Ispahan*.

From *London*.

THERE is at *London* a Native of *Aleppo* that has resided here some Years as a private Agent for some Merchants of that City, and passes for a *Jew*: They call him *Zabulon*, but his true Name is *Abdallah*, the Son of *Abderamen*. He has
revealed

revealed himself to me, and I have contracted a great Intimacy with him. There never was an honester, more friendly, or more valuable Man: But he is as much a Bigot to all the Eastern Notions, and as much a Stranger to every thing in *England*, as he was the first Hour of his Arrival. For my Part, *Mirza*, I set out with a Resolution to give up all my hereditary Prejudices, and form my Mind to bear different Opinions, as my Body to suffer different Climates. Nay, if I may say so, I begun my Travels a good while before I went abroad, by Reading, Enquiring, and Reasoning, about the Manners and Institutions of other Countries. I had lived long enough under the Yoke of an Arbritary Government, to see the Misery of it, and value Liberty: I am now come into an Island where that Liberty is happily establish'd, and where I may learn to know it by its Effects. This, *Mirza*, is the Study that I pursue, and it demands the utmost Attention I can give. In absolute Monarchies all depends on the Character of the Prince, and when that is known, you have little more to learn; but in mix'd Governments the Machine is more complex, and it requires a nicer Observation to understand how the Springs of it are dispos'd, or how they mutually check and assist each other.

WHEN

When I talk to *Abdallah* on this Subject, he tells me it is not worth my while to trouble myself about it; for that any Form of Government is good if it *be well administer'd*. But the Question is, which is *most likely* to be *well-administer'd*, that is, which has *best* secured itself, by wholesome Provisions and Restraints, against the Danger of a *bad Administration*.

LETTER XXVII.
Selim to Mirza at *Ispahan*.

From London.

As I was walking in the Fields near this City the other Morning, a disbanded Soldier somewhat in Years implored my Charity, and to excite my Compassion bared his Bosom, on which were the Scars of many Wounds all receiv'd in the Service of his Country. I gladly reliev'd his Wants, and being desirous to inform myself of every thing, fell into Discourse with him on the War in which he had served. He told me he had been present at the taking of ten or twelve strong Towns, and had a Share in the Danger and Glory of almost as many Victories. How then, said I, comes it to pass that thou art laid aside? Thy Strength is indeed in its decline, but not yet wasted; and I should think that Experience would well supply the loss of Youth. Alas! Sir, answered he, I have a good Heart and tolerable Limbs, but I want three Inches more of Stature: I am brave and able enough, thank God, but not quite handsome enough for a Soldier.

How then didst thou serve so long, returned I? in *Flanders*, Sir, said he, there were some Thousands such ill-looking Fellows, who did very well in a Day of Battle, but wou'd make no Figure at a Review.——It appears to me very strange, replied I, that thou shouldst be poor after fighting so many Years with such great Success. The Plunder of a single Town in the *East* is enough to enrich every Soldier that help'd to take it. Plunder! Sir, said he; we have no such Term in the modern Art of War. We fight for Sixpence a Day —— But when you have gain'd a Battle, do you get nothing by it? —— Yes, said he, we have the Advantage to go on and besiege a Town.——Ay, then, my honest Lad, comes your Harvest —— Then, Sir, replied he, it defends it self till we are half of us destroy'd; and when it can hold out no longer, it capitulates; that is, every Burgher saves his House, and every Soldier carries off his Baggage. — But what becomes of the conquering Army? —— Why the conquering Army has the Pleasure to besiege another Town, which capitulates alſo; and at the end of the Campaign it goes into Quarters. —— But when you enter an Enemy's Country, don't you raiſe Contributions? —— The Generals do, anſwer'd he, but military Diſcipline allows no Part of it to the common Soldiers; they have juſt Sixpence a Day as they had before.

Here ended our Converſation; and I repeat it to thee, as one of the moſt extraordinary Novelties I have met with in *Europe*. That Armies, mercenary Armies, ſhould be led on from Battle to Battle, from Siege to Siege, without any thing to animate them but the Hopes of a barren Reputation, and a Pay which is barely a Subſiſtence; that they ſhould be made to look upon the Property of their Enemies as ſacred and inviolable; that they ſhould return from a victorious Campaign no richer than they ſet out, and take the Field next Year with as much Alacrity as they did before, is ſuch a Wonder as Hiſtory cannot ſhew. No ſuch thing was ever heard of in *Aſia*, nor do I know that the two other Parts of the Globe have any Example of it. But all over *Europe*, except *Muſcovy* and *Turky*, it has been ſo for this laſt hundred Years, and there has yet happened no Mutiny on that Account. It is no leſs unaccountable that Valour, and a Capacity for Service ſhould be made to conſiſt in ſmug Looks and a certain degree

of

of Tallness. If Women were to raise and employ Troops, I should not much wonder at such a Choice; but God grant our invincible Sultan an Army of Veteran Soldiers, though there were not a Man among them above five Foot high, or a Face that wou'd not frighten an Enemy with the very Looks of it!

LETTER XXVIII.

Selim to Mirza at *Ispahan*.

THERE is a Set of People in this Country, whose Activity is more useless than the Idleness of a Monk. They are like those troublesome Dreams which often agitate and perplex us in our Sleep, but leave no Impression behind them when we wake. I have sent thee an Epitaph made for one of these Men of Business, who ended his Life and Labours not long ago.

Here lies ⸺ ⸺ who lived Threescore and ten Years in a continual Hurry. He had the Honour of sitting in six Parliaments, of being Chairman in twenty five Committees, and of making three hundred and fifty Speeches. He attended constantly twice a Week at the Levies of twelve different Ministers of State;

and writ for and against them one thousand Papers. He compos'd fifty new Projects for the better Government of the Church and State. He left behind him Memoirs of his own Life in five Volumes in Folio.

Reader, if thou should'st be moved to drop a Tear for the Loss of so CONSIDERABLE A PERSON, it will be a SINGULAR Favour to the Deceas'd; for no body else concerns himself about it, or remembers that such a Man was ever born.

LETTER XXIX.
SELIM *to* MIRZA *at* Ispahan.

From *London.*

I Went with my Friend the other Day to a great Hall, where all the Courts of Law were sitting together: Behold, said he, the Temple *of Justice,* the Sanctuary of Privilege and Right, which our mightiest Monarchs have not been able to violate with Impunity. Behold the lowest of our Commons contending here with the highest of our Nobles, unawed by their Dignity or Power. See those venerable Sages on the Bench, whose Ears are deaf to Sollicitation, and their Hands untainted with Corruption.

See

See also those twelve Men, whom we call the *Jury*, the great Bulwark of our Property and Freedom. But then cast your Eyes on those Men in Black that swarm on every Side: These are the Priests of the Temple, who, like other Priests, have turned their Ministry into a Trade: They have perplexed, confounded, and encumbred Law, in order to make themselves more necessary, and to drain the Purses of the People. —— I have heard, said I, that the Laws of *England* are wisely *Framed* and impartially *administred*. The old *Gothick* Pile we are now in, replied my Friend, will give you a just Idea of their *Structure:* The Foundations of it are deep and very lasting; it has stood many Ages, and with good Repairs may stand many more; But the Architecture is loaded with a multiplicity of idle and useless Parts; when you examine it critically, many Faults and Imperfections will appear; yet upon the whole it has a mighty awful Air, and strikes you with Reverence and Respect. Then as to the Administration of our Laws, the Difference between us and other Countries is little more than this, that there they sell Justice *in the Gross*, and here we sell it *by Retail*. In *Persia* the Cadi passes Sentence for a round Sum of Money; in *England* the Judge indeed takes nothing after he comes to be a Judge; but the Attorney, the Advocate, every Officer and Retainer on the Court, raise treble that Sum upon the Client. The Condition of Justice is like that of many Women of Quality: They themselves are above being bought, but every *Servant* about them must be *Feed*, or there is no *getting at them.* The disinterested Spirit of the Lady is of no Advantage to the Suitor; he is undone by the Rapine of *her Dependants.*

LETTER XXX.
Selim to Mirza at *Ispahan.*

WHAT is peculiar to this Country, continued he, in judicial Proceedings, is, that no Power of Equity is lodged either in the Breast of Judge or Jury, but they are to direct and determine altogether by the Letter of the Law.

In *France*, and other Parts of *Europe*, the Judge is trusted with a discretionary Power to vary from the Law in certain Points, according to the Dictates of his Conscience, and the Reason of the Case. But in *England*, Conscience, Reason, Right, and Justice are confined to the Words of the Act of Parliament, and the established Sense thereof.

No doubt this is productive of many Hardships; Particulars must often suffer by
it;

it; yet in the main it is a wholsome Limitation, and beneficial to Liberty. For it is generally found, that in other Conntries the Judge's Confcience depends wholly on the King's, and the Rule of Equity is a very uncertain Meafure, which Paffion, Prejudice, or Intereft can change: So that many of the Grievances we complain of in the courfe of Juftice here, are interwoven with the Conftitution of our Government, and not to be removed without endangering, or, perhaps, deftroying it. Latter Times have gone off a little from this Strictnefs of adhering to the Letter, by encouraging Applications to the Court of Chancery, which is a Court of Equity, but tied down to certain regular Methods of Proceeding, and as clofe a Conformity to the known Meaning and Purpofe of the Law as is confiftent with its Inftitution. The Bufinefs of this Court is vaftly greater than formerly it was. Anciently the Chancellor himfelf was nothing more than *Regifter* to the King, with a Power to advife him in fuch Matters as came within the Compafs of the Writings entrufted to his Cuftody: But by Degrees he became Keeper of the Great Seal, and the higheft Officer of the Realm. And indeed if there was not placed in the Houfe of Peers a Judicature fuperior to his, fo much of the Property of the Subject would depend on the Opinion of the Chancellor, that the Parliament would have Reason to claim a Right which they demanded in the Reign of *Edward* the Third, of nominating this Officer themselves.

I desired to know how the Lords behaved in this ultimate Trial of all Causes.

With great Caution and Uprightness, answered he: The Spirit of Party, or the Influence of the Court, has not yet mixed it self in their Decisions; and happy will it be for this Country if they are as scrupulous in *every Capacity* as they are in their *Judicial one*.

LETTER XXXI.
Selim to Mirza at *Ispahan*.

From *London*.

A *French* Gentleman was boasting the other Day in a Company where I was, of the Academies founded by the late King for the Support and Reward of Arts and Sciences.

You have a pleasant Way (said he) here in *England*, of encouraging a Man of Wit. When he is dead, you build him a fine Tomb, and lay him among your Kings; but while he is alive, he is as ill receiv'd at Court, as if he came

came with a Petition againſt the Miniſtry. Wou'd not the Money you have laid out upon the Monuments of two or three of your Poets, have been better beſtow'd in giving them Bread when they were living, and wanted it? This might have been formerly the Caſe, replied an *Engliſhman*, but it is not ſo now. A Man of true Genius is at preſent ſo much favour'd by the Publick, his Works are ſo greedily bought up, and ſo many People fond of ſerving him every way, that he has no need to depend upon a Court for Protection and Subſiſtence.

And let me add, that the Honours which are paid to a deceas'd Man of Wit, have ſomething in them more generous and diſintereſted, than Penſions beſtow'd on ſlaviſh Terms, and at the Price of continual Panegyrick. We have a *very great Poet* now *alive*, who may boaſt of one Glory to which no Member of the *French* Academy can pretend, *viz*. That he never flattered any Man *in Power*; but has beſtow'd immortal Praiſes upon *thoſe*, whom, for fear of offending Men *in Power*, no Poet in *France* would have dared to praiſe.

LETTER XXXII.

SELIM to MIRZA at *Ispahan*.

From *London*.

THERE is a *Christian Doctor*, who at my first Arrival here took the Trouble to visit me very often, with no other View, as I could find, but merely to make a *Christian* of me; in which Design he has been single hitherto, such a Zeal being very much out of Fashion.

BUT, what is most extraordinary, I was told the other Day, that his *Preferment in the Church* had been lately *stopp'd* at the Instance of the *Mufti of this City*, on a Supposition of his being turn'd *Mahometan*, and that all the Proof brought against him was the Commerce he formerly had with me.

WHEN I heard this, I waited on the *Mufti*, and offer'd to testify that the Doctor was a Christian, as far as I cou'd judge by all I saw of him, during the Time of our Acquaintance: But he refused to admit my Testimony in this Case, because, as he said, I was myself *a Misbeliever*, and insisted
on

on the Doctor's suppos'd *Apostacy*, as an undoubted Fact, which *shock'd* him beyond measure.

IF he is a *Mussleman*, said I, he must be *Circumcis'd*: Why don't you end the Dispute by shewing *that*? There is a *Visible Mark* of Orthodoxy in our Religion; but I shou'd be glad to know what is the *Visible Mark* of yours. If it be *Meekness*, or *Charity*, or *Justice*, or *Temperance*, or *Piety*, all these are most *conspicuous* in the *Doctor*: But I find that none of these can *prove* him to be a *Christian* ———— What therefore is the *Characteristick* of his *Accusers?* and *how* do they *prove* themselves to be *Christians?*.

LETTER XXXIII.

SELIM to MIRZA at *Ispahan*.

From *London*.

THE Principles and Practice of Toleration prevail very strongly in this Country: I myself have felt the Effects of it very much to my Advantage: The better sort of People are no more offended at the Difference of my Faith from theirs, than at the

the Difference of my Dress: The Mob, indeed, seem surprized at me for both, and can't comprehend how it is possible to make such Mistakes, but they rather contemn than hate me for them; and I have yet been affronted by Nobody but a drunken Priest, who denounc'd Damnation against me, for refusing to pledge him, *To the Prosperity of the Church of England*, in a Liquor forbidden by our Law.

This has not always been the Temper of the *English*. They have formerly waged War against *Mahometans*, only because they were so; they have kindled Fires against Hereticks, tho' what was Heresy in one Age has been Orthodoxy in another; nay, they have involved their Country in all the Miseries of Civil Discord upon Points of no greater Moment, than whether a Table ought to be placed in the Middle of the Church, or at one End of it.

I must own to thee, *Mirza*, there is nothing I abhor so much as Persecution: It seems to me no less ridiculous in its Principles, than dreadful in its Effects. One wou'd think, that the great Diversity of Opinions among Mankind, should incline Men a little to suspect that their own may possibly be wrong; but to pursue all others with Rage and Violence, instead of Pity or Persuasion, is such a Strain of Pride and Folly as Enthusiasm itself can scarce account

for

for. I have read in a famous *Spanish* Author of a certain Madman who rambled about *Spain* with Sword and Lance, and whomsoever he met with in his Way he requir'd to acknowledge and believe, that his Mistress *Dulcinea del Toboso* was the handsomest Woman in the World. It was in vain for the other to reply, that he had no knowledge at all of *Dulcinea*, or had a particular Fancy to another Woman; the Madman made no Allowances for Ignorance or Prejudice, but instantly knock'd him down, and never left beating him till he promis'd to maintain the Perfections of the said Lady above all her Rivals. Such has been the Conduct of many Priests and Priest-rid Princes in propagating their spiritual Inclinations: Each had his several *Dulcinea*, and resolved that every body should admire her as much as himself; but as this was not easily brought about, the Controversy was determin'd by Force of Arms: Nay, tho' it happen'd that all admir'd the same, they wou'd even quarrel about the Fashion of her Cloaths, and most bloody Battles have been fought to decide which Colour became her best. Alas, *Mirza*, how absurd is all this! the Beauty of True Religion is sufficiently shewn by its proper Lustre; it needs no Knight Errant to combat for it; nor is any thing so contrary to the Nature of Affection as Constraint. Whoever is compell'd pell'd to profess a Faith without Conviction, tho' it was but indifferent to him before, must grow to think it odious; as Men who are forc'd to marry where they do not approve, soon change Dislike into Aversion.

―― I will end this Subject with putting thee in mind of a Ceremony which is celebrated once a Year by the common People of *Persia*, in Honour of our Prophet *Ali*. There are two Bulls brought forth before the Crowd, the strongest of which is call'd *Ali*, and the weaker *Osman*: They are made to fight, and as *Ali* is very sure to get the better, the Spectators go away highly satisfied with this happy Decision of the Dispute between Us and the Heretical *Turks*.

Just in this Light I regard all Religious Wars. Whether the Combatants are two Bulls or two Bishops, the Case is exactly the same, and Mankind are as simple to concern themselves for the one as for the other ――

LETTER

LETTER XXXIV.

SELIM to MIRZA at *Ispahan.*

From *London.*

THERE is nothing more astonishing to a *Mussleman* than many Particulars relating to the State of Matrimony, as it is managed in *Europe*: Our Practice of it is so totally different, that we can hardly think it possible for Men to do or suffer such Things as happen here every Day.

THE following Story, which was given me for a true one, will set this in a very full Light: I wish thou may'st find it as entertaining, as I am sure thou wilt find it new. ——

IN the Reign of *Charles* the First, King of *England*, lived two Gentlemen, whose true Names I will conceal under the feign'd ones of *Acasto* and *Septimius*. They were Neighbours, their Estates lay together, and they had a Friendship for each other, which had grown up from their earliest Youth.

ACASTO had an only Son, whom we will call *Polydore*, and *Septimius* an only Daughter named

named *Emilia*. Though the Boy was but fourteen Years old, and the Girl but twelve; the Parents were so desirous of contracting an Alliance between their Families, and of uniting the two bordering Estates, that they married them before either was of Age to consummate the Marriage, or even to understand the Nature of their Contract. As soon as the Ceremony was perform'd, they sent the young Gentleman abroad, to finish his Education.

After four Years which he had spent in *France* and *Italy*, he was recall'd by the News of his Father's Death, which made it necessary for him to return to *England*.

Emilia, who was now about sixteen, begun to think he had been absent long enough, and receiv'd him with a great deal of Satisfaction. She had heard a fine Character of him, from those who knew him in his Travels; and when she saw him, his Person was so improv'd that she thought herself the happiest of Women in being his Wife.

But his Sentiments for her were very different.

There was in his Temper a Spirit of Contradiction, which cou'd not bear to have a Wife impos'd upon him.—— He complain'd, that his Father had taken Advantage of his tender Age, to draw him into an Engagement, in which his Judgment
cou'd

cou'd poffibly have no Part. He confeft that he had no Objections to the Perfon or Character of *Emilia*; but infifted on a Liberty of Choice, and declar'd that he look't upon his Marriage to be forc'd and null. In fhort, he abfolutely refufed to confummate, in fpite of all the Endeavours of their Friends, and the Conjugal Affection of the poor young Lady, who did her utmoft to vanquifh his Averfion.—— When fhe found that all her Kindnefs was thrown away, the natural Pride of her Sex made her defire to be feparated from him, and fhe join'd with him in a Petition for a Divorce. The firft Parliament of the Year *Forty* was then fitting: The Affair was brought before them, and it was believ'd, that a Divorce wou'd have eafily been obtain'd at their mutual Demand. But the Bifhops oppos'd it with great Violence, as a Breach of the Law of God, which they faid wou'd admit of no Divorce, but in Cafes of Adultery. They were anfwered, that the Marriage was not *compleat*; and that the ceremonious Part, which was all that had paft between them, might as properly be difpens'd with by the Legiflature, as any other Form of Law. That the young Gentleman's Averfion was *invincible*, and inconfiftent with the Obligation laid upon him: That therefore it wou'd not well become the Fathers of
the

the Church, to put him under a manifest Temptation of committing Adultery: And that nothing cou'd be imagin'd more unjust, than to condemn the Lady to perpetual Virginity, under the Notion of a Marriage, which, it was plain, was a meer Illusion.———
These Arguments seem'd convincing to all the World except the Bishops; but they persisted in their *usual Unanimity*, and were so powerful by the *Favour* of the *Court*, that they carried their Point in the House of Lords; and the unfortunate *Polydore* and *Emilia* were declared to be *one Flesh*, though no Union had ever been between them, either in Body or in Mind.—— The Husband immediately paid back his Wife's Portion to her Father; and firmly resolv'd that from that time forwards he wou'd never see her more. His natural Obstinacy was irritated by the Constraint that was put upon him, and he took a Pride to shew the World that there was no Power Ecclesiastical or Civil, which could oblige him to act like a married Man against his Inclination. The poor Lady retir'd to a Seat of her Father's in the Country, and endeavour'd by long Absence from her Husband to forget that he had ever pleas'd or offended her.—— Two Years afterwards the Civil War broke out between the King and Parliament. *Polydore* was so enraged against the Bishops for obstructing his
Divorce,

Divorce, that it determin'd him in chusing of his Party, and made him take up Arms against the King. *Septimius* the Father of *Emilia*, was as zealous a Royalist, to which his Hatred of *Polydore* contributed as much as any thing; for it was hardly possible that two such bitter Enemies shou'd be of the same Side. In the Course of the War, the King being worsted, the Estates of many of his Party were confiscated; and *Septimius* having been one of the most active, was also one of those that suffered most. He was compelled to retire into *France* with what he cou'd save out of the Wreck of his Estate; and carried with him his Daughter, who was quite abandon'd by her Husband and his Family.

In the mean while, the Army of the Parliament begun to form itself into different Factions: *Cromwell* at the Head of the Independants, acquir'd by Degrees such an Influence, that the Presbyterians were no longer a Match for him: *Polydore*, who was devoted to that Sect, threw up his Commission in Discontent; and happily for his Reputation had no Share in those violent Proceedings, which ended in the Destruction of the King, and the ancient Constitution.

He continued quite unactive for some Years; but at last growing weary of a Life that agreed so ill with his Vivacity, he determin'd to go and serve in the Low-Countries under the

the Great Prince of *Conde*, who in the Year 1654 commanded the Armies of *Spain* against his Country.—— Two Reasons inclin'd *Polydore* to this Party; First, The Desire he had to learn his Trade under a General of so great Reputation; and, Secondly, Because *Cromwell* had refus'd to enter into an Alliance with that Prince, though most agreeable to the Interests of *England*.—— He found his Highness employ'd in besieging *Arras*, and was receiv'd by him with high Marks of his Esteem. During the Siege he often signaliz'd his Courage, and supported the Opinion that was spread all over *Europe* of the Valour of the Parliament-Officers. But the Marshal *Turenne*, with *La Ferté* and *Hoquincourt*, having attackt the Besiegers in their Lines, reliev'd *Arras*, and wou'd have destroy'd the *Spanish* Army if the Prince of *Conde* had not saved them by a Retreat, which was one of the greatest Actions of his Life. In this Battle, *Polydore* was taken Prisoner, and sent to *Paris* with many other *Spanish* Officers, to continue there till they shou'd be ransom'd or exchang'd. In the Journey, he contracted a great Intimacy with the Count *d'Aguilar*, Brigadier under the Count *de Fuensaldagna*, and one of the first Gentlemen in *Spain*. As they travell'd together several Days, they very naturally acquainted one another with the principal Incidents of their Lives.

Polydore,

Polydore related to *Aguilar* the whole Story of his Marriage with *Emilia*, and declaim'd with great Heat against the Folly of tying two People thus together, who wish'd nothing so much as to be loose.

No Doubt, said the Count, it is most absurd; but to say the Truth, I find nothing very reasonable in the whole Affair of Marriage as we have made it. I don't know what it may be to other Men, but to me it seems horribly unnatural, to be confin'd to any single Woman, let her be ever so agreeable.

If I had *Chose* a Woman *Freely*, answer'd *Polydore*, I cou'd be always constant to her with Pleasure; but to have a Companion *for Life forc'd* upon me, I had rather row in the Gallies than submit to it.

You are mistaken, my dear *Polydore*, replied the Count, in fancying it so easy to be constant even to a Wife of one's own chusing. I have had some Experience of that kind, and know that the first choice is only good till we have made a second.

To prove this to you, I need only give you the History of my Amours. —— That you may not think I am telling you a Romance, I will begin where Romances always end, with the Article of my Marriage. I was married at four and twenty to a Lady, whom I chose for her Beauty and good Sense, without troubling myself
about

about her Fortune, which was but small. The three or four first Years that we lived together, was the happiest Period of my Life: I preserved all the Ardour of a Lover with the Freedom and Tenderness of a Husband. She loved me still more fondly than I did her; and if I had not left her till she gave me Occasion, I believe I shou'd have been constant to this Day.——But I was not able to hold out any longer: All her Charms were become so familiar to me, that they cou'd not make the least Impression; and I went regularly to her Bed as I did to Supper, with an Appetite quite pall'd by too much Plenty. In this dull Way I drudged on for a tedious Twelvemonth, till the Sight of a Relation of my Wife's, who came opportunely to lodge in my own House, rouz'd me out of my Lethargy. It was a beautiful Creature of eighteen, just taken out of a Convent to be married. She knew nothing of the World, but had a natural Quickness that went further than Experience. However, as there was something a little awkward in her exterior Carrriage, the Countess *d' Aguilar* thought it proper to keep her with her for some Time before her Marriage, till she had instructed her how to behave herself in Publick. I thought my Instructions might be of use to her as well as my Wife's, to teach her how to behave

behave herself in *Private*; and had the good Fortune to make them more agreeable.

SHE liked me better and better every Lesson, and in Proportion, as her Passion encreas'd for me, she conceiv'd a stronger Aversion for the Man who was design'd to be her Husband: And indeed she had no great Reason to be fond of him, for he was a peevish, stupid, bigotted old Fellow, who did nothing Day or Night but pray and scold. Her Friends press'd the Conclusion of her Marriage, and as unwilling as she was to come into it, she cou'd not resist their Importunities. Yet to comfort me, she very fairly let me know, that she wou'd give her Virginity to me in spite of all their Teeth; and moreover, that I shou'd have it on the *wedding Night*. I represented to her the Improbability of her performing *such* a Promise at *such* a Time; but she bid me trust to her Management and I shou'd be satisfied.

THE Wedding-Night came; and when the Company was retired, the Bridegroom was surpriz'd to see the Bride dissolved in Tears. He beg'd to know the Cause of her Affliction; but she wou'd not tell him, except he swore that when he knew it he wou'd do his utmost to remove it.

THE poor Man, in the Vehemence of his Love, assured her that he wou'd do any thing to make her easy, that was not contrary

trary to the *Honour of a Cavalier*, or the *Injunctions of our Holy Mother Church.*

No, said she, the Thing I require of you will recommend you extremely to the *Church*, as it is only to give me leave to accomplish a Vow I made to the Blessed Virgin, in a Fit of Sickness when my Life was in great Danger.

Heaven forbid, my pretty Child, replied the Don, that I shou'd hinder you from performing a sacred Vow, to the hazard of your Soul.

Well then, said she, I will own to you, that in my Fright, I vow'd that if I cou'd but get well again and live to be married, I wou'd consecrate my Wedding Night to the Blessed Virgin, by passing it in the Bed of my waiting Woman the virtuous *Isabella*. And this very Morning while I slept, our Lady appeared to me in a Dream, and threaten'd me with another Fit of Sickness if I did not keep my Word.—

If it be so, replied the Husband, there is no doubt but *the Virgin* must be *serv'd* before *me*; and so, my Dear, I wish you a good Night.

Now you must know, that the virtuous *Isabella* was trusted with all the Secrets of her Mistress, and had gone between us through the whole Course of our Amour.

Accordingly Madam went to Bed to her waiting Woman, who had taken care to inform me of this Defign, and conceal'd me in a Clofet within her Chamber; from whence, as foon as every body was afleep, I was admitted to the Place of *Ifabella*, and receiv'd the full Acquittance of a Promife I little expected to fee perform'd.——

THE Singularity of this Adventure fo delighted me, that I cou'd not help in the Vanity of my Heart, difcovering it to the Duke *de l'Infantada*, the moft intimate of my Friends. He was very thankful for the Confidence I repos'd in him, and to reward me for it, betray'd it inftantly to my Wife, whom, it feems, he had long made Love to without Succefs. As he thought that the greateft Obftacle to his Defires was her Fondnefs for me, he hoped to remove it by convincing her of my falfenefs; but though the News of it had like to have broke her Heart, it was not capable to change it.

SHE reproached me in a Manner that made my Fault appear much more inexcufable.—— I might complain, faid fhe, of the Affront you have done my Honour in debauching my Relation; but alas! I am only fenfible to the Injury you have done my Love. You are grown weary of me, and I know it is impoffible to regain your Heart, fince the fingle Reafon of your Diflike muft ftill continue, which is, That I am your Wife. If any Part of my Behaviour had offended you, I might have chang'd it to your

your Satisfaction; but this is a Fault, which in spite of all my Care, will grow worse every Day.—— I endeavour'd to pacify her by Assurances of my future Fidelity; and really I was so affected by her Behaviour, that I seriously meant to keep my word.— But our Inclinations are very little in our Power: My Resolution soon yielded to the Charms of the Countess *Altamira*, one of the handsomest Women about the Court, but the vainest, the most interested, and the most abandond. She made it a Point of Honour to seduce me, out of a Desire to mortify my Wife, with whom she had quarrel'd upon some female Competition of Precedency or Dress.

Her Avarice was equal to her Pride, and she made me pay dearly for her Favours, though her Husband was one of the richest Men in *Spain*. I hardly ever went to her without a Present of some kind or other, and my Fortune begun to suffer by my Expence; yet I was so bewitch'd to her, that though I heartily despis'd her, I cou'd not help loving her to Madness.

One Day, when I came to see her after an Absence that had rais'd my Desires to the highest Pitch; she receiv'd me with a Sullenness and Ill-humour that tortur'd me beyond Expression. I conjur'd her to acquaint me with the Cause of it, and she told me, 'That the last time she was at
'Court,

'Court, she had seen the Countess *d'Agui-*
'*lar* with a Diamond Necklace on, which
'I had given her the Day before: That
'my making such Presents to another
'Woman in the midst of our Intrigue,
'was an Insult she was determin'd not to
'bear; and that since I was grown so fond
'a Husband, she cou'd not but make a
'Conscience of disturbing our conjugal
'Felicity.'

I offer'd her any Satisfaction she wou'd ask; and the malicious Devil had the Impudence to tell me, that nothing cou'd satisfy her, but my taking away that Necklace from my Wife, and giving it to her.——— I entreated her to accept another of twice its Value; but she replied, that her Honour was concern'd; and in short she wou'd have that, and that alone.——— Overcome with her Importunities, I went home, and stole it for her; but made her promise me solemnly to be very cautious, that my Wife shou'd never see it in her Possession.

About three Days after, Word was brought me, that the Countess *d'Aguilar* had fainted away in the Anti-chamber of the Queen, and was gone Home in great Disorder to her Mother's the Countess of *Pacheco*.

I went immediately thither in such a Fright, as convinc'd me I lov'd her better than I thought I did; but imagine my

E 2 Con-

Confusion, when she inform'd me, that she had fainted at the Sight of her own Diamonds on the Neck of the Countess *Altamira*. She added, that it was no Mystery to her, nor to any Body else, how that Lady came by them; and that to save her self the Mortification of any more such publick Affronts, she wou'd no longer live with me as my Wife, but leave me at full Liberty to please myself, as my licentious Inclination shou'd direct.

I us'd my utmost Eloquence to prevail on her to come home to me again; but she remain'd inflexible, and said no more to all my Protestations, but that if her past Conduct had not been able to fix my Heart, she despair'd of doing it for the future.

AFTER living without her half a Year, I was order'd to my Regiment in *Flanders*, and was very glad of an Occasion to leave *Madrid*, where the Regret of her Separation was such a Pain to me, that it entirely sunk my Spirits. Since my Arrival in the Army, I have writ to her three or four Letters, but she disdain'd to make me any Answer; and I have Reason to believe, that her high Spirit has by this time got the better of her Love.

FOR my part, I endeavour to amuse myself the best I can with other Women; and I desire, my dear *Polydore*, that we may be always reciprocal Confidants of
every

every Intrigue that we engage in during our Stay in *France*.——

POLYDORE thank'd him, and assur'd him, that on his Part, he should meet with no Reserve. When they came to *Paris*, his first Care was to enquire, what was become of *Septimius* and *Emilia*, whom he had heard no Account of for many Years: He was inform'd, that *Septimius* was dead, and his Daughter gone from *Paris*. His Curiosity made him write to his Friends in *England*, to ask if she was there? They answer'd him, That every Body believ'd she was dead in *France*, having receiv'd no News of her a great while. *Polydore* was mightily pleas'd with this Account, and fancy'd himself very happy in being a Widower, though he had given himself no Trouble to support the Character of a Husband.—— The two Friends had not resided long at *Paris*, before they were exchang'd for some *French* Officers: who were taken Prisoners by the Prince of *Conde*. They return'd to the Army, but the Season not permitting them to come to any Action, they agreed to pass the Winter at *Brussels*, in the Court of the Archduke. They had not been there above a Month, before *Aguilar* acquainted his *English* Friend, that he had begun an Intrigue with a *French* Lady, who liv'd in a very retir'd Manner, which he believ'd was owing to her

Circumstances: That he had seen her two or three times, by Means of a Woman at whose House she lodg'd, whose good Offices he had secur'd by a handsome Bribe. He added, that he wou'd carry *Polydore* to see her the next Visit that he made. Accordingly they went together to Madamoiselle *Dalincourt* (for that was the Name of *Aguilar*'s new Mistress.) At their coming in, *Dalincourt* seem'd much surpriz'd, changed Colour, and was not able to speak a Word. The Count, alarmed at her Disorder, suspected some Lover had been with her, and told her with an Air of Discontent, that he was sorry he came at so wrong a Time. She endeavour'd to shake off her Confusion, and reply'd, that he was always very welcome: But that the Gentleman he brought with him had so much Resemblance of a Brother of her's, who was kill'd in *Flanders*, that at first Sight she cou'd not help being struck with it in the Manner they had seen: She added, that if the Gentleman was as like her Brother in Mind, as he was in Form, she shou'd be mightily pleas'd with his Acquaintance. She spoke this with such an Air of Sincerity, that the Count began to think his Jealousy was without Foundation.

After some general Discourse, she applied to *Polydore*, and ask'd him how long he had been engag'd in the *Spanish* Service, with
many

many other more particular Enquiries, which seem'd to intimate a Defire to know him better. *Polydore* was very glad of it, in Hopes to ferve his Friend; and the Count, who had no Sufpicions on that Side, did his utmoft to engage them in a Friendfhip which he imagin'd wou'd turn to his Advantage.

At Night, when the two Gentlemen were at home together, *Aguilar* afk'd his Companion, what he thought of *Dalincourt*'s Perfon and Underftanding? Better of the laft than the firft, anfwer'd he, tho' both are certainly agreeable. I can't help thinking, continu'd he, that her Perfon is not quite new to me; but I can't recollect where I met with her, except it was at *Paris*, when I was there a Boy.——You will do well to improve your Acquaintance now, replied the Count; and, to give you an Opportunity of doing it, I'll fend you there To-morrow to make my Excufes for being obliged to hunt with the Archduke, inftead of waiting upon her, as I intended. I know, my dear *Polydore* will employ all his Wit and Eloquence to fet his Friend's Paffion in the beft Light, and while he is with her, I fhall have lefs Uneafinefs in being away. *Polydore* promis'd him all the Services he cou'd do him, but faid, he wifh'd he had got a Miftrefs too, to make the Party even.

THE next Day he went to her, and said a great deal in Praife of *Aguilar*, to difcover what fhe thought of him: She anfwer'd him with Terms of a cold Efteem, but nothing that gave him the leaft Encouragement to believe fhe was in Love. He then endeavour'd to perfuade her of the Violence of the Count's Paffion for her; but fhe affur'd him, that this was the only Subject fhe did not care to hear him talk of. —— He return'd to his Friend quite difcouraged at her Manner of proceeding, and told him there was nothing to be hop'd for. The Count fhew'd him a Letter he had juft receiv'd from his Confidante, the Lady of the Houfe; which advis'd him not to think of gaining *Dalincourt* by a timorous Refpect; but to offer her at once a handfome Settlement, which the Straitnefs of her Fortune would make her liften to much more kindly than fhe did to his fine Speeches.

THIS indeed may do fomething, faid *Polydore*; for I found by her Difcourfe, that fhe had been reduced, by a Series of Misfortunes, to a Condition very much beneath her Birth. ——— In Conclufion, they agreed to make a Trial, whether fhe was to be bought or no; and *Polydore* was made the Bearer of a Letter which contain'd a very liberal Propofal. She read it, look'd at *Polydore* fome Time without faying a Word,

Word, and at last burst out into a Flood of Tears.

I THOUGHT, said she, recovering her Voice, that it had not been in the Power of my ill Destiny to make me more unhappy: But I now find, that my Misfortunes have sunk me lower than I ever was aware of, since two Gentlemen, whose Esteem I wish'd to gain, think so meanly of me, as to imagine me a proper Person to receive *such a Letter*. But know, Sir, that I am as much a Stranger to Infamy, as I am to Happiness; and have a Spirit superior to all the Wrongs that your insolent Sex can put upon me. Had not you disgrac'd your self by the scandalous Employment of endeavouring to seduce me with a Dirty Bribe, I shou'd have been happy in seeing you often here; but must now desire you to trouble me no more, and to tell your Friend, as my Answer to his Letter, that I wou'd sooner *give* myself to a Footman, than *sell* myself to a Prince. ———

POLYDORE was infinitely struck with this Reception: Every Word she utter'd pierc'd him to the Heart; and he look'd upon her as a Miracle of Virtue, such as he never had any Notion of before. ——— He return'd to the Count in great Confusion, and acquainted him with the ill Success of his Commission. *Aguilar*, more in Love with her than ever, writ a most

sub-

submissive Letter to beg her Pardon, but she instantly sent it back unopen'd. When he found all his Courtship was ineffectual, he left *Brussels* in Despair, and retired to a Villa of one of his Friends, where he resolved to stay till the Opening of the Campaign. In the mean while *Polydore*, who continued still at *Brussels*, was in a Situation little easier than his Friend. Madamoiselle *Dalincourt* took up all his Thoughts; he repeated to himself a thousand times the last Words he heard her speak, and admir'd the Spirit that appear'd in them to a degree of Adoration.

Not being able to bear her Absence any longer, he sent to beg that he might see her once again, upon a Business wholly relating to himself. She admitted him, and begun the Conversation, by strictly forbidding him to name the Count in any thing he had to say to her.—— I have no Inclination to name him, replied he, for I wou'd willingly forget that I ever knew him. I am sensible that I wrong him, in declaring to you, that I love you more than Life; yet, as his Passion is quite destitute of Hope, why shou'd not I sollicit you for a Heart to which he has no Pretensions? But, be my Conduct right or not in Regard to Him, to You, Madam, it shall ever be most honourable. I come to offer you my whole Fortune upon such Terms,

Terms, as your Virtue need not blush at: I am a Widower, and free to marry whom I please; my Estate is sufficient for us both, and I am happy to think it in my Power, to raise you to that Rank which you were born to. This, Madam, is the only Reparation by which I can attone for the Affront I did your Character; and, if you refuse to accept of it, my Despair will be equal to my Love. ———

The Lady answer'd him with Blushes, That she was highly sensible to the Sentiments he express'd for her; that she lik'd his Person, and admir'd his Understanding; but that, to her Misfortune, she was married already; and therefore cou'd say nothing to his Proposal. ——— Good Heaven, cried *Polydore*, You are married! And who then is your Husband? The most unworthy of Mankind, answer'd she; One, who has abandon'd me to the Malice of my Fortune, and does not know at this Time what is become of me, nor trouble himself about it. ——— He is indeed unworthy, replied the Lover, who is possess'd of such a Treasure, and can neglect it. But, Madam, employ me in your Revenge: Command my Sword to pierce the Monster's Heart, and tear it from his Bosom. ——— No, said she, your Safety is more dear to me than the Desire of Revenge. All I ask of you is, to swear that you will never be like that Husband; but continue to love me equally when you know me better: Upon this Condition, I will grant you all the Favours which my Duty will allow, and perhaps, your future Conduct may prevail upon me to throw off all Restraint.——

The happy *Polydore* swore every Thing she desir'd, and she permitted him to see her when he pleas'd; but, being inform'd by him, of the Treachery of her Friend at whose House she lodg'd, they agreed to make their Appointments at another Place.

They continued this Commerce for some Time without any Interruption, till the Count *d'Aguilar* had Notice of it from his Confidante, who perceiv'd it in Spite of all their Caution.

Never was Rage equal to his at this Discovery. He writ to *Polydore*, reproaching him with his Breach of Friendship in the bitterest Terms, and requir'd him to meet him with his Sword behind the Walls of a Nunnery that was situated about two Leagues out of *Brussels*. *Polydore* accepted of the Challenge, and met him at the Place appointed: He attempted to justify himself, but the Count had not the Patience to hear him out: They fought with great Fury a good while, till the Fortune of *Polydore* prevail'd, and the Count fainted away with the Loss of Blood from two or three Wounds which he had receiv'd. The other
seeing

seeing him fall, thought him dead, and made off with the utmoſt Precipitation.

Juſt at that Inſtant came by a Coach and Six, which was driving towards the Nunnery: A Lady who was in it ſeeing a Gentleman lye weltring in his Blood, ſtopp'd her Coach, and went to try if ſhe could aſſiſt him: At the Sight of the Face ſhe fetch'd a Scream, and fell upon the Body in a Swoon. Her Servants concluding it was ſome Body ſhe was much concern'd for, carried them both into the Nunnery, where the Lady ſoon came to herſelf, and the Count alſo begun to ſhew Signs of Life, his Spirits being agitated by the Motion. He was immediately put to Bed, and a Surgeon ſent for, who declared his Wounds to be dangerous, but not mortal. While they continued uncertain of his Cure, the Lady who brought him into the Nunnery, waited conſtantly Day and Night at his Bedſide, and nurs'd him with a Care that wou'd not yield to a Moment of Repoſe. As her Face was always cover'd with a Veil he took her to be one of the Nuns, and was aſtoniſh'd at a Charity ſo officious. When he grew better his Curioſity encreas'd, and he ardently preſs'd her to let him know to whom he ow'd ſuch great Obligations. Are you a Nun, Madam? ſaid he: I hope you are not; for it wou'd afflict me infinitely, if I was never to ſee you more,

after

after leaving a House where you have done me so many Favours. —— The Lady for whom you fought, answer'd she, will make you soon forget the Loss of me; and tho' I am not a Nun, you will never see me out of the Limits of these Walls.

How, Madam! said he, was you not *out* of them, when you found me on the Ground, and saved my Life?

Yes, replied she; I was returning from a Visit to a Convent in the Town: But I will take Care not to stir from hence while you are at *Brussels*, because you are the Man in the World I would avoid.

This Speech so surpriz'd him, that for some Time he was not able to make her any Answer. At last he told her, that her Actions and her Words entirely disagreed, and that he cou'd not think himself so hateful to her as she said, when he reflected how kindly she had us'd him.

These Riddles shall be clear'd to you, answer'd she, when you are perfectly recover'd: Till then content yourself with knowing that I cannot hate you, but am as much determin'd to avoid you, as if I cou'd.

Thus ended a Conversation which left the Count in a Perplexity not to be described.

He saw her no more for a few Days; but when she heard that his Strength was
quite

quite return'd, she came to him one Morning, and spoke thus:

IF you wou'd know who she is that was so afflicted when your Life was in Danger; that nurs'd you so carefully in your Illness; and is resolv'd to quit you for ever when you are well; think of your former Gallantries at Madrid, of your present Passion for a Mistress that despises you, and your Ingratitude to a Wife that always lov'd you; think of all this, and you will not wonder any longer at my Actions or my Words.——*Yes*, Aguilar, *I am that Wife, whose Fate it is to be acquainted with all your Infidelities, and to smart for all your Follies.*

As she said this, she lifted up her Veil, and shew'd the astonish'd Count a well known Face, which he little expected to have seen in *Flanders*. All the Passions that can agitate the Heart of Man, Shame, Remorse, Love, Gratitude, Esteem, invaded his in that Moment. He threw himself at her Feet, and with many Tears implor'd her to forgive him.

SHE rais'd him, and assur'd him of her Pardon, nay, more, of her Affection: *But my Person*, said she, *I am determin'd, shall be ever seperated from you. I have had too many Proofs of your Inconstancy to hope that any Obligations can engage you: You will* never be faithful to me alone, and I difdain to fhare you with another. It is Happinefs enough for me that I have been the Inftrument of preferving your Life, though you rifqued it for the Sake of another Woman; and all the Return I ask of you is, to think of me fometimes with Kindnefs, but never to attempt to fee me more.

AGUILAR was on the Rack to hear her talk in fo refolute a Stile; but he flatter'd himfelf it was owing to her Jealoufy of Madamoifelle *Dalincourt*: Being impatient to make her eafy on that Head, he difpatch'd one of his Servants with a Letter to acquaint that Lady with his Recovery. He begg'd her earneftly to come to him at the *Nunnery*, and, if poffible, to bring her Lover along with her. *Polydore* had abfconded a few Days, till he heard that the Count was out of Danger, after which he continued very publickly his Addreffes to *Dalincourt*.

WHILE the Meffenger was bringing them to the *Nunnery*, *Aguilar* demanded of his Wife, by what Accident fhe came into *Flanders*?

You know, faid fhe, that after my Difcovery of your Amour with the Countefs *Altamira*, I retir'd to my Mother's Houfe, and remain'd there till your Departure for the Army.

SOON afterwards, I had the Misfortune to lofe my Mother, and what particularly

ag-

aggravated my Grief, was the Knowledge that her Concern at your ill Usage of me had hasten'd her Death.

These Afflictions made *Madrid* so uneasy to me, that I cou'd not bear to stay in it any longer. Luckily about that time I receiv'd a Letter from my Cousin *Donna Eugenia de Montalegre*, a Religious of this House, to inform me of her being elected Abbess: It instantly occurr'd to me, that no Place cou'd be more proper for my Retreat, than a Monastery, of which she was the Head: So, as soon as I cou'd settle my Affairs, I left *Spain*, and put myself into a Pension under the Government of *Donna Eugenia*; in which manner I have liv'd ever since.

She had scarce finish'd this Account, when they were interrupted by the Arrival of *Polydore* and *Dalincourt*. Madame d' *Augilar* changed Colour at the sight of her; but her Husband embracing *Polydore*, assur'd him, that he no longer lookt upon him as a Rival, but was glad to resign his Mistress to a Friend who so well deserv'd her. Then he related to him the Manner in which his Wife had tended and preserv'd him, and express'd so much Gratitude, so much Love, that if any thing cou'd have shaken her Resolution, this wou'd certainly have done it.—— Madamoiselle *Dalincourt* seem'd much affected at this Relation, and told

told the Countess, she was infinitely concern'd that she had been the innocent Cause of her Husband's Danger; but that she hoped this Accident wou'd be a Means of making them happy for the future, and put an End to his Infidelities, and her Resentment.

My Happiness too, added she, is now at Stake; and I have need of your Friendship to support me in a Discovery which I tremble to begin, but which, in Justice to my Honour, I am obliged to delay no longer.

At these Words she knelt down, and taking hold of *Polydore*'s Hand, *Behold, said she, my dear Husband, in that* Dalincourt *whom you have sworn to love eternally, behold your Wife* Emilia, *that* Emilia, *whom you left a Bride, and a Virgin at sixteen; whom you imagin'd dead, and who will not live a Moment, if you refuse to acknowledge and receive her.* ———

You cannot now complain that I am a Wife impos'd upon you; you chose me freely out of pure Inclination; our Parents had nothing to do in it; Love only engag'd us, and from Love alone I desire to possess you. This is my Claim, and if you are willing to allow it, I am blest to the Height of all my Wishes.

Polydore gaz'd on her with a silent Admiration; he examin'd every Feature

over

over and over, then throwing his Arms round her Neck, and almost stifling her with Kisses: *Are you really Emilia?* (cried he) *and have I confirm'd my former Marriage by a new Choice, by a Choice which I never will depart from, and which makes me the happiest of Men? O my Angel, what Wonders do you tell me! How is it possible that I find you here at* Brussels, *when I thought you in your Grave? Explain all this to me, and let me know how much I wrong'd you formerly, that I may try to repair it all by my future Conduct.*

Count *Aguilar* and his Lady joining with him in a Desire to know her History, she related it as follows.

The HISTORY of
Polydore and *Emilia.*

YOU may remember, *Polydore*, that as soon as we were parted, I went to live in the Country with my Father, being asham'd to appear in publick after the Affront your capricious Aversion had put upon me.

My Pride was deeply wounded, but with Shame I own it, my Love was the Passion that suffer'd most. I was bred up to consider you

you as my Husband; I had learn'd to love you from a Child, and your Person was so wonderfully agreeable, that I cou'd not look upon you with Indifference. Nay, such was my Partiality in your Favour, that I cou'd not help admiring you for your Spirit in asserting the Freedom of your Choice, and justified you in my Heart for a Proceeding which openly I was oblig'd to disapprove. In this wretched State of Mind I remain'd some Years, till the unfortunate Event of the Civil War depriv'd my Father of his Estate, and drove him out to seek Refuge in a foreign Country. We settled at *Paris*, where with three or four Thousand Pounds, which we found Means to carry off, Part in Money, and the rest of it in Jewels, we maintain'd ourselves well enough in a private Way, which pleas'd my Melancholy better than any other. In this Retreat, where we saw no Company, but two or three *French* Women that lodg'd in the House with us, I amus'd myself with learning the *French* Tongue, which I had some Knowledge of before I came to *France*; and by speaking nothing else for three or four Years, I became so very perfect in it, that it was difficult to discover by my Accent that I was not born at *Paris*. I mention this, because it has since been of Use to me, in making me pass more easily upon you for the *French* Woman I personated.—

nated.——The third Year of our Residence at *Paris*, my Father became acquainted with a Widow-Lady, the true Madame *Dalincourt*, whose Name has since made me full Amends for many Injuries I have to charge her with in the Sequel of my Story. This Woman was a Native of *Brabant*, but married a *French* Gentleman, who dying young, left her in very narrow Circumstances. She had a Sister much younger than herself, but not so handsome, who liv'd with her at *Paris*.

My Father was at that Time near three-score, and the Widow turn'd of forty; yet her Charms were still powerful enough to engage him in a Passion for her, which nothing but Dotage cou'd excuse. It went so far, that she drew him in to marry her, and to settle upon her Three Thousand Pounds, leaving me no more than the Worth of my own Jewels, which scarce amounted to a Thousand. But her Avarice was not satisfied with all this. There was a *French* Nobleman who had long courted me for a Mistress, and not finding me so complying as he wish'd, thought the best Way was to buy me of my Mother-in-law, whom he knew to be capable of such a Bargain. He offer'd her a Present of Two Thousand Crowns to introduce him by Night to my Apartment. The wicked Creature accepted of his Bribe, and taking her Opportunity when

when my Father was gone into the Country, brought him late one Night into my Chamber, where she imagin'd he wou'd find me fast asleep. But it happen'd that I and Madamoiselle *Du Fresne*, the Sister of *Dalincourt*, had been engag'd in reading a Romance, which kept us up beyond our usual Hour; and as her Room was on the other side of the House, not to disturb the Family in passing through, she went to Bed to me. The Romance run so strongly in my Head that I cou'd not sleep for thinking of it; and perceiving that the Moon shone very brightly, I got up, slipp'd on a Night-Gown, and went out to take a Walk in a little Garden that lay contiguous to my Chamber. I had not been there above half an Hour before I heard *Du Fresne* call out for Help; and coming in to her Assistance, saw my Lover struggling with her at such Advantage, that I was almost afraid I came too late. I join'd my Cries to her's, and the Noise we made so alarm'd the Marquis, that he thought it best to retire as soon as possible; especially when he discover'd his Mistake, and that my infamous Mother-in-law had put him to Bed to her own ugly Sister instead of me.

But, to be reveng'd of her for what he took to be a Design of imposing upon him, he reveal'd to us the Part she had in this Affair, and bid me tell her, that he

did

did not think the Enjoyment of Madamoiselle *Du Frefne* worth a quarter of the Money he had given her.——After making this Confeſſion he went off, and was hardly got ſafe out of the Houſe, when two or three of our Servants came in to us to know what was the Matter. The Story ſoon reach'd my Father's Ears; and I was ſo angry at my Stepmother for her Intention againſt my Honour, that in the Heat of my Paſſion I told him all that the Marquis had reveal'd; and *Du Frefne* confirm'd it; which Imprudence we had both Reaſon to repent of. My Father was ſo ſhock'd and afflicted at it, that it threw him into a Fever which prov'd mortal. He was no ſooner dead, but his loving Widow turn'd her Siſter and me out of Doors, and it was with great Difficulty that I carried off my Money, and neceſſary Apparel. In this Diſtreſs, which was the greateſt I ever knew, *Du Frefne* propos'd to me to go with her to *Bruſſels*, where ſhe had an old Aunt whom ſhe expected ſomething from, and that wou'd be willing to receive us. I gladly accepted her Propoſal, my Spirit being too high to return to *England* in the Condition I was reduced to. When we came to *Bruſſels* we found that her Aunt was dead, but had left her the beſt Part of what ſhe had, which amounted to a reaſonable Subſiſtence. We agreed that I ſhou'd board

with

with her under the Name of Madamoiselle *Dalincourt*, and pretend I was a Relation of her former Brother-in-law's; she not caring to say any thing of the last Alliance which had been attended with such ill Consequences to us both. Upon this Foot I liv'd with her very quietly, till the Count *d'Aguilar* found me out, and by corrupting my mercenary Friend, obtain'd more frequent Access to me than I desir'd.

You remember the Disorder I was in when he brought you first to see me: I knew you instantly; for my Love had trac'd your Image too strongly in my Mind to be effaced by any Length of Time; whereas your Indifference quickly made you lose all Memory of me, and the Alteration of almost fifteen Years had changed my Person entirely from what it was when you saw me last.—— I thought I shou'd have died with the Surprise, and was going, as soon as I cou'd speak, to discover myself to you; but perceiving that you did not remember me, I check'd myself, and invented a Pretence to cover my Confusion. It struck me, that I might possibly make some Advantage of the Disguise in which you saw me; at least, I was sure of the Satisfaction of conversing with you freely, and knowing what had happen'd to you since our parting. When you came to me again as the Confident of the Count *d'Aguilar*, it was no

small

small Revenge and Pleasure to me, to see you ignorantly helping another Man to debauch your own Wife; and I cou'd have found in my Heart to have let you succeed in your friendly Mediation, as a Punishment for the Injuries you had done me: But my Virtue soon rejected that Temptation, and I thought of nothing but how to gain your Esteem.

When you brought me the base Proposal from Count *Aguilar*, it appear'd to me such a Mark of your Contempt, that I fully resolv'd not to see you any more. But when you express'd a Repentance of that Fault, and declar'd a respectful Passion for me, even to the offering me Marriage, I yielded to the Dictates of my Love, and admitted you to all Freedoms but one alone. That I told you your future Conduct might obtain; and I believe, said she blushing, you will hardly now have the same Reluctance to accept it as you had formerly. But tho' I had thus engaged you by your Promise, and still more by your Inclination, my Happiness was far from being fix'd. While the Name of *Emilia* was conceal'd, I cou'd not tell how the Knowledge of it might affect you. It was still in your Power to make me miserable, by being angry with my innocent Deceit; but since you have been so good to approve it, and acknowledge me for your Wife, I shall make

make it my whole Study and Ambition, to deserve that Title; and never think of my past Misfortunes, but to inhance my present Happiness.

Thus *Emilia* ended her Narration, and receiv'd the Compliments of Count *Aguilar* and his Lady, who both express'd the highest Joy at her good Fortune.

Polydore, on his Side, endeavour'd to persuade the Countess to follow the Example of *Emilia*, and be reconcil'd to her Husband. She answer'd him coldly, That she had had too much Experience of the Temper of the Count, to trust to a sudden Fit of Fondness, which wou'd wear itself out in a few Months. That she was neither so young, nor so handsome now, as before their Separation; how then could she flatter herself, that he wou'd like her better when she was really less amiable? That what she had done for him might secure her his Esteem, but she had receiv'd abundant Proof that his Esteem cou'd but ill secure his Love. I know, said she, the Weakness of my Heart: Were I to live with him again, I shou'd be jealous of him, even tho' he did not give me Cause; and that wou'd certainly make us both unhappy. It is better for me to leave him to his Pleasures, and endeavour to secure my own Tranquility, by retiring from a World which I am unfit for.

Poly-

POLYDORE finding it in vain to argue with her, and admiring the Greatness of her Mind, took his Leave of the Count, and return'd to *Brussels*, where his Marriage with *Emilia* was *consummated almost twenty Years after it was contracted.*

LETTER XXXV.

SELIM to MIRZA at *Ispahan*.

From *London*.

I WENT Yesterday with one of my Acquaintance to see a Friend of his who has a House about twenty Miles from *London*. He had formerly been a Citizen and Tradesman, but growing rich on a sudden by some lucky Hit in the more profitable Trade of Stock-jobbing, he as suddenly set up for a Judge in Architecture, Painting, and all the Arts which Men of Quality wou'd be thought to understand, and built this House as a Specimen of his Learning. When we came in, though it was in the Midst of Winter, we were carried into a Room without a Fire-place; and which *look'd*, if possible, still colder than it *felt*. I suppose, said I, this *Stone-Vault* that we are in is design'd to be *the Burying-place* of the Family; but I shou'd be glad to see the Rooms in which they *live*, for the Chilness of these Walls is insupportable to a *Persian* Constitution.

I see, said my Companion, that you have *no Taste*, or else you cou'd not be cold in a *Saloon* so *beautiful* as this.

Before I had Time to make him any Answer, the Master of the House came in; but, instead of carrying us to a Fire, as I hoped he wou'd, he walk'd us about all his vast Apartments, then down into the Offices under Ground, and last into a Garden, where a North-East Wind, that blew very keen from off a *Heath* to which it was laid open, finish'd what the *Saloon* had begun, and gave me a Cold, which took away my Voice in the very Instant that I was going to complain of what he made me suffer. At length we ended our Observations, and sate down to Dinner, in a Room where, by good Fortune, the Rules of Architecture allow'd us to be warm: But when the Meat was serv'd, I was in great Confusion not to know how to ask for any Dish of all I saw before me; for, it seems the Gentleman eat in the *French Way*, and nothing came up to his Table in its natural Form: My Uneasiness was still greater, when, upon tasting of five or six different Compositions, I found they were all mix'd with the

Flesh

Flesh of * Hogs, which I could not touch without Pollution.

After losing my Dinner in this manner, I was entertain'd all the Evening with a Conversation between the Gentleman of the House and another Man (who, they told me, was an Architect) so stuff'd with hard Words and Terms of Art, that I cou'd not understand one Part in five of it. They talk'd much of certain Men call'd *Virtuosi*, whom, by the near Relation their Title bore to *Virtue*, I took at first to be a *Sect of rigid Moralists*: But, upon Enquiry, I discover'd that they were a Company of *Fidlers, Eunuchs, Painters, Builders, Gardeners*, and above all, Gentlemen that had *travell'd into Italy*, who immediately came home perfect *Virtuosi*, tho' they went out the dullest Fellows in the World. This Order of Men, which is pretty numerous (as I cou'd collect from the Discourse of *these two Adepts*) assume a Sort of *Legislative Authority* over the Body of their Countrymen: They bid one Man pull down his House, and build another, which he can neither pay for, nor inhabit; they take a Dislike to the Furniture of a second, and command him to change it for a different one more expensive and less commodious; they order a third to go and languish at an *Opera*, when he had rather be hallowing in a Bear-

* Larded.

a Bear-Garden: It is even fear'd they will take upon them to decide what Sort of Woman every Man shall be *in Love with*, and prescribe a particular Colour of Eyes and Hair for the only Object of *universal Inclination*.

I DESIR'D to be inform'd whether *this Jurisdiction* had been *ancient* in this Kingdom, having met with no Traces of it in History?

No, said he, it is so *modern*, that all the Laws of it are changed once in every seven Years; and that which before was *Right itself*, becomes at once *a High Crime and Misdemeanour*.

BUT, said I, does not the Parliament confirm it, at least, for its own Duration?

No, replied he, this Authority is exercis'd independent of Parliament; nay, it is even independent *of the Court*, and the Ministry must obey it as implicitly as the meanest of the People; for, all *Great Men* are desirous *to have a Taste*, and there is no other Way of coming at one.

UPON the Whole, it appears to me to be a Kind of *epidemical Madness*, and I am afraid to return to my own Country, for fear I shou'd carry it with me thither, as those who have been in *Italy* bring the Infection along with them into *England*.

LET-

LETTER XXXVI.

Selim to Mirza at *Ispahan*.

From *London*.

THERE is a Lady's House where I often pass my Time, tho' I have very little Intimacy with her; because it is really being in a *publick Place*, and making a Visit to half the Town. The first Time I went thither I congratulated her on the prodigious Number of her Friends, and told her, that she must certainly be possess'd of most extraordinary Perfections, to attract such a Variety of People, and please them all alike.—— But I soon found that in all that Crowd of Visitants there was hardly one who came thither on her Account, but that their Reason for coming was the same as her's for receiving them, because they had nothing else to do.

The last Time I was there I met a Gentleman, whose Character I was still a Stranger to, tho' I was very well acquainted with his Face.

I want to know (said I to a Lady who sate next me) what is the Merit of that

that Gentleman over-againſt us, which recommends him ſo much to all the World? It ſeems to me that he does nothing, ſays nothing, means nothing, and is nothing; yet I always ſee him in good Company!

His Character, ſaid ſhe, may be comprehended in very few Words —— He is a *good-natur'd Man.*

I am mighty glad to hear it, return'd I, for I want ſuch a Man very much: There is a Friend of mine in great Diſtreſs, and it lies in his Power to do him Service.

No, ſaid ſhe, he is of too indolent a Temper, to give himſelf the Trouble of ſerving any Body.

Then what ſignifies his *Good-nature,* anſwer'd I; or, how do you know that he *has any?*

During this Dialogue between us, the reſt of the Company had turn'd their Diſcourſe wholly upon Scandal; and few Reputations were ſpared by them, that were *good* enough to be thought *worth attacking.*

The *good-natur'd* Man ſate ſilently attentive, and with great Humanity let them abuſe his abſent Friends, as much as they thought fit.

When that was over, he begun to entertain us with his Sorrow for the Death of a Noble Perſon, who, he ſaid, had been his Patron and his Benefactor: But, methought,

thought, he talk'd of it mightily *at his Eafe*; and the Lady, who had given me his Character, whifper'd me, That, notwithftanding his Obligations and Love to *the Deceas'd*, he was now making Court to *his* worft Enemy, as obfequioufly as he ever had to *him*.

At that Inftant there came in a certain Colonel, who, as foon as he faw my Gentleman, ran up to him, and embracing him very tenderly, My dear *Jack*, faid he, thou fhalt be *drunk* with me To-night.——

You know I have been ill, faid the other gently, and *Drinking* don't agree with me.

No Matter for that, replied the Colonel, you muft pofitively be drunk before you fleep, for I can get No-body elfe to bear me Company.

The *good-natur'd Man* cou'd not refift fuch ftrong Sollicitations: He kindly agreed to the Propofal, and all the Room exprefs'd their Apprehenfions, that his *Good-nature* wou'd be the Death of him fome time or other.

LETTER XXXVII.
SELIM to MIRZA at *Ispahan*.

From *London*.

I HAD, last Night, so extraordinary a Dream, and it made such an Impression on my Mind, that I cannot forbear writing thee an Account of it.

I THOUGHT I was transported, on a sudden, to the Palace of *Ispahan*. Our mighty Lord was sitting on a Throne, the Splendor of which my Eyes cou'd hardly bear: At the Foot of it were his *Emirs*, and Great Officers, all prostrate on the Ground in Adoration, and expecting their Fate from his Commands. Around him stood a Multitude of his Guards, ready to execute any Orders he shou'd give, and striking Terror into the Hearts of all his Subjects. —— My Soul was aw'd with the Majesty of the Scene, and I said to my self, Can a King of *England* compare himself to this? Can he, whose Authority is confin'd within the narrow Bounds of Law, pretend to an Equality with a Monarch, whose Power has no Limits but his Will?

I HAD scarce made this Reflexion, when, turning my Eyes a second time towards the Throne, inſtead of the *Sophi*, I ſaw an *Eunuch* ſeated there, who ſeem'd to govern more deſpotically than he. The *Eunuch* was ſoon changed into a Woman, who alſo took the *Tiara* and the Sword; to her ſucceeded another, and then a Third: But, before ſhe was well eſtabliſh'd in her Seat, the Captain of the Guards that ſtood around us march'd up to the Throne, and ſeiz'd upon it: In that Moment I look'd and beheld the *Sophi* lying ſtrangled on the Floor, with his *Vizir*; and three of his *Sultanas*. Struck with Horror at the Spectacle, I left the Palace, and going out into the City, ſaw it abandon'd to the Fury of the Soldiers, who pillaged all its Riches, and cut the Throats of the defenceleſs Inhabitants. From thence I made my Eſcape into the Country, which was a waſte uncultivated Deſart, where I found nothing but Idleneſs and Want.

O, said I, how much happier is *England*, and how much greater are its Kings! Their Throne is eſtabliſh'd upon Juſtice, and therefore cannot be overturn'd. They are guarded by the Affections of their People, and have no military Violence to fear. They are the moſt to be honour'd of all Princes, becauſe their Government is beſt fram'd to make their Subjects rich, happy, and ſecure. ——

LET.

LETTER XXXVIII.
SELIM to MIRZA at *Ispahan*.

From London.

I HAD some Discourse To-day with an *English* Gentleman, who has an Affectation of being thought a great *Philosopher:* His Pretensions to it consist in nothing else, but refining away all the Happiness of his Life. By a great Force of Reasoning, he is arriv'd at a total *Disrelish* of *himself*, and as complete an *Indifference* to *others*. I am quite weary of living, said he to me; I have gone thro' every Thing that bears the Name of Pleasure, and am absolutely disgusted with it all: I have no Taste for Women, Wine, or Play, because I have experienc'd the Folly of pursuing them, and as for Business, it appears to me to be more *ridiculous* than any of the three. The Bustle of the Town disturbs my Quiet, and in the Country I am dying of the Spleen. I believe I shall go with you into *Persia*, only to change the Scene a little; and when I am tired of being there, take a Dose of *Opium*, and remove to the other World.

I HOPE, *Mirza*, that Thou and I shall never know what it is to be *so wise*; but
make

make the best of those Comforts and Delights which Nature has kindly bestow'd upon us, and endeavour to diffuse them as wide as possible, by the Practice of those Virtues from which they flow. ⸻

LETTER XXXIX.

SELIM to MIRZA at *Ispahan*.

From *London*.

THERE is another Gentleman of my Acquaintance, who is a *Philosopher*, but of a Species very different from him I describ'd to thee in my last.

HE is possess'd of a considerable Estate, which his Friends are as much Masters of as He: His Children love him out of a Principle of *Gratitude*, by far more endearing than that of *Duty*; and his Servants consider him as a *Father*, whom it wou'd be *unnatural* for them not to *obey*.

His Tenants are never hurt by Drought or Rain, because the Goodness of their Lord makes Amends for the Inclemency of the Sky.

THE whole Country looks *gay* about his Dwelling, and you may trace all his Footsteps by his Bounties.

Is it not strange (I have often heard him say) that Men shou'd be so delicate as not to bear a *disagreeable Picture* in their Houses, and yet force every *Face* they see about them to wear a *Gloom* of Uneasiness and Discontent?

Is there any Object so pleasing to the Eye, as the Sight of a Man whom you have obliged, or any Musick so agreeable to the Ear, as the Voice of one that owns you for his Benefactor?

SUCH are the Notions of this Man concerning *Happiness*; and it is probable they are not very *wrong*, for he himself is never *out of Humour*, nor is it possible to be so *in his Company*.

LETTER XL.

SELIM *to* MIRZA *at* Ispahan.

From *London*.

I Went last Night with my Friend to see a Lady, whose House is the favourite Resort of the most agreeable People of both Sexes. The Lady herself receiv'd me with a good Breeding, which I found was the Result of good Sense: She treated me as a *Stranger* that came *to see*, not like a *Monster* that came to be *seen*; and seem'd
more

more desirous to appear in a good Light herself to me, though a *Persian*, than to set me in a ridiculous one to her Company. The Conversation turn'd upon various Subjects, in all which she bore a considerable, but not a petulant or over-bearing Part; and with Modesty shew'd herself a Mistress of most of the living Languages, and not unacquainted with ancient and modern History.

The rest of the Company had their due Share of the Conversation, which was carried on with Spirit and good Manners: One Gentleman in particular distinguish'd himself, by the Superiority of his Wit, accompanied with so much Delicacy and Politeness, that none who heard him, felt themselves hurt by that *Pre-eminence*, which he alone seem'd not to be conscious of.

His Wit was all founded on good Sense; it was Wit which a *Persian* cou'd comprehend as easily as an *Englishman*; whereas most that I have met with from other Men, who are ambitious of being admir'd for that Accomplishment, is confin'd not only to the Taste of their own Countrymen, but to that of their own peculiar Set of Friends. When this Gentleman had entertain'd us for an Hour or two, with the justest, as well as liveliest Remarks both on Persons and Things that I ever heard, he went away; and to comfort us for losing him, there came in *the Man of great good Nature*, whom I describ'd to thee in one of my former Letters.

This *courteous Person* hearing all of us very warm in Praise of the *other's* Wit, join'd in with us, but ended his Panegyrick on it, with a plain, though indirect Insinuation, that there was a *Satirical Turn in it*, which render'd it very *dangerous*, and that the Gentleman cou'd not possibly be so witty, but at the Expence of his good Nature.

I cou'd not help being quite angry at so impertinent and ill-grounded a Reflection, on a Man for whom I had conceiv'd a great Esteem, and desir'd to know why he suppos'd him to be *Ill-natur'd*, only because he was not *Dull*. Has he abused, said I, any worthy Man? Has he defamed any Woman of good Character? If all the Edge of his Wit is turn'd on those who are justly the Objects of Ridicule, his Wit is as great a Benefit to *private Life*, as the Sword of the Magistrate is to *Publick*.

My Gentleman fearing to be drawn into a Dispute, which he cou'd not carry on without exposing the secret Envy of his Heart, chang'd the Discourse; and for the rest of his Stay among us, which was not very long, kept a most strict Silence, and gave no other Indications of Life, but that of laughing whenever any Body laugh'd; and Nods and Gestures of Approbation to whoever spoke.

THE Moment he was gone, I told my Friend, that I did not much wonder to see that Gentleman in *mix'd Company*, where it was enough that he gave no Offence; but that, in a select Society as this was, he shou'd be receiv'd only from a general Notion of his *Good-nature*, which was supported by no one Action of his Life, seem'd to me entirely unaccountable. For even allowing his Pretensions to that Title, I was surpriz'd that such a Character shou'd be so *scarce*, as to make it so very valuable.

I can easily conceive, continued I, that the notorious Reverse of that Virtue wou'd be a good Reason *to turn* a Man *out of Company*; but I can't think, that the Possession of that Virtue, destitute of all others, is a Reason for *letting him into it*.

IF you'll keep my Secret, replied my Friend, I'll tell you the whole Truth; but if you discover me, I shall pass for *Ill-natur'd* myself. You must know then, that there are about this Town, ten thousand such Fellows as this, who, without a Grain of Sense or Merit, make their Way by reciprocally complimenting one another. Their Numbers make them formidable, especially supported, as they are, by the fair Sex.

Sex. They sneak into good Company like *Dogs* after some Man of Sense, whom they seem to belong to; where they neither *bark* nor *bite*, but *cringe* and *fawn*; so, that neither good Manners nor Humanity will allow one to kick 'em out, till at last they acquire a sort of *Right by Sufferance.* They preserve their Character, by having no Will of their own, which in reality is owing to their having no Choice: They are all possest of some Degree of Cunning, and their Passions are too low and dull to break in upon't, or hurry them into the Indiscretions of Men of Parts. Besides, they know that they are in a constant State of Probation, where the least Transgression damns them: They carry no Compensation about them, for *active* Faults won't be borne, where there are at best but *negative* Virtues. The small Number of People of Sense are forc'd to submit in this, as in many other silly Customs, to a tyrannical Majority, and lavish undeservedly the valuable Character of Good-nature, to avoid being as unjustly branded with that of Ill-nature themselves.

MIGHT not another Reason be given for it, answer'd I? Are not *Vanity* and *Self Love* the great Causes of not only the Toleration, but the Privileges these People enjoy? And don't Security from Censure, Certainty of Applause, or the Discovery of an eminent Superiority, prevail with
these

those of the best Parts to really like, what they only pretend to suffer, the Conversation of those of the worst?

VERY possibly, reply'd my Friend; at least the *Vanity* of the wisest is certainly the *Comfort* of the weakest, and seems to be given as an Allay to superior Understandings, like Cares to superior Stations, to preserve a certain Degree of Equality, that Providence intended among Mankind.

LETTER XLI.
SELIM *to* MIRZA *at* Ispahan.

I HAD Yesterday the Pleasure of a Spectacle, than which nothing is more striking to a Foreigner, because he can have a right Idea of it no where else; I saw the three Estates of the Kingdom assembled in Parliament. The King was on his Throne in all his Majesty; around him sat the Peers in their different Robes; at the Bar stood the Speaker of the Commons, attended by the House. Several Laws were offer'd to the King to receive his Assent; and the Person who brought them up to him, made Obeysances, almost as low as *those* which are us'd in *Persia*, when we approach the sublime Throne of our mighty Emperor. I took Notice of the Humility of *these*

Pro-

Prostrations to a Gentleman that came with me: The Reason of them is this, answer'd he, That here the King appears in his highest Character, and the Honours that are paid him are to his Office; but where his Person only is consider'd, such extraordinary Submissions are not practis'd. Then he made me observe, that when the Commons sent up the Subsidies granted to the King, he thank'd them for 'em, as an Acknowledgment, that he had no Power to raise them on the People without their free Consent: Anciently, added he, Supplies of Money, and Redress of Grievances went together; but such is the present Happiness of our Condition, that we have *more* Money than ever to bestow, and *no* Grievances at all to be redrest.

Pray, said I to him, who are those upon yonder Bench, whose Habit is so different from the rest, and that look as if they belong'd to another Place? Those, said he, are the Bishops, who sit here not as *Bishops*, but as *Barons*.

I suppose then, return'd I, that while these Reverend Persons *do their Duty here* as *Barons*, they take Care to appoint *others* in the *Country, to do their Duty there as Bishops*.

He was going to answer me, when the House rose, and put an End to my Enquiries.

LETTER XLII.

SELIM *to* MIRZA *at* Ispahan.

From *London*.

THIS Morning I receiv'd a Visit from the Gentleman under whose Conduct I had been at the House of Lords. After some general Discourse upon that Subject, he askt me what I thought of their Nobility.

I AM too great a Stranger, answer'd I, to have form'd a right Opinion of what they are; but if you please, I will tell you freely what I think they shou'd be.

AN *English* Nobleman shou'd be a strenuous Assertor of the Privileges of the People, because he is perpetually intrusted with the Care of them; and at the same time desirous to preserve the just Rights of the Crown, because it is the Source from which his Honour is derived.

HE shou'd have had an Estate that might have set him above Dependance, and employ the Superfluities, if such there were, not in improving Luxury, but extending Charity.

HE shou'd make his Dignity easy to his Inferiors, by the Modesty and Simplicity of his Behaviour; nor ever think himself too great for the loweſt Offices of Friendſhip and Humanity.

HE ſhou'd claim no *Privilege* that might exempt him from the ſtricteſt Rules of Juſtice; and afford his *Protection* not to Men *obnoxious to the Law*, but to every modeſt Virtue and uſeful Art.

THE Character you have drawn, replied my Friend, though it be *Rare*, yet is not *Imaginary*: Some there are to whom ſtill it may belong; and it eminently exiſts in a young Nobleman, *Grandſon* and *Heir* to a late illuſtrious Commander, whoſe *Name* even in *Perſia* is *not unknown*.

LETTER XLIII.

SELIM *to* MIRZA *at* Iſpahan.

From *London.*

ABOUT a Fortnight ago I went in Company with one of my Acquaintance, to ſee a Place in this City call'd the *Exchange*, which is the general Rendezvous of all the Merchants, not only of *England*, but the whole trading World. I never yet came into an *Aſſembly* with ſo much Reſpect as into this. Theſe, ſaid I, to my Friend, are the moſt *uſeful*, and therefore the moſt

Honourable

Honourable of Mankind. They are met here to carry on the common Happiness; their *Gains* are the *Advantage* of the Publick; and their *Labour* makes the *Ease* of human Life.

By the Character you give me of *this Circle*, replied my Friend, you don't seem to think yourself *in a Court*, though there are so many * *Kings* round about you.

I see, said I, the Images of Kings, but I see neither *Dependance* nor *Adulation*. Besides, every Body *here* has some *real Business*, which alone were sufficient to distinguish them from the Crowd that fills a Drawing-room.

I had scarce spoke these Words, when he carried me out into a *neigbouring Alley*, where I also saw some busy Faces, but which lookt methought very different from the *others*. These, said he, are a sort of *Traders*, whose whole Business is confin'd within the Compass of this Alley, where they create a kind of Ebb and Flow, which they know how to turn to good Account; but which is destructive to all Trade, except *their own*. Nay, they have sometimes rais'd such violent *Tempests here*, that half the Wealth of the Nation has been sunk by it.

THEY

---

* The *Royal-Exchange* is set round with the Statues of the Kings of *England*.

They are then a sort of *Magicians*, anfwer'd I.

A moft *Diabolical One* truly, replied he; and what is moft wonderful, *the Mafters of the Art* have the Secret to render themfelves *invifible*: Though they are always *virtually prefent here*, they never appear to vulgar Eyes; but fome of their *Imps* are frequently difcover'd, and by their Motions, the skilful in this Traffick fteer their Courfe, and regulate their Ventures.

While he was faying this to me, there came up to us an ill-lookt Fellow, and askt if we had any *Stock* to fell.

He whifper'd me in the Ear, that this was *an Imp*——I ftarted; call'd on *Mahomet* to protect me, and made the beft of my Way out of the Alley.

LETTER XLIV.

Selim to Mirza at *Ifpahan*.

From *London*.

That *Abdallah*, whom I mention'd in a Letter is gone from *England*; thou wilt be affected with the Virtue of the Man, when I tell thee the Caufe of his Departure. He fent laft Week to defire I wou'd come to him; I came, and found him oppreft with the deepeft Sorrow. Ah, *Selim*,

Selim, said he to me, I muſt leave thee; I muſt go, and diſcharge my Duty to the beſt of Fathers; I muſt give my All for him to whom I owe it. At theſe Words, he put a Letter into my Hand, which he had juſt receiv'd the Day before: I found by it, that his Father, who was a Merchant, in a Voyage from *Grand Cairo* to *Aleppo*, was taken by a Cruizer of the Iſle of *Malta*, and being unable himſelf to pay his Ranſom, had writ to his Son to do it for him. Thou knoweſt, ſaid he to me, that I am not rich: To raiſe the Sum demanded for my Father's Liberty, I muſt ſell all my Effects, and leave myſelf without the Means of a Subſiſtance, except what my Labour can procure me. But my own Diſtreſs is not what concerns me moſt: The Fear of Poverty cannot fright me from my Duty; I only grieve for the Fate of my poor Wife, whom the Ruin of my Fortune will expoſe to Indigence and Shame. 'Tis for her ſake that I have ſent for you; and I conjure you by all our Friendſhip, by the Prophet and the God whom we adore, not to refuſe met he firſt Favour I ever askt. —— When he had ſaid this, he open'd the Door of another Room, where I ſaw a beautiful Woman in the *Turkiſh* Habit, who with a Modeſty peculiar to our *Eaſtern* Ladies, endeavour'd to conceal herſelf from my Regards. Come hither *Zelis*, ſaid my Friend, and ſee the

Man whom I have chosen to protect you: See him who must shortly be your Husband in the room of the unfortunate *Abdallah*. Then turning to me, and weeping bitterly, This, cry'd he, O *Selim*, is the Grace for which I am a Suppliant: Permit me to give her to a Man, who I know will use her well; I am resolv'd to divorce her this very Instant, according to the Power allow'd me by our Law, if you will consent to take her for your Wife. If the Charms of her Person are not sufficient to recommend her to you, know that her Mind is still fairer and more accomplish'd. I brought her with me into *England* three Years ago, in all which time, she has hardly stirr'd out of my House, nor desired any Company but mine. It is impossible to be happier with a Wife, than I have been with her: Nothing shou'd ever have prevail'd on me to part with her, but the Desire to separate her from my Misfortunes, and to procure her a Maintenance agreeable to her Birth and Merit, which I am no longer able to provide for her myself.

He had scarce ended, when the Lady tearing her Hair, and beating the whitest Breast I ever saw, implored him not to think of a Separation, more painful to her than any Misery that Poverty cou'd reduce her to.

After

After many passionate Expressions of her Love, she declared, that she wou'd accompany him to *Malta*, and beg her Bread with him afterwards if it was necessary, rather than stay behind in the most affluent Condition. But he positively refused to let her go, and insisted upon giving her to me, as the only Expedient to make him easy. I continued some time a silent Witness of this extraordinary Dispute; but at last seeing him determin'd to divorce her, I told him, I wou'd accept her as a Treasure committed to my Hands, not for my own Use, but to secure it for my Friend: That she shou'd remain with me under the Character of my Wife, but I wou'd always be a Stranger to her Bed; and if at his Return he found himself in Circumstances sufficient to maintain her, I wou'd restore her back again to him untouch'd; or in Case they shou'd mutually desire it, carry her with me to my *Seraglio* in the *East*. They were both much comforted with this Assurance, and *Zelis* consented to stay with me, since *Abdaliah* commanded it. The poor Man embarkt for *Malta* the following Week, with his whole Fortune on Board for his Father's Ransom, and left me so touch'd at his filial Piety, that I made an Offer to pay part of it my self; but he told me I had done enough for him in taking Care of what was dearest to him

him upon Earth, and refus'd any further Succour from me.

NB. *This Story is resumed* Letter 79.

LETTER XLV.
SELIM to MIRZA at *Ispahan*.

From *London*.

I LATELY fell into Discourse with an *Englishman*, who has well examin'd the Constitution of his Country: I beg'd him to tell me what he thought of the present State of it. Two principal Evils, answer'd he, are making Way for arbitrary Power, if the Court shou'd ever be inclin'd to take Advantage of them, *viz.* Corruption and *Eloquence*: The last is, if possible, more mischievous than the first; for it seduces those whom Money cou'd not tempt. It is the most pernicious of all our Refinements, and the most to be dreaded in a free Country. To speak Truth is the Privilege of a Freeman; to do it roundly and plainly, is his Glory: Thus it was, that the ancient *Romans* debated every thing that concern'd the Common-wealth, at a time when they best knew how to govern, before *Greece* had infected them with Rhetorick:

rick: As nothing was propounded to them with Disguise, they easily judg'd what was most for their Honour and Interest. But the Thing call'd Eloquence is of another Kind: It is less the Talent of enforcing Truth, than of imposing Falshood; it does not depend on a true Kdowledge of the Matter in Debate, for generally it aims at nothing more than a specious Appearance; nor is Wisdom a necessary Quality in the Composition of an Orator; he can do without it very well, provided he has the happy Facility of discoursing smoothly, and asserting boldly. I own to thee, *Mirza*, this Account surpriz'd me; we have no Knowledge in the *East* of such an Eloquence as this Man describ'd: It is our Custom to speak naturally and pertinently, without ever imagining that there was an Art in it, or that it was possible to talk finely upon a Subject which we do not understand.

Pray Sir, said I, when these Orators you tell me of have been caught two or three times *in a Lie*, don't you treat them with the utmost Contempt? Quite the contrary, answer'd he, the whole Merit and Pride of their Profession is to *deceive*: They are to lay false Colours upon every thing, and the greater the Imposition is, the greater their Reputation: The Orator who can only persuade us to act against some of our lesser Interests, is *but a Genius of the second Rate*; but he who can compell us by his Eloquence to violate the most essential, is *an able Man indeed*, and will certainly *rise very high*. I suppose, it may be your Custom in *Persia* to bestow Employments on such Persons as have particularly qualified themselves for them; you put the Care of the Army and the Marine into the Hands of Soldiers and Seamen; you make one Man Secretary of State, because he has been bred in foreign Courts, and understands the Interests of your neighbouring Princes; to another you trust the Revenue, because he is skilful in Oeconomy, and has prov'd himself above the Temptation of embezzling what passes through his Hands. Yes, replied I, this is surely the right Method, and I conclude it must be yours. No, said he, we are above those vulgar Prejudices; such Qualifications are not requisite among us; to be fit for all or any of these Posts, one must be *a good Speaker in Parliament.* How! said I, because I make a fine Harangue upon a Treaty of Peace, am I therefore fit to superintend an Army? We think so, answer'd he: And if I can plausibly defend a Minister of State from a reasonable Charge brought against him, have I thereby a Title to be taken into the Administration? Beyond Dispute, in this Country, answer'd he. Why then, by *Mahomet,* said I, your

your Government may well be sick: What a distemper'd Body must that be, whose Members are so monstrously out of joint, that there is no one Part in its proper Place! If my Tongue shou'd undertake to do the Office of my Head and Arms, the Absurdity and the Impotency wou'd be just the same.

YET thus, said he, we go on, lamely enough I must confess, but still admiring our own wise Policy, and laughing at the rest of the World.

You may laugh, replied I, as you think fit: But if the *Sultan*, my Master, had among his Counsellors such an *Orator* as you describe, a Fellow that wou'd prate away Truth, Equity and Common-Sense; by the Tomb of our holy Prophet, he wou'd make a *Mute* of him, and set him to watch over the *Seraglio* instead of the *State*.

AT these Words, I was oblig'd to take my Leave, and our Discourse was broke off till another Meeting.

LETTER XLVI.

SELIM *to* MIRZA.

THE next Day I saw my Friend again, and he resum'd the Subject of Eloquence. You can't imagine, said he to me,

me, of what fatal Consequence this Art of Haranguing has been to all free States: Good Laws have been eſtabliſh'd by wiſe Men, who were far from being eloquent; and eloquent Men, who were far from being wiſe, have every where deſtroy'd or corrupted them. Look into Hiſtory, you will find, that the ſame Period which carried Eloquence to its Perfection, was almoſt always mortal to Liberty. The Republicks of *Greece,* and that of *Rome* did not ſee their moſt celebrated Orators, till the very Moment that their Conſtitutions were overturn'd. And how indeed ſhou'd it be otherwiſe? When once it becomes a Faſhion to advance Men to Dignity and Power, not for the good Councils that they give, but for an agreeable Manner of recommending bad ones; it is impoſſible that a Government ſo adminiſter'd can long ſubſiſt. Is any Thing complain'd of as amiſs? Inſtead of Redreſs, they give you an Oration: Have you propos'd a good and needful Law? In Exchange for that you receive an Oration. Has your natural Reaſon determin'd you upon any Point? Up gets an Orator, and ſo confounds you, that you are no longer able to reaſon at all: Is any right Meaſure to be obſtructed, or wrong one to be advanc'd? There is an Orator always ready, and it is moſt charm-
ingly

ingly perform'd to the Delight of all the Hearers.

I DONT know, said I, what Pleasure you may find in being deceiv'd; but I dare say shou'd these Gentlemen undertake to instruct a Merchant in his Business, or a Farmer in his Work, without understanding either Trade or Husbandry, they wou'd only be laught at for their Pains; and yet when they attempt to persuade a Nation to commit a thousand senseless Faults, they are listen'd to with great Attention, and come off with abundance of Applause. But for my Part, I think they deserve nothing but Hatred and Contempt, for daring to play with such sacred Things as Truth and Justice, in so wanton and dissolute a Manner.

MOST certainly, answer'd he, they are very dangerous to all Society; for what is it that they profess? Don't they make it their Boast, that they have the Power to sooth or to inflame; that is, in proper Terms, to make us partial, or to make us mad? Are either of these Tempers of the Mind agreeable to the Duty of a Judge? I maintain, that it wou'd be just as proper for us to decide a Question of Right or Wrong, after a Debauch of Wine, or a Doze of Opium, as after being heated or cool'd, to the Degree we often are, by the Address of one of these skilful Speakers.

WISELY

WISELY was it done by the *Venetians* to banish a Member of their Senate, (as I have read they did) only becauſe they thought he had too much Eloquence, and gain'd too great an Aſcendant in their Councils by that bewitching Talent. Without ſuch a Caution there is no Safety; for we are led, when we fancy that we lead; and the Man that can maſter our Affections, will have but little Trouble with our Reaſon. —— But to ſhew you the Power of Oratory, in its ſtrongeſt Light, let us ſee what it does with Religion: In it ſelf it is ſimple and beneficent, full of Charity and Humility; and yet, let an eloquent Preacher get up into a Pulpit, what monſtrous Syſtems will he draw out of it! What Pride, what Tyranny will he make it authorize! How much Rancour and Malignity will he graft upon it! If then the Laws of God may be thus corrupted by the Taint of Eloquence, do we wonder that the Laws of Men cannot eſcape? No, ſaid I, no Miſchiefs are to be wonder'd at, where the Reaſon of Mankind is ſo abus'd.

LETTER XLVII.
Selim to Mirza.

THE Conversation I repeated to thee in my last, was heard by a Gentleman that sat near us, who, I have been told, has found his Account so much in Eloquence, as to be interested in the Defence of it: Accordingly, he attackt my Friend, and told him, he was afraid he had forgot his History, or he wou'd have recollected, that *Demosthenes* and *Cicero*, the two greatest Orators that ever were, employ'd their Rhetorick in the Service of their Country. I might perhaps, answer'd he, make some Objections to the Integrity of both; but allowing what you say, it amounts to no more than this, that Eloquence may be of Service to Mankind in the Possession of very good Men; and so may arbitrary Power, of the greatest Service; but yet we say in *England*, that it is wiser not to trust to it; because, as it is generally managed, it becomes a most grievous Oppression. And, I am sure, I can shew you in History as many Orators that have abus'd their Eloquence, as Kings that have abus'd their Authority: For besides the Wickedness
common

common to Human-nature, the Vanity of making a bad Cause appear a good one, is in itself a dangerous Temptation: When a Man sees he is able to impose upon the Judgments of others, he must be a very honest and very modest one indeed, if he never does it wrongfully. Alas, Sir, return'd his Antagonist, the Generality of Men are too weak to bear Truth! They must be cheated into Happiness, —— I am sure they are often *cheated out of it*, replied my Friend: Nor can I wholly agree to your Proposition in the Sense you understand it: It may be necessary for the Government of Mankind, not to tell them the *whole* Truth; something may be proper to be hid behind the Veil of Policy; but it is seldom necessary to tell them *Lies*.

THESE *pious Frauds*, are the Inventions of very *impious Men*; they are the Tricks of those, who make the publick Good a Pretence for serving their private Vices. Let us consider how Mankind was govern'd in those Ages and States, where they are known to have been the happiest. How was it in *Athens*, while the Laws of *Solon* preserv'd their Force? Was it then thought necessary to Lie for the Good of the Commonwealth? No,---the People were truly inform'd of every thing that concern'd them, and as they judg'd by their natural Understanding, their Determinations were right,

right, and their Actions glorious: But when their Orators had got the Dominion over them, and they were *deceiv'd* upon the Principle you establish, what was the Consequence? Their Leaders became factious and corrupt, and they who had given Liberty to the rest of *Greece*, most shamefully yielded up their own. In *Rome* the Case was much the same: As long as they were a great and free People, they understood not these political Refinements. All Governments in their first Institution were founded in Truth and Justice, and the first Rulers of them were generally honest Men; but, by length of Time, Corruption is introduced, and Men come to look upon those Frauds as necessary to Government, which their Forefathers abhorr'd as destructive to it. It does not, said I, belong to me, to decide in this Dispute; but it seems to be highly important, that *this Power of Deceiving for the Publick Good* shou'd be lodg'd in safe Hands. And I suppose, that such among you as are trusted with it, are very *constant* and *uniform* in their Principles; they never vary from themselves: What with them is the declar'd and essential Interest of the Nation *Now*, will certainly be so *next Year*: Disgrace or Favour can make no Difference.

LET-

LETTER XLVIII.

SELIM to MIRZA at *Ispahan*.

From *London*.

I WAS the other Day in Company with a Clergyman, who has the Education of several young Noblemen committed to his Care: A Trust of this Importance made me regard him as one of the most *considerable* Men in *England*. This Sage (said I to myself) has much to answer for: The Virtue and Happiness of the next Age will in a great Measure depend on his Capacity. —— I was very desirous to enter into Discourse with him, that I might know if he was equal to his Office, and try'd all the common Topicks of Conversation; but on none of these was I able to draw a Word from him: At last, upon some Point being started, which gave him Occasion to quote a *Latin* Poet, he open'd all at once, and pour'd forth such a Deluge of hard Words, compos'd out of all the learned Languages, that though I understood but little of his Meaning, I could not help admiring his Elocution.

As his Scholars were many of them born to an hereditary Share in the Legiſlature, I concluded he muſt be thoroughly acquainted with the *Engliſh* Conſtitution, and able to inſtruct them in the Knowledge of it: But upon aſking him ſome Queſtions on that Subject, I found to my very great Surprize, that he was more a Stranger to it than myſelf, and had no Notions of Government, but what he drew from the *imaginary Republick* of a *Greek* Philoſopher. Well, ſaid I, you at leaſt inſtruct your Scholars in *Græcian* and *Roman Virtue*; you light up in them a *Spirit of Liberty*; you exerciſe them in *Juſtice* and *Magnanimity*; you form them to a Reſemblance of the *great Characters* they meet with in ancient Authors. Far from it, ſaid a Gentleman in Company---They are accuſtom'd to *tremble at a Rod*, to tell *Lies* in excuſe of trifling Faults, to *betray their Companions*, to be *Spies* and *Cowards*: The natural Vigour of their Spirits is reſtrain'd, the natural Ingenuity of their Tempers varniſh'd over, the natural Bent of their Genius curb'd and thwarted: The whole Purpoſe of their Education is to acquire ſome *Greek* and *Latin* Words; by this only they are allow'd to try their Parts; if they are backward in this, they are pronounc'd Dunces, and often made ſo from Diſcouragement and Deſpair.

I shou'd think, said I, if *Words* only are to be taught them, they shou'd learn to speak *English* with Grace and Elegance, which is particularly necessary in a Government where Eloquence has obtain'd so great a Sway. That Article is never thought of, answer'd he: I came myself from the College a perfect Master of one or two dead Languages, but cou'd neither write nor speak my *Own*, till it was taught me by the Letters and Conversation of *a Lady about the Court*, whom luckily for my *Education* I fell in Love with.

I have heard, said I, that it is usual for young Gentlemen to finish their Studies in other Countries; and indeed it seems necessary enough by the Account you have given me of them here: But if I may judge by the greatest Part of those whom I have seen at their Return, the *foreign Masters* are no better than the *English*, and the *foreign Mistresses* not so good. Were I to go back to *Persia* with an *English* Coat, an *English* Footman, and an *English* Cough, it wou'd amount to just the Improvement made in *France*, by one half of the Youth who travel thither. Add to these, a Taste for Musick, replied the Gentleman, with two or three Terms of Building and of Painting, and you wou'd want but *one Taste more* to be as *accomplish'd*, as the finest Gentleman that *Italy* sends us back.

LETTER XLIX.

Selim *to* Mirza.

FROM considering the Education of *English* Gentlemen, we turn'd our Discourse to that of *English* Ladies. I askt a married Man that was in Company, to instruct me a little in the Course of it, being particularly curious to know the Methods which cou'd render a Woman in this Country so different a Creature from one in *Persia*. Indeed Sir, said he, you must ask *my Wife*, not me that Question: These are Mysteries I am not allow'd to pry into: When I presume to give my Advice about it, she tells me the Education of a Lady is above the Capacity of a Man, let him be ever so wise in his own Affairs. I shou'd think, said I, that as the Purpose of Womens Breeding is nothing else, but to teach them to *please Men*; a *Man* shou'd be a better Judge of *that* than any Woman in the World. But, pray Sir, what in General have you observ'd of this *mysterious Institution?* I don't enquire into the Secrets *behind the Altar*, but only the outward Forms of *Discipline* which are expos'd to the Eyes of all the World. Why Sir, replied he, the
first

first great Point which every Mother aims at, is to make her Girl *a Goddess* if she can.

A GODDESS! cry'd I, in great Astonishment. ——

YES, said he; you have none of them in the *East*; but here we have five or six in every Street: There never were more *Divinities* in *Ægypt*, than there are at this time in the Town of *London*. In order therefore to fit them for *that Character*, they are made to *throw off human Nature*, as much as possible, in their Looks, Gestures, Words, Actions, Dress, *&c.* —— But is it not apt to return again ? said I. —— Yes, replied he, it returns indeed again, but strangely distorted and deform'd. The same Thing happens to their *Minds* as to their *Shapes*; both are *crampt* by a violent Confinement, which makes them swell out *in the wrong Place*. You can't conceive the wild Tricks that Women play from this habitual Perversion of their Faculties: There is not a single Quality belonging to them, which they do not apply to other Purposes than Providence design'd it for: Hence it is, that they are *vain* of being *Cowards*, and asham'd of being *Modest*: Hence they *smile* on the Man whom they dislike, and *look cold* on him they love; hence they kill every Sentiment of their own, and not only *Act with the Fashion*, but really *Think with it*.

All

All this is taught them carefully from their Childhood, or elfe it wou'd be impoffible fo to conquer their natural Difpofitions.

I don't know, faid I, what the Ufe is of thefe Inftructions; but it feems to me that in a Country, where the Women are admitted to a familiar and conftant Share in every active Scene of Life, particular Care fhou'd be taken in their Education, to *cultivate their Reafon*, and *form their Hearts*, that they may be equal to the Part they have to Act. Where great Temptations muft occur, great Virtues are requir'd; and the *giddy Situations* they are plac'd in, or love to place themfelves, demand a more than ordinary Strength of Brain. In *Perfia* a Woman has no Occafion for any thing but Beauty, becaufe of the Confinement in which fhe lives, and therefore that only is attended to; but *here*, methinks, good Senfe is fo very neceffary, that it is the Bufinefs of a Lady to improve and adorn her Underftanding with as much Application as the other Sex, and, generally fpeaking, *by Methods much the fame.*

LETTER L.

SELIM to MIRZA at *Ispahan*.

From *London*.

I WAS this Morning with some Gentlemen of my Acquaintance, who were talking of the Attempt that had been made not long ago of setting up a Press at *Constantinople*, and the Opposition it had met with from the *Mufti*. They applied to me to know what I thought of it, and whether in *Persia* also, it was our Religion that deprived us of so useful an Art.

I TOLD them, that Policy had more part than Religion in that Affair: That the Press was a very dangerous Engine, and the Abuses of it made us justly apprehend ill Consequences from it.

YOU are in the Right, said one of the Company, for this single Reason, *because your Government is a despotick one*. But, in a free Country the Press may be very useful, as long as it is under no Correction; for it is of great Consequence, that the People shou'd be inform'd of every thing that concerns them; and without Printing, such Knowledge cou'd not circulate, either so easily or so fast. And to argue against any Branch of Liberty from the ill Use that may be made of it, is to argue against Liberty itself, since all is capable of being abus'd. Nor can any part of Freedom be more important, or better worth contending for, than that by which the Spirit of it is *preserved*, *supported*, and *diffus'd*. By this Appeal to the Judgment of the People, we lay some Restraint upon those Ministers, who may have found Means to secure themselves from any other *less incorruptible Tribunal*; and sure, they have no Reason to complain, if the Publick exercises a Right, which cannot be denied without avowing, that their Conduct will not bear Enquiry. For though the best Administration may be attackt by Calumny, I can hardly believe it wou'd be hurt by it, because I have known a great deal of it employ'd to very little Purpose, against Gentlemen, in Opposition to Ministers, who had nothing to defend them but the Force of Truth.

The Gentleman who spoke thus, was contradicted by another of the Company, who, with great Warmth, and many Arguments, maintain'd; 'That if the Press 'was put under the Inspection of some 'discreet and judicious Person, it wou'd 'be far more beneficial to the Publick.'

I Agree to it, answer'd he, upon one Condition, *viz*. That there may be likewise wife *an Inspector for* THE PEOPLE, as well as one for the *Court*; but if *nothing* is to be licens'd on one side, and every thing on the other, it wou'd be vastly better for us to adopt the Eastern Policy, and allow *no Printing here at all*; than to leave it under so *partial a Direction*.

LETTER LI.

SELIM *to* MIRZA *at* Ispahan.

From *London*.

THE same Gentleman, who, as I told thee in my last, argued so strongly for the Liberty of the Press, went on with his Discourse in the following Manner.

IF we have so much Reason to be unwilling, that what we *Print* shou'd be under the *Inspection* of the Court; how much more may we complain of a new Power assumed within these last fifty Years by all the Courts in *Europe*, of *inspecting private Letters*, and invading the *Liberty of the Post*? The Secrecy and Safety of Correspondence, is a Point of such Consequence to Mankind, that the least Interruption of it wou'd be criminal, without an evident *Necessity*; but that of Course, from one Year to another, there shou'd be a constant Breach of it publickly

publickly avow'd, is such a Violation of the Rights of Society, as one cannot but wonder at *even in this Age*.

You may well wonder, said I to him, when I myself am quite amaz'd to hear of such a Thing; the like of which, was never practis'd amongst *Us*, whom you *English* reproach with being *Slaves*. But I beg you to inform me what it was, that cou'd induce a free People to give up all the Secrets of their Business and private Thoughts, to the Curiosity and Discretion of a Minister, or his inferior Tools in Office?

They never gave them up, answer'd he; but those Gentlemen have exercis'd this Power by their own Authority, under Pretence of discovering Plots against the State. —— No Doubt, said one of the Company, it is a great Advantage and Ease to the Government, to be acquainted at all times with the Sentiments of considerable Persons, because it is possible they may have some ill Intent. —— It is very true, replied the other, and it might be still a *greater* Ease and Advantage to the Government to have a *licens'd Spy* in every House, who shou'd report the most private Conversations, and let the Minister thoroughly into the Secrets of every Family in the Kingdom. This wou'd effectually detect and

prevent

prevent Conspiracies; but wou'd any Body come into it on that Account?

Is it not making a bad Compliment to a Government, to suppose, that it cou'd not be secured without such Measures, as are inconsistent with the End for which it is design'd?

But such in General is the wretched Turn of modern Policy: the most sacred Ties are spurn'd at, to promote some present Interest, without considering how fatal it may prove in its remoter Consequences, and how greatly we may want those useful Barriers we have so lightly broken down.

LETTER LII.

Selim to Mirza at *Ispahan*.

From *London*.

THOUGH the *English* are a very warlike People, yet military Virtues and Abilities are neither so much consider'd or encourag'd by them, as many others of vastly less Importance: They seem to forget, that on these alone must depend the Security of the rest, and that every civil Excellence is useless, unless it be under their Protection. So careless is the Nation in this Point, that a General who has served with Reputation to himself and to his Country, shall have less Power allow'd him in the Government than a voluble Speaker in Parliament, or a drudging Pleader at the Bar. Nay, even in his own Province, at the Head of an Army, he shall be curb'd and thwarted by twenty People, who are got into military Employments, by the *peaceful Merit* of unbounded Complaisance, and who by virtue of their Posts in a War Office, take upon them to direct his Operations, and criticise his Conduct. Hence it has often been seen that *in the Camp*, where an absolute Authority is most necessary, there was neither *Obedience* nor *Subordination*; while in *another Place*, where they never shou'd be suppos'd, they were most regularly *establish'd* and *maintain'd*. There was, indeed, a *great General* in a late Reign, who kept himself superior to all *these Gentlemen*, during the Course of a twelve Years War; and therefore made it a very Glorious One; but it was not his *Merit* nor his *Success*, that set him above their Censures; it was wholly owing to a fortunate Relation he happen'd to have *with the first Minister*.

And this very General was afterwards disgrac'd in the midst of all his Glory, by the Cabals of a Man of no great Parts, and a Woman

LETTERS *from a*

a Woman, who had juſt *Wit enough* to influence *Another* that had *none*.

VERY different was the Conduct of the *French* King, in Regard to thoſe who fought his Battles in that War: Far from diſgracing them in their Triumphs, he rewarded them even in their Defeats; thinking the Zeal with which they ſerved him was a Merit, which though it cou'd not procure them the *Smiles* of *Fortune*, very juſtly entitled them to *His*.

SUCH a Policy as this, at the long run, muſt infallibly make a Prince victorious: For who wou'd not die to ſerve ſo good a Maſter? And how formidable is an Army that is animated by Sentiments of *Affection* as well as *Glory*.

BUT, I don't know how it comes to paſs, that the *Engliſh* Nation, whichhas often made a great Figure *in the Field*, and generally a very poor one *in the Cabinet*, is ſo laviſh of Favour and Rewards to *unſuccefsful Negotiators*, and ſo ſparing of them to its moſt fortunate Commanders.

LETTER LIII.

Selim *to* Mirza.

I AM return'd to this City, from which I have made a long Excursion, and am going to give thee an Account how I have past my time. A Friend of mine, who lives in a part of *England*, distant from the Capital, invited me to spend the Summer at his House: My Curiosity to see something new, and a natural Love to Fields and Groves at this Season of the Year, made me glad to accept of his Proposal.

THE first Thing that struck me in leaving *London*, was to find all the Country cultivated like one great Garden. This is the genuine Effect of that happy Liberty which the *English* enjoy: Where Property is secure, Industry will exert itself; and such is the Force of Industry, that without any particular Advantages of Soil or Climate, the Lands about this City are of a hundred times greater Profit to their Owners, than the best temper'd and most fertile Spots of *Asia* to the Subjects of the *Sophi* or the *Turk*.

ANOTHER Circumstance which engaged my Attention throughout all my Journey,

Journey, was the vaft Number of fine Seats that adorn'd the Way as I travell'd along, and feem'd to exprefs a certain *rural Greatnefs* extreamly becoming a free People. It lookt to me, as if Men who were poffeft of fuch magnificent Retreats, were above depending on a Court, and had wifely fix'd the Scene of their Pride and Pleafure in the Center of their own Eftates, where they cou'd really make themfelves moft confiderable. And indeed, this Notion is true in Fact ; for it has always been the Policy of Princes that wanted to be abfolute, to draw Gentlemen away from their Country Seats, and place them about a Court, as well to deprive them of the Popularity which Hofpitality might acquire, as to render them cold to the Intereft of the Country, and wholly devoted to themfelves. Thus we have often been told by our Friend *Ufbec*, that the Court and Capital of *France* is crowded with Nobility ; while in the Provinces, there is fcarce a Manfion-houfe that is not falling to Ruin ; an infallible Sign of the Decay and Downfall of the Nobility itfelf. Thofe who remember what *England* was forty Years ago, fpeak with much Uneafinefs of the Change they obferve in this Particular ; and complain, that their Countrymen are making hafte to copy the *French*, by abandoning their Family Seats, and living too conftantly in Town; but this

this is not yet sensible to a Foreigner. Thou may'st expect the Sequel of my Journey in other Letters.

LETTER LIV.

Selim *to* Mirza.

IT happen'd when I set out from *London,* that the Parliament, which had sat seven Years, was just dissolv'd, and Elections for a new one were carrying on all over *England*. My first Day's Stage had nothing in it remarkable, more than what I observ'd to thee in my last. But when I came to the Town where I was to lodge, I found the Streets all crowded with Men and Women, who gave me a lively Idea of what I have read of the ancient *Bacchanals*. Instead of Ivy, they carried Oaken Boughs, were exceeding drunk and mutinous; but at the same time mighty zealous for Religion. My *Persian* Habit drew them all about me, and I found they were much puzzled what to make of me. Some said, I was a *German* Minister, sent by the Court to corrupt the Electors; upon which Suggestion, I had like to have been torn to Pieces; others fancied me a *Jesuit*; but at last they agreed I was a *Mountebank*, and

as such conducted me to my Inn with great Respect. When I was safely deliver'd from this Danger, I took a Resolution to lay aside my foreign Dress, that I might travel with less Disturbance; and fell into Discourse upon what had past with a Gentleman that accompanied me in my Journey. It seem'd to me very strange, that in an Affair of so great Importance as the choice of a Guardian for their Liberties, Men shou'd drink themselves out of their Reason. I askt, whether Riots of this kind were common at these times. He answer'd, that the whole Business of the Candidates was to pervert and confound the Understandings of those that chuse them, by all imaginable ways: That from the Day they begun to make their Interest, there was nothing but Idleness and Debauchery among the common People: The Care of their Families is neglected; Trades and Manufactures are at a Stand; and such a Habit of Disorder is brought upon them, that it requires the best part of *seven* Years to settle them again. And yet, continued he, this Evil, great as it is, may be reckon'd one of the *least* attending these Affairs. Cou'd we bring our Electors to content themselves with being made drunk for a Year together, we might hope to preserve our Constitution; but it is the *sober, considerate Corruption*, the cool bargaining for a
Sale

Sale of their Liberties that will be the certain undoing of this Nation, whenever a wicked Minister shall be the Purchaser.

LETTER LV.

SELIM to MIRZA.

THE next Day brought us into a County Town, where the Elections for the City and the Shire were carrying on together. It was with some Difficulty that we made our Way through two or three Mobs of different Parties, that oblig'd us by Turns to declare ourselves for their respective Factions. Some of them wore in their Hats Tobacco Leaves, and seem'd principally concern'd for the Honour of that noble Plant, which they said had been attackt by the Ministry; and in this I heartily join'd with them, being myself a great Admirer of it's Virtues, like most of my Countrymen. When we came to our Inn, I entertain'd myself with asking my Fellow-Traveller Questions about Elections. The Thing was so new to me, that in many Points I cou'd not believe him. As for Instance, when he told me that in former Times the Counties and Boroughs us'd to *pay* the Members they sent to Parliamen for the Expence of their Journey and Attendance; but that now thofe Wages were withdrawn, and on the contrary, *the Candidates paid the Electors*; it feem'd to me incomprehenfible, that an Age fo mercenary in other Cafes, fhou'd be grown fo difinterefted in this. —— It lookt alfo very odd, that a Corporation fhou'd take fuch a fudden Liking to a Man's Face, whom they never faw before, as to prefer him to a Family that had ferv'd them time out of Mind; yet this, I was affur'd, very often happen'd, and what was ftranger ftill, on the Recommendation of another Perfon, who was no better known to them himfelf. My Inftructor added, that there was in *England* ONE MAN, fo extreamly *Popular*, though he never affected *Popularity*, that a Line from him, accompany'd with two or three Bits of a particular Sort of Paper, was enough to direct half the Nation in the Choice of their Reprefentatives.

IT wou'd be endlefs, to repeat to thee, all the Tricks which he told me other Gentlemen were forc'd to ufe to get themfelves elected. One Way of being well with a Corporation, is to *kifs* all their *Wives*. My Companion confeft to me, that he himfelf had formerly been oblig'd to go through this laborious Sollicitation, and had met with fome old Women in his Way, who made him pay dearly for their Intereft.

But these Methods, (said he) and other Arts of Popularity, are growing out of Fashion every Day. We now court our Electors, as we do our Mistresses, by sending a Notary to them with a Proposal: If they like the Settlement, it is no Matter how they like the Man that makes it; but if we disagree about *that*, other Pretensions are of very little Use. And to make the Comparison the juster, the Members thus chosen have no more Regard to their venal Constituents, than Husbands so married to their Wives. I askt, if they had no Laws against Corruption. Yes, said he, very strong Ones, but Corruption is stronger than the Laws. If the Magistrates in *Persia* were to sell Wine, it would signify very little that your Law forbids the drinking it. Upon the whole, he gave me to understand, that some of their Parliaments had not been much better Representatives of the Nation, than some of their Kings of God Almighty, whom they arrogantly pretended to represent.

LETTER LVI.

Selim to Mirza.

ON the third Day our Travels were at an End, and I arriv'd at my Friend's House with all the Pleasure which we receive from Retirement and Repose, after a Life of Tumult and Fatigue. I was as weary of Elections, as if I had been a Candidate myself, and cou'd not help expressing my Surprize, that the general Disorder on these Occasions, had not brought some fatal Mischief on the Nation.—— That we are not undone by it, replied my Friend, is entirely owing to the happy Circumstance of our being an Island. Were we seated on the Continent, every Election of a new Parliament wou'd infallibly draw on an Invasion.—— It is not only from Enemies abroad that you are in Danger, answer'd I: One wou'd think that the Violence of domestick Feuds shou'd of itself overturn your Constitution, as it has so many others; and how you have been able to escape so long, is the Wonder of all who have been bred up under absolute Monarchies: For they are taught, that the superior Advantage of their Form of Government consists in the

Strength

Strength of Union; and that in other States, where Power is more divided, a pernicious Confusion muft enfue.—— They argue rightly enough, faid the Gentleman who came along with me, but they carry the Argument too far. No Doubt, Factions are the natural Inconveniencies of all free Governments, as Oppreffion is too apt to attend on arbitrary Power. But the Difference lies here, that in an abfolute Monarchy, a Tyrant has nothing to reftrain him; whereas Parties are not only a Controul on thofe that Govern, but on each other; nay, they are even a Controul *upon themfelves* as the Leaders of them dare not give a Loofe to their own particular Paffions and Defigns, for fear of hurting their Credit with thofe whom it is their Intereft to manage and to pleafe. Befides, that it is eafier to infect a Prince with a Spirit of Tyranny, than a Nation with a Spirit of Faction; and where the Difcontent is not general, the Mifchief will be light. To engage a whole People in a Revolt, the higheft Provocations muft be given; in fuch a Cafe, the Diforder is not chargeable on thofe that defend their Liberties, but on the Aggreffor that invades them. Parties in Society, are like Tempefts in the natural World; they caufe, indeed, a very great Difturbance, and when violent, tear up every thing that oppofes them; but then they purge

purge away many noxious Qualities, and prevent a Stagnation which wou'd be fatal: All Nations that live in a quiet Slavery, may be properly said to stagnate; and happy wou'd it be for them, if they were rous'd and put in Motion, by that Spirit of Faction they dread so much; for let the Consequences of Resistance be what they wou'd, they can produce nothing worse than a confirm'd and establish'd Servitude: But generally such a Ferment in a Nation throws off what is most oppresive to it, and settles by Degrees, into a better and more eligible State. Of this, we have receiv'd abundant Proof; for there is hardly a Privilege belonging to us, which has not been gain'd by popular Discontent, and preserv'd by frequent Opposition. I may add, that we have known many Instances, where Parties, though ever so inflam'd against each other, have united, from a Sense of common Danger, and join'd in securing their common Happiness. This I think ought to free us from the Reproach of sacrificing our Country to our Divisions, and make those despair of Success, that *hope by dividing to destroy us.*

LETTER LVII.

Selim to Mirza.

FOR the first Month of my being in the Country, we did nothing from Morning till Night, but dispute about the Government. The natural Beauties round about us were little attended to, so much were we taken up with our Enquiries into political Defects. My two Companions disagreed in many Points; though I am persuaded they both meant the same Thing, and were almost equally good Subjects, and good Citizens. I sometimes fancy'd, that I had learnt a great Deal in these Debates; but when I came to put my Learning together, I found myself not much wiser than before. The Master of the House was inclin'd to the side of the Court, not from any interested or ambitious Views, but, as he said, from a Principle of *Whiggism:* This Word is one of those Distinctions, which for little less than a Century have divided and perplext this Nation. The opposite Party are call'd *Tories*. They have as strong an Antipathy to each other, as the Followers of *Osman* to those of *Hali*. I desired my Friend to give me some certain

Mark by which I might know one from the other. The *Whigs*, said he, are they that are *now in Place*, and the *Tories* are they that are *out*. I understand you, return'd I, the Difference is only *there*; so that if they who are now *Tories*, were *employ'd*, they wou'd instantly become *Whigs*, and if the *Whigs* were remov'd, they wou'd be *Tories*. Not so, answer'd he, with some Warmth: There is a great Difference in their Principles and their Conduct. Ay, said I, let me hear that, and then I shall be able to chuse my Party. The *Tories*, said he, are for *advancing* the *Power* of the *Crown*, and *raising* the Pride and Riches of the *Clergy*. They *garbled* our Army, *lost* our Honour, and were *assistant* to the Greatness of *France*.

You surprize me, replied I; for I have heard *all this* imputed to *some*, who, you assure me, are *good Whigs*; nay, the very Pillars of *Whiggism*.

I'll explain that Matter to you immediately, said the Gentleman that came down with me: Whiggism is an *indelible Character*, like *Episcopacy*: For as he who has once been *a Bishop*, though he no longer perform any of the Offices and Duties of his Function, *is a Bishop* nevertheless; so he who has once been a Whig, let him act never so contrary to his Principles, *is* nevertheless *a Whig*; and as all true Church-men are oblig'd in
Conscience

Confcience to *acknowledge* the firft, fo all true Whigs are in Duty bound to *fupport* the laft.

VERY well, faid I; but are there none who differ from this *Orthodox Belief?* Yes, faid he, *certain obftinate People*; but like other *Diffenters*, they are punifh'd for *their Separation*, by being excluded from *all Places of Truft and Profit.*

A HEAVY Punifhment indeed, anfwer'd I! But I have obferv'd, that all *Sects* are apt to *ftrengthen* and *encreafe* by *Perfecution*.

LETTER LVIII.

SELIM to MIRZA at *Ifpahan*.

From London.

I WENT with my Country Friend fome Days ago, to make a Vifit in a neighbouring County, to the Prelate of that Diocefe. His Character is fo extraordinary, that not to give it to thee, wou'd be departing from the Rule I have laid down, to let nothing that is *fingular* efcape my Notice. In the firft Place, he *refides* conftantly on his Diocefe, and has done fo for many Years: He asks nothing of the Court for

for himſelf or Family: He hoards up no Wealth for his Relations, but lays out the Revenues of his See in a decent Hoſpitality, and a Charity devoid of Oſtentation. At his firſt Entrance into the World, he diſtinguiſh'd himſelf by a Zeal for the Liberty of his Country, and had a conſiderable Share in bringing on the Revolution that preſerv'd it. His Principles never alter'd by his Preferment: He never proſtituted his Pen, nor debaſed his Character by Party Diſputes or blind Compliance. As he is at too great a Diſtance from the Scene of Action, to judge himſelf of what is doing, he has not thought fit to put his *Conſcience in the keeping of another.* Though he is ſerious in the Belief of his Religion, he is moderate to all who differ from him: He knows no Diſtinction of Party, but extends his good Offices alike to Whig and Tory; a Friend to Virtue under any Denomination; an Enemy to Vice under any Colours. His Health and old Age, are the Effects of a temperate Life and a quiet Conſcience: Though he has now ſome Years above Fourſcore, no Body ever thought he liv'd too long, unleſs it was out of an Impatience *to ſucceed him.*

THIS excellent Perſon entertain'd me with the greateſt Humanity, and ſeem'd to take a peculiar Delight in being uſeful and inſtructive to a Stranger. To tell thee the Truth, *Mirza*, I was so affected with the Piety and Virtue of this Teacher *; the Christian Religion appear'd to me so amiable in his Character and Manners, that if the Force of Education had not rooted *Mahometism* in my Heart, he wou'd certainly have made a Convert of me.

❀❀❀❀❀❀❀❀❀❀❀❀❀❀❀❀❀❀❀❀❀

LETTER LIX.

Selim *to* Mirza.

MY long Stay in the Country, gave me Leisure to read a good deal; I applied myself to History, particularly that of *England*; for rightly to understand what a Nation *is*, one shou'd previously learn what it *has been*. If I complain'd of the different Accounts which are given by the *English* of themselves in their present Circumstances, I have no less Reason to complain of their Historians: Past Transactions are so variously related, and with such a Mixture of Prejudice on both Sides, that it is as hard to know Truth from their Relations, as Religion from the Comments of Divines. The great Article in which they

---

* The Translator supposes, that the Author means Dr. *Hough*, the present Bishop of *Worcester*.

they differ moſt, is the ancient Power of the Crown, and that of the Parliament: According to ſome, the latter is no more than an Incroachment on the former; but according to others, it is old as the Monarchy itſelf.

This Point is debated with great Warmth, and a Multitude of Proofs alledged by either Party: Yet in truth, it is of very little Conſequence to the preſent Intereſts of the State. If Liberty were but a Year old, the *Engliſh* wou'd have juſt as good a Right to claim and to preſerve it, as if it had been handed down to them from many Ages: For allowing that their Anceſtors were Slaves, through Weakneſs or Want of Spirit; is *Slavery* ſo *valuable an Inheritance* that it never muſt be parted with? Is a long Preſcription neceſſary to give Force to the natural Rights of Mankind? If the Privileges of the People of *England* be *Conceſſions* from the Crown, is not the Power of the Crown itſelf a *Conceſſion* from the People. Thou ſeeſt therefore, that all this mighty Controverſy is rather Matter of Speculation, than of Uſe: However, I have endeavour'd to clear it up for my own Satisfaction, and deſign to give thee my Notions on that Subject, in ſome Letters where I conſider it more at large. I will finiſh this, by making one Remark on the Uncertainty of Hiſtory, *viz.* That

That those Accounts which are writ by Men concern'd in the Transactions they relate, though their Authority be generally most allow'd, are perhaps still more unlikely to be true, than those that are drawn from ancient Records, and common Fame; because Vanity and Self-love are more dispos'd to disguise the Truth, than the Publick to make wrong Judgments, or a diligent Collector to alter Facts.

LETTER LX.

Selim to Mirza.

IT is a usual Piece of Vanity in the Writers of every Nation, to represent the original Constitutions of their respective States, as founded on deep laid Systems and Plans of Policy, in which they imagine that they discover the utmost Reach of human Wisdom; whereas, in truth, they are often the Effects of downright Chance, and produc'd by the Force of certain Circumstances, or the simple Dictates of Nature itself, out of a Regard to some present Expediency, and with little Providence to the future.

Such was the Original of the celebrated *Gothick* Government, that was formerly spread

spread all over *Europe*, and though much defac'd by Time, is still distinguishable *here*. Notwithstanding the Admiration, which those who treat of it, affect to express of its wise Contrivance, it is plain, that it was casually establish'd; that it was produc'd not in a Cabinet, but a Camp; and owes much less to the Prudence of a Legislator, than to the Necessity of the Times which gave it Birth.

THE People that introduc'd it into *Britain*, and every where else, were a multitude of Soldiers, unacquainted with any thing but War: Their Leader, for the better carrying of it on, was invested with a sort of regal Power, and when it happen'd that the War continu'd long, he acquir'd a prescriptive Authority over those who had been accustom'd to obey his Orders; but this Authority was directed by the Advice of the other Officers, and dependant on the Good-liking of the Army, from which alone it was deriv'd: In like Manner, the first Revenues of this Leader, were nothing more than a Title to a larger Share in the common Booty, or the voluntary Contributions of the Soldiers out of the Wealth acquir'd under his Command. But had he attempted to take a Horse or Cow, or any Part of the Plunder from the meanest Soldier, without his free Consent, a Mutiny wou'd certainly have ensu'd, and the Violation

lation of Property been reveng'd. From these Principles, we may naturally draw the whole Form of the *Saxon* or *Gothick* Government. When these Invaders were peaceably settled in their new Possessions, the General was chang'd into a King, the Officers into Nobles, the Council of War into a Council of State, and the Body of the Soldiery itself into a general Assembly of all the Freemen. A principal Share of the Conquests, as it had been of the Spoils, was freely allotted to the Prince, and the rest by him distributed according to Rank and Merit among his Troops and Followers, under certain Conditions agreeable to the *Saxon* Customs. Hence the different Tenures, and the Services founded upon them; hence the Vassallage, or rather Servitude of the conquer'd, who were oblig'd to Till the Lands which they had lost, for the Conquerors who had gain'd them, or at best, to hold them of those new Proprietors on such hard and slavish Terms, as they thought fit to impose. Hence likewise, the Riches of the Clergy, and their early Authority in the State: for those People being ignorant and superstitious in the same Degree, and heated with the Zeal of a new Conversion, thought they cou'd not do too much for their Teachers, but with a considerable Share of the conquer'd Lands, admitted them to a large Participation of

Domi-

Dominion itself.—— Thus, without any settled Design or speculative Skill, this Constitution in a manner form'd itself; and perhaps it was *the better* for that Reason, as there was more of Nature in it, and little of *political Mystery*, which wherever it prevails, is the Bane of publick Good. A Government so establish'd, cou'd admit of no Pretence of a superior Nature in the Person of a King, or an unalterable Right in the Succession. It cou'd never come into the Heads of such a People, that they were to submit to a bad Administration for Conscience sake; or, that their Liberties were not every Way as sacred as the Prerogative of their Prince. They cou'd never be brought to understand, that there was such a thing as Reason of State distinct from the common Reason of Mankind; much less, wou'd they allow pernicious Measures to pass unquestion'd, or unpunish'd, under the ridiculous Sanction of that Name.

LETTER LXI.
Selim to Mirza.

I GAVE thee in my last a short Account of the first Rise and Constrvction of the *Saxon* Government, on very plain and simple Foundations. It was a mix'd State, and consequently limited, but the Limitations were not well ascertain'd: The different Powers that compos'd it, were mutually Checks upon each other; but to what Degree those Restraints were to be exercis'd, did not always sufficiently appear. The Nobles found the King too imperious, and the King the Nobles too incroaching; the Commons had Rights and Privileges, but with little Ability to make them good, unless when particular Conjunctures supply'd them with an extraordinary Force. The Clergy aw'd alike both King and Nobles, at once protecting the Commons, and oppressing them: They protected them for their own Interest against the Crown upon certain Occasions; but opprest them with infinite Exactions, and a Denial of all Justice against themselves. In this State the Government continued for a considerable Length of Time, till the Wisdom of two or three great Kings corrected many of its Errors, and brought the whole Machine into better Order; but the violent Invasion of the *Danes*, and much more that of the *Normans*, like a foreign Weight roughly laid upon the Springs, disturb'd and obstructed its proper Motions: Yet by Degrees, it recover'd itself again; and how ill soever the *Saxon* People might be treated, under the Notion of a Conquest, the *Saxon* Constitution was unsubdued. The new Comers relish'd Slavery no better than the old Inhabitants, and gladly join'd with them upon a Sense of mutual Interest, to force a Confirmation of their Freedom and the ancient Laws. Indeed, there was so great a Conformity between the Government of *Normandy* and that of *England*, the Customs of both Nations were so much the same, that unless the *Normans* by conquering this Island had lost their original Rights, and fought on Purpose to degrade themselves and their Posterity, it was impossible their Kings cou'd have a Right to absolute Power. When therefore they attempted to assume it, they were vigorously oppos'd. Civil Wars ensu'd, which ended to the Disadvantage of the Crown; but the Misfortune was, that in all these Struggles, *the Nobles treated for the People*, not the People *for themselves*; and therefore their Interests were much neglected, and the Advantages

vantages gain'd by the Nobles grew as heavy a Burthen to them as the very Powers they had taken from the King. It then became the Interest of the King to raise the People in Opposition to the Nobility; and they felt the Effects of this Jealousy, far more to their Advantage than they had done the Friendship of the Nobles; for in Process of Time, they grew a Match for them and the Crown itself; by which happy Alteration in their Circumstances, the whole Frame of the Government was chang'd, and a new Ballance of Power introduc'd, better pois'd than it ever was before. Yet many principal Causes that brought about this great Revolution were purely accidental, and the Consequences of them unforeseen by those who laid them; so great a Share has Fortune in the Events which are generally attributed to Policy.

LETTER LXII.

SELIM *to* MIRZA.

THOU wilt be surpriz'd to hear that the Period when the *English* Nation enjoy'd the greatest Happiness was under the Influence of *a Woman*. As much as we *Persians* shou'd despise a female Ruler; it was not till the Reign of Queen *Elizabeth*, that this Government came to an equal Ballance, which is the true Perfection of it.

To shew what this happy Situation was, it will be necessary to give thee some Idea of what Parliaments had been till her Time.

The Assembly of the People under the *Saxons*, was more properly *a Diet* than a *Parliament*. All the Freemen had a Right to be present there; but how far they had to *Vote* in it, is uncertain. It is probable, that in most Affairs they were determin'd by the Advice and Authority of the principal or leading Men.

After the Invasion of the *Normans*, these Assemblies seldom met, and by Degrees, wholly lost their former Shape: The Commons were no longer present in them; and when *afterwards* they came thither by *Deputation*, (not promiscuously, as before) the People were no great Gainers by it; for the whole Strength of the Government resided in the Barons and the Clergy, who did what they pleas'd in all Affairs. The Proceedings of the Commons cou'd not be free in their *Representative Body*, while they were feeble and opprest in their *Collective*. The Laws of Vassallage, and the Immunities of the Church hung heavy upon them,

and

and hinder'd them from acting with any Vigour. Without the Nobles or Clergy on their Side, they durst refuse nothing to the Crown, and so strong was their Dependancy upon them, that we find in most of the Civil Wars, they blindly follow'd the Passions of both, and made or unmade Kings as they directed. But in return for their Services they got their Liberties confirm'd, and many of their Grievances redrest; they reveng'd themselves on the Ministers that opprest them, and obtain'd good Laws for the Common-wealth. Nor indeed, did any Parliament, *freely chosen*, ever consent to establish Slavery by Law, but their Rights continued always *unretracted*, though *weakly* maintain'd.

Such was the Condition of the House of Commons for many Centuries, and that it was not able to support itself at all under so many Disadvantages, shews a great natural Strength in its Constitution. That Strength was exerted by Degrees; its Privileges were considerably enlarg'd, and it became in Fact, as well as Name, a third Part of the Legislature. The Laws of Vassallage were broken through; the Estates of the Nobles were made alienable; the Weight of Property was transferr'd to the Side of the People. Many Accidents concurr'd to the same Effect. A Reformation in Religion was begun, by which that mighty Fabrick of Church Power, erected on the Ruins of publick Liberty, and adorn'd with the Spoils of the Crown itself, was happily attackt and overturn'd. The immense Possessions of the Clergy were taken away, and most of them bestow'd upon *the Commons*. They had now the greatest Share of the Lands of *England*, and a still greater Treasure in their Commerce, which they were beginning to extend and improve. Their Riches secured their Independancy; the Clergy fear'd them, and the Nobles cou'd not hurt them. In this State, Queen *Elizabeth* found *the Parliament:* The Lords and Commons were nigh upon a Level, and the Church in a decent Subordination. She had Skill enough to give to each its proper Weight, and yet keep her own Authority entire: She was the Head of this well-proportion'd Body, and supreamly directed all its Motions. Thus, what in 'mix'd Forms of Government seldom happens there was; no Contest for Power in the Legislature; because no part was so high as to be uncontroul'd, or so low as to be opprest. The great End of Government was attain'd in the Satisfaction of the People, and every other Happiness follow'd *that*, as every Misfortune and Disgrace is sure to attend on their Discontent.

LETTER LXIII.

SELIM to MIRZA.

I ENDED my last Letter with the Felicity of *Elizabeth*'s Reign: Very different was that of her Successor *James* the First: for his Character and Conduct were the reverse of hers. He endeavour'd to break the Ballance of the Government by her so wisely fixt; and begun a Struggle for Power with his People, without one Quality that cou'd render him capable of going through with it to his Advantage: He had neither Courage, Ability, nor Address: He was contemn'd both at Home and Abroad; his very Favourites did not love him, though he sacrificed every thing to them: Yet by the single Force of Luxury, he so weaken'd the Spirit of the Nation, that he made great Advances towards effecting the Point he aim'd at, *viz.* rendering himself absolute: And that he did not compleat it, was rather owing to the Indigence to which he had reduc'd himself, and want of personal Resolution, than any Difficulties he met with. The Clergy, whom he corrupted among the rest, were very assistant to him, by preaching up

Notions which they seem to have borrow'd from *our* Religion, of a Right Divine in Kings, and other such *Mahometan* Tenets, that had never been heard of in this Country. And they were reciprocally assisted by the King in the Introduction of certain Ceremonies, of little use but to encrease their own Authority. But there were many who disliked these Innovations, and their Opposition hinder'd them from spreading quite so far as the Court desir'd. These obstinate Protestants and Patriots were branded with the Name of Puritans, and much hated by *James*, and *Charles* his Son, who upon the Decease of the former, succeeded to his Kingdoms and Designs. He had many better Qualities then his Father, but as wrong a Judgment, and greater Obstinacy. He carried his Affection for the Clergy, and Abhorrence of the Puritans, to an Excess of Bigottry and Rage. He agreed so ill with his Parliaments, that he soon grew weary of them, and resolv'd to be troubled with no more: None were call'd for several Years together, and all that time he govern'd as despotically as the *Sophi* of *Persia*. The Laws were either openly infring'd, or explain'd in the Manner he directed: He levied Money upon his Subjects against Privileges expresly confirm'd by himself. In short, his Passion for Power might have been fully gratified, if his more prevailing

prevailing one to Bigottry had not engag'd him in a senseless Undertaking, of forcing the same Form of Worship upon his Subjects in *Scotland*, as he had declar'd himself so warmly for in *England*. It is safer to attack Men in their Civil Rights, than their Religious Opinions: The *Scots*, who had acquies'd under Tyranny, took up Arms against Persecution. Their Insurrection made it necessary to call a Parliament; it met, but was instantly dissolv'd by the intemperate Folly of the Court. All Hopes of of better Measures were put an End to, by this last Provocation. The *Scots* marched into *England*, and were receiv'd by the *English*, not as Enemies, but as Brothers and Allies: The King, unable to oppose them, was compell'd to ask the Aid of another Parliament. A Parliament met, inflam'd with the Oppressions of fifteen Years: The principal Members of it were Men whom the Necessity and Danger of the Times had render'd equally able and determin'd: They resolv'd to make use of the Opportunity to redress their Grievances, and secure their Liberty; the King granted every thing that was necessary to either of those Ends; but what perhaps was really Concession, had the Appearance of Constraint, and therefore gain'd neither Gratitude nor Confidence: The Nation cou'd no longer trust the King, or if it might, particular

Men cou'd not, and the Support of thofe particular Men was become a National Concern: They had expos'd themfelves by ferving the Publick; the Publick therefore judg'd that it was bound in Juftice to defend them. Nor indeed was it poffible, when the Work of Reformation was begun, to keep People who were fore with the Remembrance of Injuries receiv'd, within the Bounds of a proper Moderation. Such a Sobriety is much eafier in Speculation than it ever was in Practife. Thus partly for the Safety of their Leaders, and partly from a Jealoufy of his Intentions, the Parliament drew the Sword againft the King: But the Sword when drawn, was no longer theirs; it was quickly turn'd againft them by thofe to whofe Hands they trufted it: The honefteft and wifeft of both Parties were out-witted and over-power'd by Villains: Yhe King perifh'd, and the Conftitution perifh'd with him.

A PRIVATE Man, whofe Genius was call'd forth by the Troubles of his Country, and form'd in the Exercife of Faction, ufurp'd the Governmant. His Character was as extraordinary as his Fortune: He was Enthufiaft enough to be agreeable to the Humour of the Times; and yet fenfible enough to govern his Enthufiafm by the Rules of Prudence. He trampl'd on the Laws of the Nation, but he rais'd the

the Glory of it; and it is hard to say which he deserv'd most, a Halter or a Crown.

At his Death, (which was a natural one in his height of Power) all Order was lost in the State: Various Tyrannies were set up, and destroy'd each other; but all shew'd a Republick to be impracticable. At last, the Nation growing weary of such wild Confusion, agreed to recall the banish'd Son of their murder'd King, and restor'd him without any Limitations, even such as had been legally obtain'd before the Troubles. Thus the Fruits of a tedious Civil War were lightly and wantonly thrown away, by too hasty a Passion for Repose. The Constitution reviv'd indeed again, but reviv'd *as sickly as before*: The ill Humours which ought to have been purg'd away by the violent Remedies that had been us'd, continu'd as prevalent as ever, and naturally broke out in the same Distempers. The King wanted to set himself above the Law; wicked Men encourag'd this Disposition, and many good Men were weak enough to comply with it, out of Aversion to those Principles of Resistance which they had seen so fatally abus'd.

LETTER LXIV.

Sliem to Mirza.

THE Methods purſued by Charles the ſecond, in the Conduct of his Government, were in many Reſpects different from his Father's, though the Purpoſe of both was much the ſame. The Father always *Bully'd* his Parliaments; the Son endeavour'd to *Corrupt* them: The Father obſtinately refus'd to change his Miniſters, becauſe he really eſteem'd them as honeſt Men: The Son very eaſily chang'd *his*, becauſe he thought they were all *alike* diſhoneſt, and that his Deſigns might as well be carried on by one *Knave* as by another: The Father was a Tool of the Clergy, and a Perſecutor, out of Zeal for his Religion; The Son was quite indifferent to Religion, but ſerv'd the Paſſions of his Clergy againſt their Enemies from Motives of Policy: The Father deſir'd to be abſolute at Home, but to make the Nation reſpectable Abroad; The Son aſſiſted the King of *France* in his Invaſions on the Liberties of *Europe*, that by his Help he might maſter thoſe of *England*: Nay, he was even a Penſioner to *France*, and by ſo vile a Proſtitution of his Dignity, ſet an Example to the Nobility of his Realm, to
ſell

sell *their Honour likewise* for a *Pension*; an Example, the ill Effects of which have been felt too sensibly ever since.

THUS, a Conduct the most infamous to the Prince, was also the most dangerous to the People, and Oppression was so much the more heavy, as it was not gilded with any outward Lustre.

YET with all these Vices and Imperfections in the Character of *Charles* the second, there was something so bewitching in his Behaviour, that the Charms of it prevail'd on many to connive at the Faults of his Government: And indeed, nothing is so hurtful to a Country, which has Liberties to defend, as a Prince who knows how at the same time to make himself *despotick* and *agreeable*: This was eminently the Talent of *Charles* the second, and what is most surprising, he possest it without any great Depth of Understanding.

BUT the principal Instrument of his bad Intentions, was a general Depravity of Manners, with which he took Pains to infect his Court, and they the Nation. All Virtue, both publick and private, were openly ridicul'd; and none were allow'd to have any Talents for Wit or Business, who pretended to any Sense of Honour, or Regard to Decency.

THE King made great Use of these new Notions, and they prov'd very pernicious

nicious to the Freedom, as well as Morals of his Subjects: But an Indolence natural to his Temper, was some Check to his Designs; and fond as he was of arbitrary Power, he did not pursue it any further, than was consistent with his *Pleasure* and *Repose*.

IN the following Reign, the Evil still encreast, as it had been justly apprehended.

The Spirit of *Bigottry* was added to the Spirit of *Tyranny*, and an *enterprising* Temper to a *weak* Understanding: A Change of Religion was attempted as well as of Government, which rouz'd those whom no Danger to the latter cou'd ever have alarm'd, and taught the Preachers of *Non-resistance* to *Resist*. A Revolution was evidently necessary to save the whole, and that Necessity produc'd one. ——

KING *James* the second lost his Crown, and the Nation gave it to their Deliverer the Prince of *Orange*: The Government was settled on a new Foundation, agreeable to the ancient *Saxon* Principles from which it had declin'd; and by a *Happiness* peculiar to itself, grew *stronger* from the *Shocks* it had *sustain'd*.

LETTER LXV.

SELIM *to* MIRZA.

THE first Advantage gain'd by the *English* Nation in the change of their Govern-

Government, was the utter Extinction of thofe vain and empty Phantomes of *hereditary inalianable Right*, and a Power *not subject to controul*, which King *James* the firſt had conjur'd up, to the great Diſturbance and Terror of his People. With *James* the ſecond they were expell'd, nor can they ever be brought back again with any Proſpect of Succeſs, but by *that Family* alone, which *claims from him*: For which Reaſon it will eternally be the Intereſt of the People of *England* not to ſuffer ſuch a *Claim* to prevail; but to maintain an Eſtabliſhment which is founded on the Baſis of their Liberty, and inſeperably connected with it.

As the Parliament plainly diſpos'd of the Crown in altering the Succeſſion, the Princes who have reign'd ſince that time, cou'd pretend to none but a *Parliamentary Title*, and the ſame Force as the Legiſlature cou'd give to that, it alſo gave to the Privileges of the Subject.

The Word *Loyalty*, which had long been miſapplied, recover'd its original and proper Senſe; it was now underſtood to mean no more than a due Obedience to the Authority of the King, in Conformity to the Laws, inſtead of a bigotted Compliance to the Will of the King, in Oppoſition to the Laws.

How great an Advantage this muſt be, will appear by reflecting on the Miſchiefs that have been brought upon *this* Country in particular, from the wrong Interpretation *of certain Names*. But this is not the only Benefit that ensu'd from that happy Revolution. The Prerogative of the Crown had been till then so ill defin'd, that the full Extent of it was rather stopt by the Degree of *Prudence* in the Government, or of *Impatience* in the People, than by the Letter of the Law: Nay, it seem'd as if in many Instances the Law allow'd a Power to the King, entirely destructive to itself. Thus Princes have been often made to believe, that what their Subjects complain'd of as Oppression, was a legal Exercise of their Right; and no Wonder, if in disputable Points, they decided the Question in Favour of their own Authority.

But now the Bounds of Prerogative were markt out by express Restrictions; the Course of it became regular and fix'd; and cou'd no longer move obliquely to the Danger of the general System.

Thou wilt therefore observe this Difference between the Government in the Reign of Queen *Elizabeth*, and the State of it since the Revolution; that *Elizabeth* chose to rule by Parliaments, from the Goodness of her Understanding; but Princes now are forc'd to do so *from Necessity*; because all Expedients of governing without them are manifestly *impracticable*

cable. I will explain this to thee more distinctly when I write again. In the mean while, let me a little recall thy Thoughts from past Events, and the *History of* England, to the Remembrance and Love of thy faithful *Selim*, who is not become so much an *Englishman* as to forget his native *Persia*, but perpetually sighs for his Friends and Country amidst all that engages his Attention in a foreign Land.

LETTER LXVI.

Selim *to* Mirza.

THE ancient Revenues of the Kings of *England*, consisted chiefly in a large Demesn of Lands, and certain Rights and Powers reserv'd to them over the Lands held of the Crown; by Means of which they supported the Royal Dignity without the immediate Assistance of the People except upon extraordinary Occasions. But in Process of Time, the Extravagance of Princes, and the Rapaciousness of Favourites having wasted the best part of this Estate, and their Successors endeavouring to repair it by a tyrannical Abuse of those Rights and Powers, some of them, which were found to be moſt grievous, were bought off by the Parliament, with a fix'd Eſtabliſhment for the Maintenance of the Houſhold, compos'd of certain Taxes yearly rais'd, and appropriated thereto.

But after the *Expulſion of the Stuarts* the Expence of the Government being augmented for the Defence of the Succeſſion, the Crown was conſtrain'd to apply to Parliament, not only for the Maintenance of its Houſhold, which was ſettled at the beginning of every Reign, and in every Reign *conſiderably encreaſt* ; not only for extraordinary Supplies, to which End Parliaments anciently were call'd : but for the ordinary Service of the Year.

Thus a continual Dependance on the People became neceſſary to Kings, and they were ſo truly the *Servants* of the Publick, that they receiv'd the *Wages* of it in Form, and were oblig'd to the Parliament for the Means of exerciſing their Royalty, as well as for the Right they had to claim it. Nor can this ſalutary Dependance ever ceaſe, except the Parliament itſelf ſhou'd give it up, by impowering the King to raiſe Money without *limiting the Sum*, or *ſpecifying the Services*. Such Conceſſions are abſurd in their own Nature ; for if a Prince is afraid to truſt his People with a Power of ſupplying his Neceſſities upon a thorough

Know-

Knowledge of them, the People have no Encouragement to trust their Prince, or to speak more properly, his Minister, with so blind and undetermin'd an Authority.

LETTER LXVII.

SELIM to MIRZA.

IN providing for the Maintenance of their Kings, the People of *England* have been bounteous, even beyond what cou'd justly be expected; and this shews with what Security a Prince may rely upon his Parliament: but they do not seem to be sufficiently aware how great an Addition of *real Wealth* accrues to the Crown from the Disposal of all Offices and Employments, most of which it not only may bestow, but *resume* again at *Pleasure*.

Is not this very properly a *vast Estate* in the Possession of the King, since no Prince can Eat and Drink his whole Revenue, but must lay it out in Gratifications to his Favourites, his Ministers, and his Servants. Anciently the great Officers of the State, were all of them for *Life*, and many of them chosen by the People; Those only of the Houshold were immediately

diately Dependant on the King, and as he paid them out of his own immediate Income, it was his Interest to have *as few* as was consistent with his Dignity and Service. But now, that all the Officers of the Commonwealth, both Civil and Military, are nominated by the King, and Paid *by him* with the *Money* of the *Publick*; Now that so few hold their Places by *their good Behaviour*, or any lasting Tenure whatsoever, it is plainly the Interest of the Crown, to *multiply* Offices without End, because the Court is the *richer* for all the Money that is lavished to maintain them, tho' the Publick be impoverished and undone. In other Countries, the Profit of a Tax is diminished by the charge of collecting it, but here the Court does in effect gain as much upon the produce of a Subsidy, by that part of it which goes to the Collectors, as by that which comes into the Exchequer.

How can one hope that a Prince should be desirous of reducing the National Expence, by lessening the number of Employments, when every new Salary that he gives, is a *new Fund of Wealth at his Disposal*, and the infallible Purchase of *a new Dependant* ?

LET-

LETTER LXVIII.

Selim to Mirza.

YOU have seen in my last, that from the time of King *James*'s Deposition, annual Meetings of Parliament were become necessary to the carrying on the Government. But for fear the Representatives of the People should grow by frequent Commerce, and long Habit too intimately acquainted with Courts and Ministers, it was thought expedient not long after, to pass a Law for the chusing a new Parliament, once in every three Years; which Term has been since prolong'd to seven, perhaps upon very good Foundations; but further than this, it would be most imprudent for the Nation to trust its Deputies, tho' they were much less liable than they have sometimes been, to forget what they owe to their Constituents.

Among other Advantages gain'd to Liberty at *this its happy Restoration*, a free Exercise of their Religion was allowed to those who differ from the Rites of the English Church, which has been continued and secured to them ever since, with some short interruptions, that even the *Party* which

which caused them, is now *ashamed of*. Nor has any thing contributed more than this, to the Peace and Happiness of the Government, by gaining it the Affection of all its Subjects, a Point of more importance to Society, than any speculative Opinions whatsoever.

THE Act which settled the Succession of these Realms on the Family now Reigning, is the last and greatest Bulwark of the British Freedom: It is a Covenant between the People and their Sovereign, so much the more Binding and Irrefragable, as it is founded on a true Sense of their mutual Interests, and admits of no Pretence on either side, of having been forcibly impos'd, or unwarily accepted.

THIS Succession was facilitated and secured by the Union of *Scotland* with *England*; and *Great-Britain* became infinitely stronger, by being undivded and entire.

ONE Condition of this Union, was the admitting sixteen *Scotch* Peers, chosen by the whole Body of the Peerage, into the *English* House of Lords, but upon a Tenure very different from the rest, being to sit there only for the Duration of the Parliament, at the end of which, a new Election must be made. If those *Elections* are *Uninfluenced* and *Free*, this Alteration in the *English* Constitution, may prove very much

much to its Advantage, because such a number of independant Votes, will balance *any part of the House of Peers*, over which, in any future Parliament, the Court may have obtain'd too great an Influence; but if they shou'd ever be *chosen by Corruption*, and have no hopes of *sitting there again*, except by an *unconstitutional Dependance* on the favour of a Court, then such a number added to the *others*, will grievously endanger the Constitution, and the House of Lords, instead of being, as it ought, a *mediating Power* between the Crown and People, will become a sort of *Anti-chamber to the Court*, a meer *Office* for *Executing* and *Authorising* the Purposes of a *Minister*.

I have now, my Dear Mirza, traced thee out a general Plan of the English Constitution, and I believe thou wilt agree with me upon the whole, *That a better can hardly be contrived*, the only Misfortune is, that *so good a one can hardly be preserved*.

Philosophers no doubt, may imagine very perfect Schemes of Policy, but then they should be administred by Philosophers, for if they are left to common Men, that Ideal Perfection is soon destroyed. We have seen how the Iniquity of the *Mollas* has corrupted that most holy *Form of Worship*, which came down with the Alcoran from Heaven; and if a *Form of Government*

ment also were sent down, I make no doubt but it would be turn'd into a Tyranny in the course of a few Centuries, except the same wisdom that established it, would also take care of its Execution.

LETTER LXIX.

Selim to Mirza.

IN former Reigns, when Parliaments were laid aside, for any length of time, the whole Authority of the State was lodged in the Privy Council, by the Advice and Direction of which, all Affairs were carried on. But these Counsellors being *chosen* by the King and *depending* on his Favour, were too apt to advise such Things only, as they knew would be most agreeable; and thus the Interests of the Nation were often sacrificed to the Profit and Expectations of a few Particulars. Yet still, as on extraordinary Occasions, the King might be forced to call a Parliament, the fear of it was some check to their Proceedings; and a Degree of Caution was natural to Men who foresaw they should sooner or later be called to an account. But let us suppose, that any future Prince could wholly *Influence the Election of a Parliament*, and make the

Members of it *Dependant on himself*, what would be the Difference between *that Parliament* and a Privy Counsel? Would it speak the Sense of the Nation, or of the Court? Would the Interest of the People be consider'd in it, or that of their Representatives? They would only differ in this respect, that *one*, being accountable to no body, *might be absolutely free from all Restraint*, which with the Terror of a Parliament hanging over them, the *other never could*.

This is the only imaginable Method, by which the Liberty of the *English* Nation can be attack'd hereafter; and tho' certainly this might bring it into Danger, yet the Peril is greater to the Man who shall make the Attempt: For there is a formidable Spirit in the People, that may be lull'd, but not easily laid asleep; and Corruption itself may *break*, when *swell'd too far*.

But thou wilt ask, to what end should a Court do this? Why should a King of *England* go about to destroy a Constitution, the Maintenance of which would render him both Great and Happy?

I reply, that a King indeed can have no Inducement to make such an Experiment, but a Minister may find it necessary for his own Support; and happy would it have been for many Countries, if the *Master's* Interest had been consider'd by the *Servant*,

half

half so warmly as the *Servant's* by the *Master.*

If a Man who travels thro' *Italy,* was to ask, what Advantage all the Riches in Religious Houses, are to the Saints they are Dedicated to, it would be impossible to satisfie his Demand: But the Priests, who are really Gainers by them, know that they pillage the People to good Purpose; and make use of a *venerable Name*, not from any Regard they have to it, but to *cover* and *secure* their own Extortion.

LETTER LXX.

Selim to Mirza at *Ispahan.*

From *London.*

I Came up from the Country, with the Gentleman in whose Company I went down, and as we were now become very well acquainted, the Pleasure I found in his Conversation, made me less sensible of the badness of the Roads, which else I should have murmur'd at extremely, and consider'd as a Proof of the *Disregard to publick Utility,* which seems to be growing the Characteristick of the English----At the end

End of our Journey, I obferv'd to him, with a good deal of Surprize, in how naked and defencelefs a Condition the whole Ifland appear'd to lie: Not a Town that had a Wall or Ditch about it; not a Caftle that had a fingle Cannon mounted; the very Ports and Magazines of naval Stores fo little fortified, as to be liable to an Infult.—— I don't believe, faid I, that there is a Hord of *Indian* Savages fo incapable of Defence as all this Country, were an Enemy got within it. None can get within it, anfwer'd he. —— The Sea which furrounds us is our *Wall*, and the moft impregnable of any. If that Wall (return'd I) cannot be *forc'd*, at leaft it may be *furpriz'd:* The Extent of it is too great to be fo guarded, as that no part of it fhall be open fome time or other. When I confider the Uncertainty of your Protection, I am aftonifh'd at the fulnefs of your Confidence. You do by your Country as by your Women; you expofe it to the Attacks of each Invader, and rely for its Defence on the Wind and Sea, a Security no more to be depended on, than the Inclinations of a Lady. —— We have Experience of its Safety, anfwer'd he; five or fix fuch Attempts have been made upon us, and not one of them fucceeded. —— I ftill hold to my Comparifon, replied I, of your Country to your Women: Both may have efcap'd nineteen

Attacks, and yet be carried at the twentieth; especially if we shou'd suppose any Concurrence of Passions from within, to invite the Ravisher, or weaken the Resistance. But, said he, we have an Army to defend us in Case of an Invasion; an Army maintain'd in time of Peace, and the best *aguerried* of any Troops in *Europe* that have never seen an Enemy.

True, said I; but I heard you the other Day declare very warmly for reducing them.—— I did so, answer'd he, and do so still, from a Jealousy of the use that may be made of them. They are design'd to oppose a Foreign Enemy, but they may be employ'd to *Civil* Purposes as well as *Military*; they may be submitted to the Discipline of *a Minister* as well as of *a General*; the very Rewards and Punishments which are necessary for keeping them in Order, may be under *a Ministerial Direction*; In short, they may be so twisted, turn'd, and chang'd, as to become the Troops of the *Minister*, not of the *State*.

If an Army, said I, be necessary for your *Defence*, you shou'd take Care that no Body may have Power to employ it for your *Destruction*: If that *Security* cannot be obtain'd, you must endeavour to defend yourselves without it, or at least, with as small a part of it as is possible, because *the nearest Danger is the Greatest*: But give me leave to say, that were I an *Englishman*, I shou'd be terribly uneasy at *this Dilemma*, and wish extreamly that some *Expedient* cou'd be found to lessen the Danger *on one Side*, without encreasing it *on the other*. I have been told, that in a neighbouring Republick, numerous Forces are constantly kept up, without any Danger at all to the Constitution; the single Reason of which, I take to be, that *the Republick itself is at the Head of them*, and can't be suppos'd to employ them *against itself*: But were *another Power* to *Model* and *Command* them, it is manifest, that a Danger might arise. In such a Case therefore, it shou'd seem prudent to lay *that Power* under *proper Limitations*; and methinks, wheresoever it was lodg'd, there wou'd be no Cause to oppose those Limitations, because the more *safe* it can be made, the more *durable* and *easy* it will be.

WHY have former Kings of *England* been oblig'd to part with Rights that undeniably belong'd to them, as the ancient Prerogatives of their Crown? Because the *Use* of them was *dangerous* to their People.—— Had the dangerous Part of them been *remov'd*, the beneficial might still have been *retain'd*; but by resolving to *give up neither*, they *lost both*. The Argument is yet stronger, in a Point where *Prerogative* cannot be pretended.

It is therefore the Interest of *the Governor*, as well as of *the governed, to make whatever is necessary agreeable*; and of all Mistakes in Policy, the greatest is, to *confound* what is *hurtful*, with what is *necessary*.

Far be it from me, replied my Friend, to desire to see *a standing Army* made *agreeable*.

I understand you, said I, you are afraid of the *Unpopularity* of the Sound: But when for want of that Army your Tenants Houses are burnt about their Ears, and the whole Country ravag'd and laid waste, you may chance to grow *Unpopular the other Way*, and to find that a *well regulated* Provision for your Safety and Defence, is more *agreeable* than Weakness and Desolation.

What wou'd you have us do? replied he warmly. We are liable to be hurt so many Ways, that we don't know what to avoid, or what to chuse. The best Provisions we can make for our Security, may be perverted and applied to our undoing. The Truth is, that no single Thing is perfect, and Government less perfect than any other, because compos'd of so many various Parts, and dependant on so many different Springs. The Love of Liberty is attended with *Anxieties*, which Servitude is a Stranger to; but Servitude is attended with a *Baseness* which our Nature makes us loath: It may be *easier* to sit quietly in Prison, and sollicit the good Graces of the Jailor; but a generous Mind will rather struggle through the Bars, let the Pain be what it will, as long as there is any Opening left to encourage the Attempt. And if *Those* who defend their Liberties are liable to *Errors* and *Miscarriages*, which give their *Enemies* a great Advantage over them, those *Enemies* themselves are no less liable to *Weakness* and *Mismanagement*, which often render their *most pernicious Schemes abortive*, and turn the Mischief on the Heads of the Contrivers.

LETTER LXXI.

SELIM to MIRZA at *Ispahan*.

From *London*.

THE other Morning, a Friend of mine came to me, and told me, with the Air of one who brings an agreeable Piece of News, that there was a Lady who most passionately desir'd the Pleasure of my Acquaintance, and had commission'd him to carry me to see her.—— I will not deny to thee, that my Vanity was a little flatter'd with this Meffage: I fancy'd fhe had feen me in fome publick Place, and taken a Liking to my Perfon; not being able to comprehend what other Motive cou'd make her fend for a Man fhe was a Stranger to in fo free and extraordinary a Manner. I painted her in my own Imagination very young, and very handfome, and fet out with moft pleafing Expectations, to fee the Conqueft I had made. But when I arriv'd at the Place of Affignation, I found a little old Woman very dirty, encircled by four or five ftrange Fe'lows, one of whom had a Paper in his Hand, which he was reading to her with all the Emphafis of an Author.

My coming in oblig'd him to break off, which put him a good deal out of Humour; but the Lady, underftanding who I was, receiv'd me with a great deal of Satisfaction, and told me, fhe had long had a Curiofity to be acquainted with *a Mahometan:* For you muft know (faid fhe) that I have applied myfelf particularly to the Study of *Theology*, and by profound Meditation and Enquiry have formed a Religion of my own, much better than *the vulgar one* in all Refpects. I never admit any Body to my Houfe who is not diftinguifh'd from the *common Herd of Chriftians* by fome extraordinary Notion

in

in Divinity: All thefe Gentlemen are eminently *Heretical*, each in a Way peculiar to himfelf: They are fo good to do me the Honour of inftructing me in their feveral Points of Faith, and fubmit their Opinions to my Judgment. Thus, Sir, I have compos'd a private Syftem, which muft neceffarily be perfecter than any, becaufe it is collected out of all; but to compleat it, I want a little of the *Koran*, a Book which I have heard fpoken of mighty handfomely, by many learned Men of my Acquaintance: And I affure you, Sir, I fhou'd have a very good Opinion of *Mahomet* himfelf, if he was not a little too hard upon the Ladies. Be fo kind therefore to *initiate* me in *your Myfteries*, and you fhall find me very *docile* and very *grateful*.

MADAM, replied I in great Confufion, I did not come to *England* as a *Miffionary*, and was never vers'd in *Religious Difputation*. But if a *Perfian Tale* wou'd entertain you, I cou'd tell you one, that the *Eaftern* Ladies are mighty fond of.

A *Perfian Tale!* cry'd fhe; Have you the Infolence to offer me a *Perfian Tale!* Really, Sir, I am not us'd to be fo affronted; and muft defire you to come no more within thefe Doors, for I have no Leifure to throw away upon a *Tale-teller*.

At these Words, she retir'd into her Closet, with her whole Train of *Metaphysicians*, and left my Friend and me to go away, as unworthy any further Comunion with her.

LETTER LXXII.

Selim *to* Mirza at *Ispahan.*

From *London.*

WOULDS'T thou know, *Mirza*, the present State of *Europe?* I will give it thee in very few Words. — There is *one Nation* in it, which thinks of nothing but how to *prey* upon the *others*; while the others are entirely taken up with *preying* upon *themselves.* There is *one Nation* where Particulars take a Pride in the Glory of their Country; while in *the others* no Glory is consider'd, but that of raising or improving a vast Estate. There is *one Nation* which, though able in Negotiation, puts its principal Confidence in *the Sword*; while *the others* trust wholly to *the Pen*, though incapable of using it with Advantage. There is *one Nation* which invariably pursues *a great Plan of general Dominion*; while *the others* are pursuing *little Interests*,

terests, through a Labyrinth of *Changes* and *Contradictions*. What, *Mirza*, doſt thou think will be the Conſequence? Is it not probable that *this Nation* will in the End be Lord of all the reſt, even as all the Religions of the Earth muſt at laſt be over power'd * by that of *Mahomet*, which is *ſimple, uniform*, and founded upon *Force*; whereas the reſt are rent in Pieces by their *Diviſions*, and *weak* by the very Frame of their *Inſtitutions*.

LETTER LXXIII.

SELIM to MIRZA at *Iſpahan*.

From *London*.

I WAS the other Day in a Coffee-houſe, where I found a Man declaiming upon the preſent State of *Perſia*, and ſo warm for the Intereſts of *Kouli Can*, that if it had not been for his Language and his Dreſs, I ſhou'd have took him for a *Perſian*.

SIR, ſaid I, are you acquainted with *Kouli Can*, that you concern yourſelf thus about him? No, ſaid he, I was never out

---

* The *Mahometans* are taught by the *Alcoran*, that ſooner or later all the World will be ſubmitted to their Law.

of *England*; but I love the *Persians* for being Enemies to the *Turks*.

WHAT Hurt have the *Turks* done you, answer'd I, that you bear such Enmity against them?

SIR, replied he, I am afraid they shou'd hurt the *Emperor*, whose Friend I have always declar'd myself.

I enquir'd of a Gentleman that sat by me, who this FRIEND OF THE EMPEROR's might be, and was told that he was a Dancing Master in St. *James*'s-*street*.

FOR my Part (said a young Gentleman finely drest, that stood sipping a Dish of Tea by the Fire-side) I don't care if *Kouli Kan*, and the Great *Turk*, and all the *Persians* and Emperors in *Europe* were at the bottom of the Sea, provided *Farinelli* be but safe.

THE Indifference of this Gentleman surpriz'd me more than the Importance of the other.

IF you are concern'd for *Farinelli*, said a third (who they told me was a Chymist) persuade him to take my *Drop*, and that will secure him from the Humidity of the *English* Air, which may very much prejudice his Voice.

WILL it not also make a *Man* of him *again*, said a Gentleman to the Doctor? After the Miracles we have been told it has perform'd, there is nothing more wanting

ing but *such a Cure* to compleat its Reputation.

※※※※※※※※※※※※※※※※※※※※※※※

LETTER LXXIV.

SELIM *to* MIRZA at *Ispahan.*

From *London.*

A FRIEND of mine was talking to me some Days ago, of the Spirit of Enthusiasm, which appear'd so strongly in the first Professors of our Religion; and, as he pretended, in the Prophet himself: To that chiefly he ascrib'd their mighty Conquests, and observ'd, that there needed nothing more to render them invincible, such a Spirit being constantly attended with a Contempt of Pleasure and of Ease, of Danger and of Pain.—— If, said he, the Enthusiasts of this Country in the Reign of *Charles* the first, had been united among themselves, like the *Arabians* under *Mahomet* and his Successors; I make no Doubt, but they might have conquer'd all *Europe*: But unhappily their Enthusiasm was directed to different Points; some were Bigots to the Church of *England*, some to *Calvin*, some to particular Whimsies of their own; one Set of them run mad for a Republick,

publick, others were no lefs out of their Wits in the Love of Monarchy; fo that inftead of making themfelves formidable to their Neighbours, they turn'd the Edge of their Fury againft each other, and deftroy'd all Peace and Order here at Home. Yet as much as our Anceftors fuffer'd then by the wrong Direction of their Zeal, I wifh the prefent Age may not fuffer more by the *total Want* of it among us. There is fo cold and lifelefs an Unconcern to every Thing but a narrow private Intereft; we are fo little in earneft about Religion, Virtue, Honour, or the Good of our Country; that unlefs fome Spark of the ancient Fire fhou'd revive, I am afraid we fhall jeft away our Liberties, and all that is ferious to our Happinefs. If the great Mr. *Hampden* had convers'd with our modern Race of Wits, he wou'd have been told, that it was a *ridiculous Enthufiafm*, to trouble himfelf about a trifling Sum of Money, becaufe it was rais'd againft the Privileges of the People, and that he might *thrive* better by Patience and Submiffion.

LETTER LXXV.

SELIM *to* MIRZA at *Ispahan.*

From *London.*

THERE is a new Science produc'd in *Europe* of late Years, entirely unknown to any former Age, or to any other Part of the World, which is call'd TREATY LEARNING. I have been let into a general Idea of it, by a very ingenious Friend of mine, who has acquir'd a considerable Talent in it, having serv'd an Apprenticeship of twenty Years under different Masters in Foreign Courts, and made, in a Political Sense, *the Tour of Europe.* He tells me, it is a very extensive Study; for not only *the Rights* of every Prince, but *their Inclinations to the Rights of any other* are therein set forth and comprehended. This has branch'd it self out into an Infinity of *seperate* and *secret Articles, Engagements, Counter-Engagements, Memorials, Remonstrances, Declarations*; all which the learned in this Science are requir'd to know perfectly by Heart, that they may be ready upon Occasion to apply them, or elude their Application, as the Intereſt of their Maſters ſhall demand.

He ſhew'd me ten or twelve Volumes lately publiſh'd, conſiſting only of the Treaties which have been made ſince the beginning of this Century, four or five of which were quite fill'd with thoſe of *England*.

Sure, ſaid I, this huge Heap of Negociations cou'd never have been employ'd about the Buſineſs of this little Spot of Earth for ſo ſmall a ſpace of Time as *thirty Years!* No, —— The Affairs of all *Europe* muſt be ſettled in them, *for the next Century at leaſt.* —— For the next *Seſſion of Parliament*, anſwer'd he; *theſe Political Machines* are ſeldom mounted to go longer than *that Period*, without being *taken to Pieces*, or *new-wound up.*

But how, ſaid I, cou'd *England*, which is an Iſland, be enough concern'd in what paſſes on the Continent to undergo all this Labour in adjuſting it?

O, replied he, we grew weary of being confin'd *within the narrow Verge of our own Intereſts*, we thought it lookt more *conſiderable* to *expatiate*, and give our Talents *Room to Play*. But this was not the only End of our continual and reſtleſs Agitation: It may frequently be the Intereſt of a Miniſter, if he find Things in a Calm, to *trouble the Waters*, and work up a Storm

Storm about him; if not to perplex and confound those *above him*, yet to embarrass and intimidate the *Competitors* or *Rivals* of his Power.

PERHAPS too, there might be still a deeper Motive: These Engagements are for the most part pretty chargeable; and those who are oblig'd to make them good, complain that they are much *the poorer for them*; but it is not sure, that *those who form them* are so too. ⸺

As far, said I, as my little Observation can enable me to judge of these Affairs, the multiplicity of your Treaties is as hurtful as the multiplicity of your Laws. In *Asia*, *a few plain Words* are found sufficient to settle the Differences of Particulars in a State, or of one State with another; but here you run *into Volumes* upon both; and what is the Effect of it? Why after *great Trouble* and *great Expence*, you are as far from a *Decision* as before; nay, often more puzzled and confounded. The only Distinction seems to be, that in your Law Suits, perplexing as they are, there is at last, *a Rule of Equity* to resort to; but in the other Disputes, the last Appeal is to *the Iniquitous Rule of Force*, and Princes treat by the Mouths of *their great Guns*, which soon demolish all the *Paper* on both Sides, and tear to Pieces every *Cobweb of Negociation*.

LETTER LXXVI.

SELIM *to* MIRZA at *Ispahan.*

From *London.*

I WAS lately at a Tavern with a Set of Company very oddly put together: There was a Country Gentleman, a Man of honest Principles, but extreamly a Bigot to his Religion, which was that of the Church of *Rome*; there was a Lawyer, who was moderate enough in Matters of Belief, but zealous in the Cause of Civil Liberty; there was a Courtier who seem'd not to believe any thing, and to be angry with every Body that did.

THIS last, very rudely attackt the Faith of the poor Country Gentleman, and laid open to him the Frauds of the *Roman* Priesthood, who by slow, but regular Degrees, had erected such a Tyranny over the Minds and Spirits of the People, that nothing was too gross for them to impose, or too arrogant to assume. He set forth the vast Difference between a *Bishop* in the Primitive Ages of Christianity, who was *a Receiver of Charities for the Poor*, and a *Pope*, with a tripple Crown upon his Head, and

and half the Wealth of Chriftendom in his Treafury. He lamented the Simplicity of thofe, who without looking back to the *Original* of Things, imagine that all is *Right* which they find *Eftablifh'd*; and miftake the *Corruptions of a Syftem* for the *Syftem itfelf*; He inveigh'd againft the Pufillanimity of others, who though they *fee* the Corruptions, and *deteft* them, yet fuffer them to continue *un-reform'd*, only becaufe they *have been tolerated fo long*; as if any *Evil was lefs dangerous*, by being grown *Habitual*.

He concluded, by declaiming very eloquently on the Ufe and Advantage of *Free Thinking*, that is, of doubting and examining every Article propos'd to our Belief, which alone cou'd detect thefe Impofitions, and confound the ill Purpofes of their Authors.

His Antagonift had little to reply; but intrench'd himfelf in the Neceffity of *fubmitting* to the *Authority* of the *Church*, and the Danger of allowing private *Judgment*, to call in Queftion *her* Decifions.

The Difpute wou'd have been turn'd into a Quarrel by the Zeal of *one*, and the Afperity of the *other*, had not the Lawyer very feafonably interpos'd, who, addreffing himfelf to the Advocate for Freedom, defir'd to know, whether *Liberty* in *Temporals* was not at leaft as important to Mankind, as *Liberty* in *Spirituals?* How then comes it, that you who are so warm for the Maintenance of *the Last*, are so notoriously indifferent to the First? To what shall we ascribe the mighty Difference between your POLITICAL and RELIGIOUS FAITH? and whence is it that the former is so *easy*, and the latter so *intractable?* Can *those* who are thus quicksighted in the Frauds of *Ecclesiastical Dominion*, see no juggling at all in their *Civil Rulers?* Are the *Impositions* less glaring or more tolerable, which *they* both acquiesce in and support, than those which they so violently oppose? Let us take the very Instance you have given. —— Is a *Pope* more *unlike* to a *Christian Bishop*, than a *sole Minister* to an *Officer of a free State?* If you *look back* to the *Original* of Things, what Traces will you find of *such an Office?* In what ancient Constitution can you discover the Foundations of *such a Power?* Is not this a most manifest *Corruption*, growing out of ten thousand Corruptions, and naturally productive of ten thousand more. If you say these are *Mysteries of State*, and therefore *not to be examin'd;* I am sure the *Mysteries* you attack, have at least a good a Title to your Respect; and less Mischief will attend on their remaining not subject to *Enquiry*.

OR

Or will you borrow the Arguments of your Adverſary, and plead the *Neceſſity of Submiſſion*, and the *Danger* of ſetting up *Reaſon* againſt *Authority*. If ſo, I wou'd only put you in Mind, that *all Authority flows from Reaſon*, and ought to loſe its Force in Proportion as it deviates from its Source.

It is a Jeſt to ſay, that Mankind cannot be govern'd without *theſe Impoſitions*; they were govern'd happily before *theſe* were *invented*, much more happily than they have been ever ſince: As well may it be ſaid, that Chriſtian Piety, which was eſtabliſh'd in Plain-dealing and Simplicity, muſt be ſupported by the Knavery and Pageantry introduc'd of late Ages by the Church of *Rome*. But the Truth is, that moſt Men do in the State, juſt what you complain of in Religion; they *maintain Abuſes by Preſcription*, and make the *bad* Condition Things *are in*, an Argument for letting them *grow worſe*.

I don't know, ſaid I, interrupting him, whether the Gentleman is not rather too bold in carrying his Doubts ſo far into Religion; perhaps he wou'd do better to ſubmit; at leaſt we *Mahometans* are ſo taught. But this I am ſure of, that a *blind Confidence* in *temporal* Affairs, agrees very ill with *Doubt* in *Spirituals*. A free Enquirer into Points of Speculation, ſhou'd

beyond

beyond all others be asham'd of a tame Compliance in Points of Action.

THE *unthinking* may be passive from Delusion, or at least from Inadvertency; but the *greatest Monster* and *worst Criminal* in Society, is a FREE-THING-SLAVE.

?********:************

LETTER LXXVII.

SELIM to MIRZA at *Ispahan*.

From *London*.

EVERY Nation has some peculiar Excellence, by which it is distinguish'd from its Neighbours, and of which without Vanity it may boast: Thus *Italy* produces the finest *Singers*, *England* the stoutest *Boxers*; *Germany* the profoundest *Theologians*; and *France* is incomparable for its COOKS. This last Advantage carries the Palm from all the rest, and that Nation has great Reason to be proud of it, as a Talent of universal Currency; and for which all other Countries do them Homage: On this single Perfection depends the Pleasure, the Magnificence, the Pride, nay the Reputation of every Court in *Europe*: Without a good *French Cook* there is no Embassador can possibly do his Master's Business; no Secretary

Secretary of State can hold his Office, no Man of Quality can support his Rank and Dignity. A Friend of mine who frequently has the honour to Dine at the Tables of *the Great*, for which he pays no higher price than *his Vote in Parliament*, has sometimes obliged me with the Bill of Fare, and (as near as he cou'd) an Estimate of the Charge which these genteel Entertainments are attended with. I told him, that their Dinners put me in mind of what I had heard about their Politicks: They are *Artificial*, *Unsubstantial*, and *Unwholsome*, but at the same time most *ruinously Expensive*. Sure, said I, your *Great Men* must have *Digestions* prodigiously sharp and strong, to carry off such a load of various Meats as are serv'd up to them every Day! They must not only be made with *Heads* and *Hearts*, but with *Stomachs* very *different* from other People!

Not in the least, answered he—They seldom touch any of the Dainties that are before them: Those Dainties, like the Women in your Seraglio's, are more intended for *Ornament* than *Use*. There is always a plain Dish set in a Corner, a homely joint of *English* Beef or Mutton, on which the Master of the Feast makes his Dinner, and two or three choice Friends, who are allowed to have a Cut with him, out of special Grace and Favour, while the rest

rest are languishing in vain for such a Happiness, and piddling upon Ortolans and Truffles.

I HAVE seen a poor Country Gentleman sit down to one of these fine Dinners, with an extream dislike to the *French* Cookery; yet, for fear of being counted Unpolite, not daring to refuse any thing that was offer'd him; but cramming and sweating with the struggle between his Aversion and Civility.

WHY then, said I, this continual Extravagance? Why this number of Victims daily sacrificed to the Dæmon of Luxury? How is it worth a Man's while to undo himself, perhaps to undo his Country, that his Board may be grac'd with Pates of Perigord, when his Guests had rather have the Fowl from his Barn-door? Your comparison of the Seraglio will not hold; for tho' indeed there is an unnecessary Variety, yet they are not *all* serv'd up to us *together*; we content ourselves with *one* or *two* of 'em at a Meal, and reserve the rest for future Entertainments. I concluded, with repeating to him a Story, which is taken out of the Annals of our Kings.

SCHAH ABBAS, at the beginning of his Reign, was more luxurious than became so great a Prince. One might have judged of the vastness of his Empire, by the Variety of Dishes at his Table: Some were sent him from the *Tigris* and *Euphrates*,

others

others from the *Oxus* and *Caspian* Sea. One Day, when he gave a Dinner to his Nobles, *Mahomet Ali*, Keeper of the three Tombs, was placed next to the best Dish of all the Feast, out of respect for the Sanctity of his Office: But instead of falling too, and eating heartily, as *Holy Men* are wont to do, he fetch'd a dismal Groan, and fell a Weeping. *Schah Abbas*, surpriz'd at his Behaviour, desir'd him to explain it to the Company: He wou'd fain have been excus'd; but the *Sophi* order'd him on pain of his Displeasure, to acquaint them with the cause of his Disorder.

KNOW then, said he, O Monarch of the Earth, that when I saw thy Table cover'd in this manner, it brought to my mind a Dream, or rather Vision, which was sent me from the Prophets whom I serve: On the seventh Night of the Moon *Rhamazan*, I was sleeping under the shade of the sacred Tombs, when, methought, the Holy Ravens of the Sanctuary bore me up on their Wings into the Air, and in a few Moments conveyed me to the lowest Heaven, where the Messenger of God, on whom be Peace, was sitting in his luminous Tribunal, to receive Petitions from the Earth. Around him stood an infinite throng of Animals, of every species and quality, which all join'd in preferring a Complaint against thee, *Schah Abbas*, for destroying them wantonly and tyran-

tyrannically, beyond what any Neceffity cou'd juftify, or any natural Appetite demand.

It was alledged by them, that ten or twelve of them were often murder'd, to compofe one Difh for the nicenefs of thy Palate; fome gave their Tongues only, fome their Bowels, fome their Fat, and others their Brains, or Blood. In fhort, they declared, fuch conftant Wafte was made of them, that unlefs a ftop was put to it in time, they fhould perifh entirely by thy Gluttony. The Prophet hearing this, bent his Brows, and order'd fix Vultures to fetch thee alive before him: They inftantly brought thee to his Tribunal, where he commanded thy Stomach to be open'd, and examined whether it was bigger or more capacious, than thofe of other Men: When it was found to be juft of the common fize, he permitted all the Animals to make Reprifals on the Body of their Deftroyer; But before one in ten thoufand cou'd get at thee, every particle of it was devoured; fo ill-proportion'd was the Offender to the Offence.——

This Story made fuch an Impreffion on the *Sophi*, that he would not fuffer above one Difh of Meat to be brought to his Table ever after.

LETTER LXXVII.

To IBRAHIM MOLLAC at *Ispahan*.

From *London*.

YES, holy *Mollac*, I am more and more convinc'd of it; Infidelity is certainly attended with a Spirit of Infatuation. The Prophet hurts the Understandings of all those who refuse to receive his holy Law; He punishes the Hardness of their Hearts, by the Depravation of their Judgments. How can we otherwise account for what I have seen since my Arrival among Christians?

I HAVE seen a People, whose very Being depends on Commerce, suffer *Luxury* and the *heavy Load of Taxes* to ruin their Manufacturers at home, and turn the Ballance against them in foreign Trade!——

I HAVE seen them Glory in the Greatness of their Wealth, when they are reduc'd every Year to carry on the Expences of the Government, by robbing the very *Fund* which is to ease them of a Debt of *Fifty Millions!*

I HAVE seen them *fit out Fleets, augment their Forces,* express continual *Fears* of an *Invasion*; and all the while hug themselves in the Notion of being blest with a *profound and lasting Peace!*

I HAVE seen them wrapt up in full Security, upon the flourishing State of *Publick Credit*, only because they had a *prodigious Stock of Paper*, which now indeed, they circulate as Money; but which the first Alarm of a Calamity, may in an Instant make *meer Paper* of again!

I HAVE seen them constantly busied in *passing Laws* for the better Regulation of their *Police*, and never taking any Care of their *Execution*; loudly declaring the Abuses of their Government, and quietly allowing them to encrease!

I HAVE seen them distrest *for want of Hands* to carry on their Husbandry and Manufactures, yet permitting some thousands of able Men to *beg* about their Streets, or breeding up ten times that Number to be *Lazy*, under a Notion of being *Learned!*

I HAVE seen them make such a *Provision for their Poor*, as wou'd relieve all their Wants if well applied, and suffer a third Part of them to *Starve* from the Roguery and Riot of those entrusted with the Care of them!

But the *Greatest* of all the *Wonders* I have seen, and which most of all proves their *Infatuatiion*, is that *they profess* To MAINTAIN LIBERTY BY CORRUPTION!

LETTER LXXVIII.

Selim to Mirza at *Ispahan*.

From *London*.

I FELICITATE Thee, *Mirza*, on thy new Dignity; I bow myself reverently before thee, not with the Heart of a Flatterer, but a Friend: The Favour of thy Master shines upon thee; he has rais'd thee to the right Hand of his Throne; the Treasures of *Persia* are committed to thy Custody: If thou behavest thyself honestly and wisely, I shall think thee much *Greater* from thy *Advancement*; if otherwise, much *Lower* than before. Thou hast undertaken a Charge very important to thy Prince, and to his People; both are equally concern'd in thy Administration, both have equally a Right to thy Fidelity. If ever thou shalt separate their Interests, if thou shalt set up the one against the other, know, it will end in the Ruin of *Both*. Do not imagine, that thy Master will be richer by draining his Subjects of their Wealth: Such *Gains* are *irreparable Losses*; they may serve a present sordid Purpose; but dry up the Sources of Opulence for Futurity. I wou'd recommend to thy Attention and Remembrance, the Saying of a famous *English Treasurer* in the happy Reign of Queen *Elizabeth*. *I don't love*, said that truly able Minister, *to see the Treasury swell like a distemper'd Spleen, when the other Parts of the State are in a Consumption.* —— Be it thy Care to prevent such a Decay; and, to that End, not only save the Publick all unnecessary Expence, but so *digest* and *order* what is needful, that *Perplexity* may not serve to cover *Fraud*, nor *Incapacity* lurk behind *Confusion*. Rather submit to any Difficulty and Distress in the Conduct of thy Ministry, than *Anticipate* the Revenues of the Government without an absolute Necessity; for such Expedients are a *temporary Ease*, but a *permanent Destruction*.

In relieving the People from their Taxes, let it also be thy Glory to relieve them from the infinite Number of *Tax Gatherers*, which, far worse than the *Turkish* or *Russian* Armies, have *harrast* and *plunder'd* our poor Country.

As thou art the Distributor of the Bounties of the Crown, make them the Reward of Service and of Merit; not the
Hire

Hire of *Parasites* and *Flatterers* to thy Master, or *thyself*. But above all, as thou art now *a publick Person*, elevate thy Mind beyond any *private View*; try to enrich the Publick before thyself and think less of establishing thy Family at the Head of thy Country, than of setting thy Country at the Head of *Asia*.

If thou can'st steadily persevere in such a Conduct, thy Prince will want *Thee* more than Thou dost *Him*: If thou buildest thy Fortune on *any other Basis*, how high soever it may rise, it will be tottering from the *Weakness of its Foundation*.

He alone is a *Minister of State*, whose Services are *necessary to the Publick*; the rest are *the Creatures of Caprice*, and feel *their Slavery* even *in their Power*.

LETTER LXXIX.

Selim *to* Mirza at *Ispahan*.

From *London*.

THE virtuous *Abdallah* is return'd to *England*, after having been absent fourteen Moons. I yesterday restor'd to him his lovely *Zelis*, the *Wife* whom he had given me at his Departure, and whom

I had treated like a *Sister*. Nothing ever was so moving as the Scene, when I join'd their Hands again, after a Separation, which they had fear'd wou'd prove eternal. The Possession of the finest Woman in the World, could not give me so much Pleasure as this Act of Humanity and Justice: I made two People happy who deserv'd it; and am secure of the Affections of them both to the last Moment of their Lives. When the Transports of their Joy were a little over, *Abdallah* gave me the following Relation of all that had happen'd to him since he left us.——

The HISTORY of *Abdallah*.

YOU know that I sail'd from *England* with an Intent to redeem my Father from Captivity: As soon as I came to *Malta*, I went and threw myself at the Feet of the Grand Master, beseeching him to take the Ransom I had brought, and set my Father free.

He answer'd me, that the Person for whom I sued, was no longer in a Condition to be ransom'd, being condemn'd to die for Treason the next Day. I was ready to die myself at this Account; and desiring to know the Particulars of his Offence, was inform'd, that being unable to redeem himself, he was put to the Oar like a common Slave,

Slave, without any Regard to his Innocence or Age: That during an Engagement with a *Turkish* Ship, he had perſuaded the other Slaves to quit their Oars, and fight againſt the Chriſtians; but, that being overpower'd, he was brought to *Malta*, and condemn'd to be *broke upon the Wheel*, as an Example to the other Captives in the Gallies: That this dreadful Sentence was to be executed upon him, the Morning after my Arrival, and no Ranſom cou'd be accepted for his Life.

O Heaven! ſaid I, did I come ſo far to no other Purpoſe, but to be Witneſs of the Death of my wretched Father, and a Death ſo full of Horror? Wou'd the Waves of the Sea had ſwallow'd me up, before I reach'd this fatal and accurſed Shore! O *Abderamen!* O my Father, what avails to thee the Piety of thy Son? How ſhall I bear to take my Leave of thee forever, at our firſt Meeting after an Abſence which ſeem'd ſo long? Can I ſtand by, and give thee up to Torments, when I flatter'd myſelf that I arriv'd to bring thee Liberty? Alaſs! my Preſence will only aggravate thy Sufferings, and make the Bitterneſs of Death more inſupportable.

IN this Extremity, I offer'd the Grand Maſter, not only to pay down all the Ranſom I promis'd him before, but to yield myſelf

myself a voluntary Slave, and serve in the Gallies all my Life, if *Abderamen*'s might be spared.

He seem'd touch'd with my Proposal, and inclin'd to pity me; but was told by a Jesuit, who was his Confessor, that an Example of Severity was necessary; and that he ought to pardon my Father on no Terms but renouncing *Mahometism*, and turning *Christian*.

No, cry'd I, if *That* is to be the Price of a few unhappy Years, better both of us shou'd perish than accept them.—— But can you, said I to the Priest, who profess an Holiness superior to other Men, can you obstruct the Mercy of your Prince, and compel him to destroy a wretched Man, whose only Crime was the natural Love of Liberty? Is this your Way of making Converts to your Faith, by the Terror of Racks and Wheels, instead of Reason?——

My Reproaches signify'd nothing but to incense him, and I quitted the Palace in Despair. I was going to the Prison to see my Father, for the first and last Time, when a *Turkish* Slave accosted me, and bade me follow him.—— I refused to do it, but he assured me it was of Moment to the Life of *Abderamen*. I follow'd him, and he led me by a Back-way to a Woman's Apartment in the Palace.—— I continued there till past Midnight without seeing anybody, in Agitations

tations not to be conceiv'd: At laſt there came to me a Lady richly dreſs'd in the Habit of my own Country. After looking at me attentively ſome Time, O *Abdullah*, ſaid ſhe, have you forgot *Zoraide*, the Siſter of *Zelis?*

THESE Words ſoon brought her to my Remembrance, tho' I had not ſeen her for many Years: I embraced her tenderly, and deſired to know what Fortune had carry'd her to *Malta?*

I NEED not acquaint you, anſwer'd ſhe, that I am of one of the beſt Families in *Cyprus*, and that I was married young to a rich Merchant of *Aleppo*. I had by him two Children, a Son and Daughter; and liv'd very happily ſome Years, till my Huſband's Buſineſs carrying him to *Cyprus*, I perſuaded him to let me go, and make a Viſit to my Relations in that Iſland. In our Paſſage a violent Storm aroſe, which drove us Weſtward beyond the Iſle of *Candia*; and before we cou'd put into any Harbour, a *Malteſe* Pyrate attack'd us, kill'd my Huſband, and carried me to *Malta*. My Beauty touch'd the Heart of the Grand Maſter, which is the more ſurprizing, as I took no Pains to ſet it off; thinking of nothing but the Loſs I had ſuſtain'd: He bought me of the Knight whoſe Prize I was; and I thought it ſome Comfort in my Captivity, that I was deliver'd from the Hands that had been ſtain'd in my Husband's Blood. The Passion of my new Lord was so excessive, that he us'd me more like a Princess than a Slave. He cou'd deny me nothing that I ask'd him, and was so liberal, that he never approach'd me without a Present. You see the Pomp and Magnificence in which I live; my Wealth is great, and my Power in this Place superior to any-body's. Hear then, *Abdallah*, what my Friendship has done for you, and remember the Obligation you have to me. I have employ'd all my Interest with my Lover to save the Life of *Abderamen*: He has consented to it, and moreover, to set him free upon the Payment of the Ransom you propos'd. But, in Recompence for the Aid which I have given you, you must promise to assist me in an Affair that will, probably, be attended with some Danger. I assured her, there was nothing I wou'd not risque, to do the Sister of *Zelis* any Service.

You shall know, said she, what it is I require of you, when the Time comes to put it in Execution; till then remain at *Malta*, and wait my Orders.

At these Words she deliver'd to me a Pardon under the Seal of the Grand Master, and bid me carry it instantly to my Father; I was so transported that I cou'd not stay to thank her; I ran, I flew to the Prison of *Abderamen*, and shewing the Order I brought with

with me to his Guards, was admitted to the Dungeon where he lay.

THE poor old Man expecting nothing but his Death, and believing I was the Officer that came to carry him to the Place of Execution, fainted away before I had Time to discover to him either my Person or my Errand. While he lay in that State of Insensibility, I unbound his Chains, and bore him into the open Air, where, with a good deal of Difficulty he recover'd. O my Father! said I to him (when I perceived that his Senses were return'd) do you not know your Son *Abdallah*, who is come hither to save your Life, who has obtain'd your Pardon, and redeem'd you from Captivity? —— The Surprize of Joy that seiz'd him in that Instant at my Sight and Words, was too sudden and violent for his Age and Weakness to support. He struggled some Time to make an Answer; but at last, straining me in his Arms, and muttering some half-form'd Sounds, he sunk down, and expired on my Bosom.——

WHEN I saw that he was dead, I lost all Patience, and covering myself with Dust bewailed my Folly, in not telling him my good Tidings by Degrees.

BY this Time it was broad Day, and the whole Town being inform'd of my Affliction, was gather'd about me in great Crowds. The Grand Master himself taking Pity of me, me, sent to tell me, that he wou'd permit me to bear away my Father's Body to *Aleppo*, and excuse me the Ransom I had offer'd, since Death had deliver'd him without it. This Indulgence comforted me a little, and I wou'd have embarqued immediately for the *Levant*, if I had not been stopp'd by my Promise to *Zoraide*. Several Days pass'd without my hearing any News of her; I had already hired a small Vessel, and put on board the Remains of *Abderamen*, when late one Night I was waked out of my Sleep by *Zoraide* in the Habit of a Man, who told me, that she was come to claim my Promise. I ask'd what she requir'd me to do? To carry me to *Aleppo*, answer'd she, that I may see my dear Children once again, and enrich them with the Treasures which I have gain'd from the Bounty of my Lover. Those Treasures are useless to me without them; in the midst of all my Pomp and outward Pleasure I am perpetually pining for their Loss; the Mother's Heart is unsatisfied within, nor will it let me enjoy a Moment's Peace, till I am restored to them in my happy native Land. As she said this, she shew'd me some Bags of Gold, and a Casket fill'd with Jewels of great Value. Part of these, continued she, shall be yours, *Abdallah*, provided you set Sail this very Night, and take me along with you. The Weather is tempestuous, but that

Cir-

Circumstance will favour my Escape; and I had rather venture to perish in the Sea, than live any longer from my Family.

The Sense of the Obligation I had to her made me consent to do what she desired, much more than the Jewels which she promis'd me. As I had a Permission from the Grand Master to go away as soon as I thought fit, I put to Sea that Night without any Hindrance, and the Wind blowing hard off the Shore, in a little while we were out of sight of *Malta*. The Water was so rough for two or three Days, that we thought it impossible our Barque could weather it out; but at length the Storm abating, we pursued our Voyage with a very fair Wind, and arrived safe in the Port of *Scanderoon*. *Zoraide* was transported with the Thought of being so near *Aleppo*, and her Children; she embraced me in the most affectionate Manner, and express'd a Gratitude for the Service I had done her far beyond what it deserv'd. But how great was her Disappointment, and Affliction, when we were told by the People of *Scanderoon*, that the Plague was at *Aleppo*, and had destroy'd a third Part of the Inhabitants!

Ah! wretched *Zoraide*, cry'd she weeping, where are now all thy Hopes of being blest in the Sight of thy two Children? Perhaps, those two Children are no more; or, if they still live, it is in hourly Expectation

tation of dying with the reſt of their Fellow Citizens. Perhaps, at this Moment they begin to ſicken, and want the Care of their *Mother* to tend upon them, when they are abandon'd by every other Friend.

THUS did ſhe torture herſelf with dreadful Apprehenſions, and often turning her Eyes towards *Aleppo*, gave herſelf up to all the Agonies of Grief.

I SAID every thing I cou'd think of to relieve her, but ſhe wou'd not be comforted.

THE next Morning the Servants I had put about her, came, and told me, that ſhe was not to be found: They alſo brought me a Letter which inform'd me, that not being able to endure the Uncertainty ſhe was in about her Children, ſhe had ſtollen away by Night, and was gone to *Aleppo*, to ſhare their Danger with them. That if ſhe and her Family eſcap'd the Sickneſs, I ſhou'd hear from her again; but that if they died, ſhe was reſolved not to ſurvive them. She added, that ſhe had left me a Box of Diamonds worth two thouſand Piſtoles, being a fourth Part of the Jewels which ſhe had brought from *Malta* by my Aſſiſtance.

YOU may imagine how deeply I was affected at reading this Letter. I reſolved to ſtay at *Scanderoon* till I had ſome News of her; notwithſtanding my paſſionate Deſire

fire to return to *Zelis*. I had waited five Weeks with great Impatience, when we receiv'd Accounts that the Infection was quite ceas'd, and the Commerce with *Aleppo* restor'd again. I immediately went to visit my native Town, but alas! I had little Pleasure in the sight of it, after so dismal a Calamity. My first Enquiry was about *Zoraide* and her Children. They carried me to her House, where I found her Son, a Youth of sixteen. When I made myself known to him he fell a weeping, and told me his Mother and Sister were both dead. I very sincerely join'd with him in his Grief, and offer'd to restore to him the Jewels she had given me. No, *Abdallah*, said he, I am rich enough in what I inherit from my Father and *Zoraide*. But these Riches cannot comfort me for her Death, nor any Time wear out of my Remembrance the uncommon Affection which occasion'd it. O *Abdallah!* what a Mother have I lost, and what a Friend are you deprived of? When she came hither, continued he, from *Scanderoon*, my Sister and I believ'd we had seen a Spirit: But when we found it was really *Zoraide*, our Hearts melted with Tenderness and Joy. That Joy was soon over; for, the third Day after her Arrival at *Aleppo*, I found myself seiz'd with the Distemper. She never quitted my Bedside during my Illness, and to the Care
she

she took of me I owed my Life: But it proved fatal to *her* and my poor Sister, who both caught the Infection by nursing me; and having weaker Constitutions were not able to struggle with it so well. My Sister died first, and *Zoraide* quickly follow'd: When she perceiv'd herself just expiring, she call'd me to her, and bid me endeavour to find you out at *Scanderoon*, and let you know, that she bequeathed to you the Portion she had intended for my Sister, amounting to five thousand Pieces of Gold, as to the Man in the World she most esteem'd: She added, That to you she recommended me with her latest Breath, imploring you to take care of me for her Sake, and the Sake of her Sister *Zelis*.——

THE poor Boy was not able to go on with his Story any further. I accepted the Legacy, and did my utmost, to discharge worthily the Trust conferred upon me: But my first Care was to bury *Abderamen* with all the Pomp that our Customs will admit. After some Time spent in settling the Affairs of my Pupil, and my own, I took a Passage on board an *English* Ship, and arrived happily in *London*.

I AM now possest of a Fortune that is sufficient to maintain *Zelis* in the Manner I desire, and have nothing more to ask of Heaven but an Opportunity of repaying

you,

you, O *Selim*, the Friendship and Goodness you have shewn me.

LETTER LXXX.

SELIM to MIRZA at *Ispahan*.

From *London*.

I AM going, in the Confidence of Friendship, to give thee a Proof of the Weakness of Human Nature, and the unaccountable Capriciousness of our Passions. Since I deliver'd up *Zelis* to her Husband, I have not enjoy'd a Moment's Peace. Her Beauty, which I saw without Emotion while she continued *in my Power*, now she is *out of it*, has fired me to that Degree that I have almost lost my Reason. I cannot bear to see her in the Possession of the Man to whom I gave her: If Shame, if Despair did not hinder it, I should ask him for her again.—— In this Uneasiness and Disorder of my Mind, there remains but one Part for me to take: I must fly from her Charms and my own Weakness; I must retire to my *Seraglio* in *Persia*, and endeavour, by the Attractions of *Variety*, to efface the

Impreſſion ſhe has made. I have more than compleated the four Years I propoſed to ſtay in *England*; and am now determin'd to embarque for the *Levant* the Beginning of next Month. It is my fix'd Reſolution to go away, without giving *Zelis* the leaſt Intimation of the Cauſe of my Departure: *Abdallah* ſhall never know that I am his *Rival*; it would take too much from the Character of a *Friend*. Thou art the only one to whom I dare confide my Folly; and ſince it has hurt nobody but myſelf, I hope thou wilt rather pity than blame me for it.

LETTER LXXXI.

Selim to Mirza at *Iſpahan*.

From *London*.

MY Ship waits for me in the Mouth of the River *Thames*, and thou mayſt expect e're long to ſee thy Friend, with a *Mind* a good deal alter'd by his Travels, but a *Heart* which to thee is ſtill *the ſame*.

It would be unjuſt and ungrateful in me to quit *this Iſland*, without expreſſing a very high Eſteem of the *good Senſe, Sincerity*, and

good

good Nature I have found among *the English*: To these Qualities I might also add *Politeness*; which certainly they have as good a Title to as *any of their Neighbours*; but I am afraid that this Accomplishment has been acquir'd too much at the Expence of other Virtues more solid and essential. Of their *Industry*, their Commerce is a Proof; and for their *Valour*, let their *Enemies* declare it. Of their *Faults* I will at present say no more, but that *many* of them are *newly introduced*, and so contrary to the Genius of the People, that one wou'd hope they might be easily rooted out. They are undoubtedly, all Circumstances consider'd, a very *Great*, a very *Powerful*, and Happy Nation: but how long they shall *continue so* depends entirely on the *Preservation of their Liberty*. To the *Constitution* of their Government alone are attach'd all these Blessings and Advantages: Shou'd *That* ever be *corrupted* or *depraved*, they must expect to become the most *contemptible*, and most *unhappy* of Mankind. For what can so much aggravate the Wretchedness of an Oppress'd and Ruin'd People, as the Remembrance of former Freedom and Prosperity? All the Images and Traces of their Liberty, which, it is probable, no Change will quite destroy, must be a perpetual Reproach and Torment to them, for having so degenerately parted with *their Birth-right*. And if Slavery is to be en-

endured, where is the Man that wou'd not rather chuse it, under the warm Sun of *Agra* or *Ispahan*, than in the Northern Climate and barren Soil of *England*?

I THEREFORE take my Leave of my Friends here, with this affectionate, and well-design'd Advice, That they shou'd vigilantly *watch over their Constitution*, and guard it by those Bulwarks which alone are able to secure *it*, *Justice*, *Vigour*, *Perseverance*, and *Frugality*.

F I N I S.

ERRATA.

PAGE 9. Line 1. Inſtead of ſqueaking Eunuchs and a Penſion, read ſqueaking Eunuchs and Corruption.

Page 21. Line 29. Inſtead of this Couple, read this Loving Couple.

Page 59. Line 12. Inſtead of as in a *Seraglio*; the Honour of the Husband is preſerv'd the Malice of the Eunuchs, read, as in a *Seraglio* the Honour of the Husband is preſerv'd by the Malice of the Eunuchs, &*c.*

Page 132. Line 31. Inſtead of Applauſed, read Applauſe.

Page 135. Line 18. Inſtead of he ſhou'd have had an Eſtate that might have ſat him above Dependance, read, he ſhou'd have an Eſtate that might ſet him above Dependance.

Page 138 Line 20. Inſtead of in a Letter, read in a former Letter.

Page 189. Line 20. Inſtead of not able to ſupport it ſelf, read able to ſupport it.

Page 228. Line 27. Inſtead a good, read as good.

Page 230. Line 6. Inſtead of FREE-THING-SLAVE, read FREE-THINKING-SLAVE.

CONSIDERATIONS

Upon the present

STATE of our AFFAIRS,

AT

Home and Abroad,

IN A

LETTER

TO A

Member of Parliament

FROM A

Friend in the Country.

LONDON:
Printed for T. Cooper, at the *Globe* in
Pater-Noster Row.
MDCCXXXIX.

[Price One Shilling.]

A
LETTER
TO A
MEMBER of PARLIAMENT
FROM A
FRIEND in the Country.

SIR,

I AM a private Gentleman of some Property in the County of —— and voted for you at the Election of this Parliament. I voted for you neither as a Whig, nor as a Tory, but as a Gentleman, whom I believed to be in the Interest of my Country. For this Reason only I preferred you to your Competitor, and *gave* you the Vote I might have *sold* to him. Since that Time I have heard with Pleasure of your Conduct, and find no Reason to repent of my Choice. You serve me well in Parliament, and I don't desire to be served by you *any where else*. I have never solicited, I never will solicit you, though

though you should come to have a better Interest at Court, for any of *those little Places*, which seem of late to have been multiplied, only to answer the Demands of Men in my Situation, as far as possible, upon Those in yours; and which are become almost the *only Subject of Correspondence* between Members of Parliament, and their *Friends in the Country*. You will therefore permit me to take the liberty now of corresponding with you on another foot, and after four Years Silence to remind you a little of what I have a right to expect from you as my Representative. The Importance of the Conjuncture will excuse my Presumption. It is not difficult for us now to speak upon these Matters: They are brought so home to our Minds, they are made so plain to our Senses, that we can't be doubtful what Opinion to form. It is hardly necessary to *reason*; it is enough to *feel*. There is a time, when wrong and mischievous Measures may be disguised; but there is a time too when they will discover themselves. While the evil Seeds are sowing Those alone are alarmed, who have Penetration enough to see Things in their Causes; but when they are grown up, and the Fruits appear, the gross of Mankind have Capacity to judge, and Spirit to complain. This, Sir, is the Circumstance of the People of ENGLAND They suffer too much to be amused: And
if

if they continue to suffer, it will not be from Error, or Insensibility, but from such Causes as I do not care to suppose. There is reason to hope that their Complaints will be redress'd; and in that hope I write this Letter to you. I shall propose to your Consideration some particular Points which we in the Country think, should make the Business of this Session; and if you agree to my Reasonings, I dare promise myself, you will not afterwards *differ from them in your Conduct.*

Sir, We are a trading Nation; and whatever affects our Trade is our nearest Concern, and ought to be our principal Care.

Of all the Branches of our Commerce that to our own Colonies is the most valuable upon many Accounts. If I am rightly informed, it is by *that alone* we are enabled now to carry on the rest. And as it is the most useful to us, so for many Reasons it naturally ought to be *the most secure.* Foreign Markets may be lost or spoilt by various Accidents: Other Nations may get in, and carry Commodities, that may be preferred to ours; or by working cheaper, may be able perhaps to undersell us *there.* And by these Means I am afraid we have found our Trade decline considerably in many parts of the World. But in our own Plantations nothing of this can happen. The Trade we have there is engrost by ourselves; all other Nations are excluded from it, and we carry it on under such Regulations as are moſt for our Advantage. In conſequence of which, it is the Nurſery of our Seamen, the Support of our Navigation, and the Life of our Manufacturers.

But of late Years our Merchants paſſing to and from our Colonies have been ſtopt, examined, plundered, and abuſed by the SPANIARDS, our Ships confiſcated, and our Seamen enſlaved, ſo that the Navigation thither is become ſo dangerous, that if an effectual ſtop be not ſoon put to theſe Practices, this moſt beneficial Commerce will be utterly loſt. The original Source of them is a Right of Sovereignty which the SPANIARDS arrogate to themſelves in the *American* Seas ; a Claim that has always been treated with Deriſion and Scorn, by every Power in Europe, and particularly by us, who were really Maſters of thoſe Seas, from the glorious Reign of Queen ELIZABETH, down to the weak one of King CHARLES the Second. And this Claim of SPAIN is ſtill ſo far from being owned by us, that though it *be a ſecret Motive*, they have not *yet* had the Inſolence to avow it openly as *the Cauſe* of their Proceedings. But they treat every *Britiſh* Ship, which they are able to maſter, as if the ſailing only in thoſe Seas was a ſufficient Cauſe of Confiſcation. They have ſeized and condemned outward-bound Ships, above a hundred Leagues from any Shore, without any Pretence at all ; and where they

are

are graciously pleased to assign Pretences for their Depredations, *those Pretences are worse than the Depredations themselves.* They pretend that every Ship, which has *Logwood, Cocoa-Nuts,* or *Pieces of Eight* aboard, is lawful Prize. Now two of these grow in our own Colonies; and the South-Sea Company, by the Assiento Contract, furnish the SPANIARDS with Negroes, which they pay for in Pieces of Eight; and as the principal Market for these Negroes is JAMAICA, this occasions the circulating a great deal of that Specie there. So that we might with full as good Reason stop the Ships of SPAIN in their Passage by JAMAICA, or our other Plantations, and confiscate them formally, if we find aboard of them either *Logwood, Cocoa-Nuts,* or *Pieces of Eight:* For this will just as well prove that *they* have been trading with *our Colonies,* as our having such Goods aboard, can prove that *we* have been trading with *theirs.* And their Manner of Trial is a Mockery of Justice, which would be highly *ridiculous,* if the Effects of it were not so *terrible.* The Cause is tried in their own Courts in AMERICA, a SPANISH Advocate is to plead for our Merchants, and the Judges themselves almost always share in the Prize. The Consequence of this is, that every Ship which is taken by them must be confiscated.

BUT supposing, for Argument's sake, that

all those Species of Goods upon which Sentence is past by this most righteous Judicature, were undeniable Proofs of an *illicit Trade*, on what Ground of the Law of Nations, or by what Article of any Treaty, have the SPANIARDS a Right *to stop or search our Ships at all* ? Where a general Trade is allowed, one Species of Goods may be prohibited; as, for Instance, Wool, or Fuller's Earth; and the exporting it may be highly penal: But did this Country ever pretend, when her Naval Power was at the Height, to stop Ships *out at Sea*, in order to search whether such Commodities were aboard? Would the little Republick of GENOA endure our doing it? Could any thing less than a Conquest bring her to submit to it? But the doing it in AMERICA is much less defensible. For where no general Trade is allowed, no one particular Species of Goods can be more *prohibited* than another, and *the Searching there* has no Object at all, and no Foundation in Reason. All the Rules therefore laid down in the Treaty of 1667, between ENGLAND and SPAIN, concerning the Method of Searching for prohibited Goods, are plainly confined to EUROPE, where a general Trade is allowed, and have no relation to AMERICA, where all Trade is forbid. For in the one Case they may be necessary, but in the other they must be useless. And it is much to be wished, that

this

this most manifest Distinction *had been better understood by our Ministers* in their treating with SPAIN; and that, by insisting on Articles which are not to our Purpose, they had not weakened those by which our Rights are secured. The Ground on which those Rights stand is the Law of Nations, which establishes a Freedom of Navigation to all, and considers the Sea as an universal Benefit, not a particular Property or Dominion of one: There is no Nation *so powerful,* none *so proud* in the World, as directly to deny this Maxim; there is none *so weak,* none *so abject* as to give it up. We have been so far from departing from it by Treaty, that in all those we have made concerning AMERICA it is expressly stipulated, and indubitably confirmed, particularly in that of 1670; which declares that *the Freedom of Navigation ought by no manner of Means to be interrupted,* and makes no other Exception to this general Rule, than a reciprocal Prohibition to both Nations in AMERICA, to come *into* the Ports and Havens of the other *to trade there* ; for in Cases of Distress, or Necessity, the same Treaty allows, *that they may come into them*, and ought to be kindly received. As to our sailing *near their Coasts*, it is not only permitted, but it is of absolute Necessity in the Course of our Voyage to and from our own Plantations in AMERICA: *How near* we shall go to them, it is impossible to fix,

fix, because it depends upon Circumstances we cannot command, as Winds, and Tides; but *very near* we must go frequently; and they reciprocally must go near to ours. No Treaty therefore has ever settled any Bounds, except the Ports and Havens of either Crown in AMERICA, within which it shall not be lawful to sail; nor can they be settled, so as not to be liable to *infinite Difficulties*, and *endless Chicane*.

It remains then certain, that in Reason, and Justice, by the Law of Nations, and by all our Treaties, the Way to and from our own Dominions in AMERICA is as free as the Passage between LONDON and BRISTOL, and that SPAIN has no more Right to stop and search our Ships in the Seas of AMERICA, than in the *British* Channel.

Indeed this Practice of *searching* is so very inexcusable, that it cannot be supported upon any Notion of Right. Nothing can warrant it but superior Force, and the famous Argument of BRENNUS, VÆ VICTIS! All Sorts of Mischiefs must arise from admitting it, or from merely suffering it, as we have sadly experienced, and no one Inconvenience can attend its being denied. Were our Ships found trading in the *Spanish* Ports and Havens themselves, even in that Case, though they ought to be *confiscated*, it is a great Absurdity to suppose they should be *searched*. For as the Ship and

and Cargo, be it what it will, is forfeited by our being there without Diſtreſs, or Neceſſity, to what intent or purpoſe is *a ſearch* to be made after any particular Species we may have aboard? But upon this Pretence to ſtop our Ships on the High Seas, is *to inſult our Underſtanding, and deſpiſe our Power*, as well as to infringe our Rights, and to deſtroy our Trade.

Thus for ſome Years Things have gone on from bad to worſe, ENGLAND complaining and remonſtrating, SPAIN chicaning and inſulting; Satisfaction ſometimes refuſed, ſometimes promiſed, never given: Our Negotiations, and our Loſſes always continuing, and *encreaſing almoſt in the ſame Proportion*: At laſt our Merchants weary of theſe uſeleſs Methods applied *a third time* to Parliament, and petitioned there for Redreſs. In the Courſe of their Examination it appeared too plain, that we had been treated by SPAIN with the utmoſt Injuſtice, the utmoſt Barbarity, and the utmoſt Contempt: And that no one effectual Step had been taken to procure Reparation of our Loſſes, Satisfaction to our Honour, or Security for our Trade. It appeared indeed, that as far as *writing* would go, our Miniſtry had tried to put a ſtop to theſe Inſults. They had ſpared no Pains, they had ſpared *no Paper*. Memorials, Repreſentations to the Court of SPAIN had been as frequent, and as little minded, as the Orders and Cedulas ſent from thence, in behalf

of

of our Merchants, to the *Spanish* Tribunals, and Governors in AMERICA. Neither produced any Effect, but to encrease the Depredations, augment our Sufferings, and amuse the Sufferers. Nay, though in Consequence of a Treaty with SPAIN, in which we served her *more perhaps than we could justify*, Commissaries were appointed to adjust these Differences, and obtain Restitution for our Losses, as a Return for *Favours received*; though they continued negotiating for some Years in SPAIN, though much was promised from this Commission, yet it does not appear, that any body got by it, *but the Commissaries themselves*.

Upon the Proof of all this it was the Sense of Parliament, that more effectual Measures ought to be pursued. And to enable his Majesty to take them, great Supplies were voted, great Armaments made; the whole Nation expected, and desired a War, if such a Peace could not be gained, as would retrieve our Honour, and secure our Trade. Soon after the Parliament rose the War appeared inevitable: Strong Fleets were fitted out, and sent to SPAIN, and the INDIES: This could not be done without a vast Expence, great Obstruction to our Trade, and Hardships on our Sailors. Yet such was the Spirit of the People, such their Resentment at the Indignities put upon the King and Nation, that they came into it chearfully; and not a Murmur was heard

heard unless against the *Spaniards*. I believe it will be difficult to find a Period in History, when this Nation was so universally, and so eagerly bent upon a War, as at that Time. They had a just Abhorrence, and a just *Disdain* of the *Spaniards*; nor did *Those*, who are known to judge the best of Foreign Affairs, apprehend any Danger, *at that Crisis*, from any *other more formidable* Power; so that all concluded we should act *with Vigour*, when it was more than probable we might act *with Success*: And the Effort we had made, the Force we had raised was very sufficient, to give us a Superiority in so just a Quarrel, a Quarrel in which all Nations trading to AMERICA had an equal Interest, and a *common Cause* with ENGLAND: It was now believed, our Administration would shew, that their former Remissness did not proceed from Fear, or Negligence; but that they curbed their Spirit till *the Point of Time*, when they might be sure to exert it with *decisive Advantages*. This their Friends gave out, and candid Men were willing to think; especially as it was said, that *one Great Person* had declared, he thought it for the Interest of a Minister to have War rather than Peace. But in the Height and Warmth of these Expectations, while all EUROPE was intent on the Motions and Operations of our Fleets, we heard of a Convention being signed, and that we might expect a speedy Accommodation of our Differences by a Peace.

Of the Terms of this Convention you will, no doubt, be apprifed at the Meeting of the Parliament, and then you will judge, whether it is proportionate to the Charge we have been at, the Opportunity we have neglected, the Wrongs we have fuftained, the Satisfaction, and Security we have a Right to expect.

I only beg leave to mark out to you *two principal Points*, upon which I think you can't miftake in forming your Judgment. If we make a Peace, it ought to be fuch, as *will remove*, in the moft effectual manner, both the *Caufe*, and *Pretence*, of the Injuries done us by the Spanifh Nation.

Now *the Pretence* for them has been folely this, that they claim a Right of ftopping and fearching our Ships, on the High Seas, or near their own Coafts; which Claim of their's is unfupported by Treaty, and directly repugnant to the Law of Nations, to the Rights of our Crown, and the Freedom of our Navigation. If therefore we clearly affert, that *They have no fuch Right*; that where we have *no Trade* with them there can be *no prohibited Goods*; that we have a Liberty to fail *as nigh* to their Coafts as the Courfe of our Voyage, the Convenience of Winds and Tides, and other Circumftances of Navigation may require; that in purfuing that Courfe, our Ships *are not to be fearched* or *ftopt* on any Account; that, *in Cafes of Neceffity*, they may even *enter their Ports*,

Ports, and that only in Cafe of *Trading there* they are to be feized; if we exprefsly affert *all this* in our Treaty of Peace, it may be a fecure and lafting one, and deferves well the Sanction of Parliament.

But if we leave this *loofe*, or if we admit of *any Limits*, within which *a Search may be made on any Pretence*, we have yielded every thing, we have no Security, all will be fubject to Difpute and Chicane; we fhall have the fame weary Round to run of Applications to MADRID, References from thence to the WEST-INDIES, and from the WEST-INDIES to MADRID again; and after the folemn Hearing of our Wrongs in Parliament, after laying open all our Wounds to the View of the World, after Declarations of Right, and lofty Threats of Refentment, after Millions fpent, we fhall be in a worfe Condition, than we ever have been yet by any former Treaty, or than we fhould have been, if we had taken no Notice of the Complaints of our Merchants, and not moved in them at all.

As to the other Point, *the Caufe* of all thefe Injuries, I take it to have been the Contempt this Nation is fallen into, from what unhappily may have feemed to our Enemies a defpicable Tamenefs and Pufillanimity in our Conduct. How far this has gone, I am afhamed to fay. Thofe, who to infult us could not prefume on their own Strength, by long obferving, or supposing they observed a Weakness in our Councils, have come to suppose it in the Nation itself: And on this Presumption they became as arrogant, as they imagined ENGLAND to be timid, and weak. They have certainly acted as if they thought we were *the meanest of Nations*, or that *the meanest of Ministers* had conducted our Affairs. This Prejudice therefore must be removed, or we shall continue to suffer, as much as we have done, and still more: For where Impunity is certain, Insolence knows no Bounds. If the Peace we make does not retrieve our Reputation, it is impossible it can last, for *it may be broke without Fear.* SPAIN can have no Reason to keep it, unless it is made on such Terms, as to convince her that the Temper, and Spirit of our Court is changed; and that we will bear no longer what we have borne so long. Should any Article of it be *dishonourable or mean*, though all the rest were advantageous, that alone would be fatal, because it would leave us exposed to endless Insults and Affronts, the certain Consequence of a Stain imprinted on our national Character. Reputation is to a People, just what Credit is to a Merchant. The first depends on an Opinion of Strength, as the latter does on an Opinion of Opulence. But, that Opinion of Opulence is a real Advantage, that Opinion of Strength is a real Security. When a contrary Notion prevails in the Case of the Merchant, when his Credit is hurt,

there

there comes a Run upon him suddenly, and by being thought insufficient, he becomes so in Reality. The same Thing may happen to a Nation from the Loss of Character. An Opinion of its Weakness may encourage Enemies, may unite them against it in a sudden Attack, may dishearten its Friends, and leave it destitute of Succour. All which might have been prevented, had due Care been taken to support the Opinion of its Strength by a spirited Conduct. I hope Attention will be had to this in our Peace with SPAIN, and that we shall on no Account yield to any Thing *scandalous*, but seek Reparation to our Honour, as well as to our Merchants. And I dare answer for *them*, that, great as their Losses are, they had rather endure them without any Compensation, than have it made in a Way, that may be disgraceful to their Country. Sure I am it would be better for *them* to lose their Money, or for us to pay it out of our own Pockets, than for the sake of Retribution to them, to admit of a Treaty, in which the Security of our Commerce is not firmly established, beyond a possibility of all future Cavils, by express Declarations of our Right *not to be searched*. For to admit of such a Treaty, would be no less an Absurdity than *to be Bribed with our own Money to our own Undoing*.

In these plain Lights, Sir, I hope you will consider this Convention, when it shall be laid before you in the Course of the Session. You will

will not, I dare say, suffer yourself to be amused with nice Distinctions, and Refinements of Policy. You will remember how useless, nay, how fatal, all these Subtilties have hitherto proved, and what they are like to produce. You will desire to see a Treaty, which shall not be *the Beginning*, but *the End of Negotiation*; which shall speak so plain, that every English Country-Gentleman, and every Spanish Governor in the INDIES, shall understand the Sense of it, as well as the *Walpoles*, and *La Quadras*.

You will not be satisfied with a present Compliance, and temporary Expedients, which are only patch-work, nor refer that to Commissaries, which requires instant Dispatch; nor suffer that to be argued which is incontestable; but demand a solid and a durable Peace, founded on real Security, and express Acknowledgment of all those Rights that have been questioned by SPAIN, either with regard to our Commerce, or *to our Possessions*. For nothing less than this *will satisfy the Nation*.

And when this is done, you will consider of the Methods, how to turn this Peace to the best Advantage, and secure it effectually for the time to come. The only Way of doing that, Sir, is, to put the Nation *in a condition to be feared*; and this can only be done, by reducing its Debt, and gradually lessening its Taxes. It

It is a melancholy thought that so much Time should have been lost from this necessary Work, since it has been in our Power. I believe it could be proved almost to a Demonstration, that ever since the Peace of UTRECHT, we might have attended to it constantly, without the least Interruption from our Neighbours abroad, who had no Desire to disturb us, till within these few Years past, when, notwithstanding *great Compliances* on our Side, the Hostilities of SPAIN have loudly called for our Resentment. In all our Quarrels during the late Reign, though it can no more be doubted that *the Interest of* ENGLAND *was the only Point considered, than that* BREMEN *and* VERDEN *were never thought of in them*, yet how far *that Interest* was rightly understood by us, is not quite so clear. To some it appears we had no Grounds for quarrelling, no more than we had upon other Occasions for negotiating, and that we might better have been quiet, if such active Abilities, as some of our Ministers were endowed with, could have been content to repose. But the entring lightly into Wars, and Alliances, in which we had no Concern, or a very distant one at most, if it was the Fault, was not the only Fault of our Government.

Those who cannot see into the Depth of our Policy, and the inscrutable Wisdom of our Councils, may be apt to think, that we have

have been no less faulty in our Way of *managing Peace*, in our Neglect of using the Advantages attending it, and in finding the Secret by an unaccountable Conduct, to make it *as expensive*, and *as ruinous* as War: That we have *purchased Dishonour* at *as dear a Rate*, as we did *Glory* in some former Reigns: That this has continued, this has fixed upon us the Difficulties, which, with tolerable Management, ought to have been conquered long ago: And that to this it is owing, not to King WILLIAM, or Queen ANNE, if we are a distrest and a declining Nation. Had it not been for this, say they, we have had Leisure enough to pay off great part of our Debt; and to encrease the Sinking Fund to such an annual Sum, as would enable the Government to maintain our Dignity, without wasting our Substance. Had *that* been done, we had been now *a mighty People*, easy at home, and formidable abroad. And though we had no Disputes with SPAIN, yet on other Accounts, it would be highly desirable for us to be *in those Circumstances*, rather than in a State of Indigence, which must be a State of Fear. For though by Reason of some lucky Circumstances at this Juncture we have no Cause to apprehend any instant Danger from FRANCE, those, who look forwards at all, have very dreadful Apprehensions. The Empire is already open to her by ALSACE, and LORRAINE,

RAINE, and there has been a terrible Alarm, that it may soon be so by LUXEMBOUGH. The Weakness of the LOW COUNTRIES is apparent to every body, and God knows how soon they may be made a Sacrifice either to *the Friendship*, or the Arms of FRANCE. If the Power of that Crown in former Times had equalled its Ambition, EUROPE had been lost; if its Ambition now shall equal its Power, it will probably accomplish what it then designed. And bad is our Condition, when our Fate is to depend on a Spirit of Conquest not prevailing in that Court.

They have wisely been doing what we ought to have done. They have by Oeconomy, by Attention to Trade, by easing their People, and husbanding well the Money they raise, laid such Foundations for their future Greatness, that if an enterprising Minister should succeed to *this*, he will find Advantages, which his greatest Predecessors, RICHELIEU, MAZARIN, COLBERT, LOUVOIS, never had, and will have reason to expect a much more glorious Success. What may then be the Circumstances of that Kingdom, and *this?* On one Side, mortgaged Revenues, Credit sunk at home and abroad, an exhausted, dispirited, discontented People: On the other, a rich and popular Government, strong in Alliances, in Reputation, in the Confidence and Affection of its Subjects. Will the Contest be equal between *these two Powers?* And what an Aggravation is it to the

D   Pain

Pain of this Thought, to reflect how easily we might have been in a Condition, to save ourselves and EUROPE from this Danger and Fear, if, for these 12 Years past, (to go no higher) our Debt had decreased, in Proportion to the Means that have been in our Hands, and no greater Expence had been incurr'd by the *Government, than the real Necessity of Affairs required. We might then have spoke to FRANCE with as much Authority, as becomes this Nation in the common Cause, especially if we had taken any Care at the same Time to set ourselves at the Head of the Protestant Interest, which is our natural Post; and has on former Occasions given great Advantages as well as Lustre to the Crown of ENGLAND. Had we pursued these Measures, we should now have nothing to dread; by pursuing them steadily we may yet be safe, we may yet be considerable, we may yet hold the Balance of EUROPE. But till a wiser Administration shall restore our Affairs, little Dignity, or Vigour, is to be expected in our Councils. Some *Appearance of Vigour* may perhaps be maintained; but it will impose on Nobody; no, *not on ourselves.* To

---

* *N. B.* Had the Sinking Fund been duly applied since the year 27 to the Payment of the national Debt, at least twelve Millions might have been paid off: The Sinking Fund would then produce at 4 *per Cent.* little less than two Millions, and were Interest reduced to 3 *per Cent.* considerably more. Upon such a Bottom as this, we might well maintain a new French War.

think

think that keeping up, at a vaſt Expence, great Fleets and Armies, with a Reſolution not to employ them, can ſecure our Reputation, is as groſs a Miſtake, as if, in private Life, a Gentleman known to be in Debt, and not diſpoſed to clear himſelf, ſhould think to cheat his Creditors, and ſupport his Credit, by encreaſing his Equipage, making ſumptuous Entertainments, and beggaring his Family with new Debts and Mortgages.

It is ſcarce to be computed what it has coſt this Nation *in well equipt* Fleets, and *well-dreſt* Troops, for ſome Years paſt; and I ſhould be glad to be told (bating the Fineneſs of the Show) what Uſe they have been of to us either at home or abroad. They give to be ſure an Air of Magnificence; but then it is well known, that we owe almoſt fifty Millions, and have been forced to apply the Sinking Fund, not to diſcharge that Debt, but *to furniſh out theſe Shows.*

In moſt parts of ENGLAND Gentlemen's Rents are ſo ill paid, and the Weight of Taxes lyes ſo heavy upon them, that thoſe who have nothing from the Court can ſcarce ſupport their Families; and thoſe in Place are hardly Savers on the Account, if what they give be balanced againſt what they receive. There are indeed ſome rich People who have Money in the Funds, and out of Tenderneſs to *them* I ſuppoſe it was, that when Intereſt was naturally, and apparently fallen to three

D 2 *per-*

per Cent. the national Debt was still continued at four, by which the Publick has lost Millions, and such an Opportunity, as it may not again be in our Power to retrieve.

Yet if Peace should be settled on a durable Foot, I hope *the worthy Gentleman*, who, two Years ago, proposed the Reduction of Interest, will renew his Motion; and that it will not be *mended* so as to be made *less eligible*, and then objected to, and *thrown out by the Amenders*. I hope too Care will be taken, that, when the Scheme shall have its effect, Reduction of Interest *and Taxes* shall go hand in hand; and that the Sinking Fund so encreased shall not be left at the Disposition of a Minister, but applied in part to take off some of the Duties, which are such a Load on Industry, and so dangerous to Freedom.

All these Particulars, Sir, deserve your serious Attention. We expect to find we have *a Peace*, not by his Majesty's Speech alone, and the congratulary Compliments of both Houses of Parliament (which during all our late Sufferings, and the Hostilities of SPAIN, have been annually made with great Encomiums on his Measures) but by *the Fruits of Peace*, a considerable lessening of our Expences, and Relief to the People at whose Charge it was gained.

We may yet recover, low as we are, with good Management. To make *a great State little*, is not so difficult indeed, as to make *a little*

little one great; yet it is not to be done immediately; and with all the Skill *some* have shewn in endeavouring it here, it will require still more Time to sink us so, as that, *with the help of Friends*, we may not rise again. The natural Strength of this Nation is great, its Resources great, and in one respect greater than ever, because the Funds *having been tried*, and found *sufficient*, the borrowing on them again, when our Debt is reduced, would be secure and easy. To reduce it therefore ought to be the principal Object of all who meddle with our publick Affairs. We shall judge of all your other Virtues now by your Frugality. The best Oeconomist for the Publick will be the best Member of Parliament, the best Counsellor of State, and the best Minister. I don't know how it has happened, but for some Time past, an ignorant Country-Gentleman might be almost provoked to say, that *our Flegm* has shewn itself only in *bearing Affronts*, and *our Spirit* only in *squandering away the Publick Money*. I suppose we shall now have no Occasion to shew our Fire, but we shall have great Occasion for a reserved and cautious Temper. Let this operate in the granting of Money, in a constant refusing of new Powers to the Crown, and watching over the Use of those already granted. Above all, beware of new Additions to the Civil List. It is a strange Circumstance, and will not sound well to Posterity, that while the

Publick

[22]

Publick loses in so many Articles, so many Gains have been of late made to the Crown: That when every Gentleman's Estate is falling in Value, the Estate of the Crown should be so much encreased, that if we were to purchase it back with fifty thousand Pounds *per ann. more than it was given for*, we should save by the Bargain. I will just take notice how great Profits have accrued to the Civil List upon the Gin-Bill only. All that had been gained by the highest Amount of the Duties on Spirits, that is, by the highest Excess of the Evil designed to be reformed was made up to his Majesty out of the Aggregate Fund, by Way of Compensation for the Loss he should sustain *upon saving the Lives of many thousands of his Subjects*. At the same Time all he might gain by the Encrease of the Brewery, and by that of the Wine Licence Duty, (which together can't be *less*, and ought to be reckoned at *more* than an equal Proportion to the Decrease on the Spirits *) is, by the Bounty of this Act, preserved to him entire, and without Account. So that *the preventing a national Mischief*, of so destructive a Nature, that, rather than suffer it to continue, the Legislature was forced to ruin many Particulars, and grievously hurt our Sugar Colonies, has *(no doubt to the Com-*

---

* *N. B.* The Share of the Civil List upon foreign Spirits is about $\frac{2}{3}$; upon home Spirits about $\frac{1}{3}$; upon Beer and Ale about $\frac{1}{4}$.

fort.

fort of the Sufferers) been so happily managed, that it may prove an Advantage to the Civil List of seventy thousand Pounds a Year, and probably more. I would only observe, that if our other popular Vices could be turned as much to account as the drinking Spirits has been, the Estate of the King of ENGLAND would be more a Gainer *by the Sins of the People*, than the Exchequer of the Pope.

But there is another Article I must not pass over in Silence, because it may probably come before the House this Session; and that is, that his Majesty has been, and still is in Possession of 50,000 *l. per ann.* which most People think was designed by Parliament for the Prince of Wales, over and above the fifty which he now enjoys. It seems evident to me by all I have heard, and read upon this Subject, that the Parliament which gave the Civil List could not intend, that his Majesty should retain for himself any part of this hundred thousand Pounds a Year; since supposing the Prince to have *it all*, and allowing his Majesty to spend one hundred thousand Pounds a Year extraordinary in *Pensions, Bounties, Secret-Service Money*, &c. he will still have, for the Support of his Houshold, a Revenue equal to that of the late King. The Expence of his Family has been *unhappily lessened*, since the Consideration of this Matter in Parliament, by no less a saving than *the whole Sum in dispute*; and as for the Charge which remains, it will be abundantly supplied out of so large an Income as six hundred thousand Pounds a Year, with the great additional Profits arising from the Gin Bill, Crown Land, Plantation Rents, and other Articles commonly known by the Name of *Licks*, &c. So that if the Prince has not the fifty thousand Pounds *per Annum*, which I apprehend he has a Right to from the Intention of Parliament out of the seven hundred and fifty thousand enjoyed by his Majesty, (exclusive of the Profits on the Articles abovementioned) if, I say, this be not given to him, upon the Birth of two Children, and the Hopes of a third, it certainly ought *to be returned to the Publick.* If his R. H. has it, it will not indeed be *lost to the Publick*; it is like to circulate freely, and the Poor will have their Share of it; but as I am arguing now upon a Principle of *saving*, I must needs say, *the Nation wants it*, and the Royal Family *all together has enough.* Let the Wealth of our Princes always encrease with that of their People: Let them share the Fruits of every publick Blessing, of every Benefit derived to us from their Government: But to have *them rich*, while *we are poor*, is, methinks, both an Indecency, and a weakening of one strong Motive to them for governing with a constant Regard to the Prosperity of their Subjects.

Sir

Sir, from what I have said to recommend Oeconomy, I would not have you imagine any Argument can be drawn, to defend a bad and dishonourable Peace, should it appear that such a one has been made with SPAIN. To make all proper Savings is the Duty of our Ministers; but an Acquiescence under Wrongs and Insults is not Oeconomy: An Acquiescence that may cost us Millions is not Oeconomy: An Acquiescence that may Ruin our Trade, the only source of our Riches, is not Oeconomy: It is not Oeconomy to neglect an Opportunity of doing ourselves Justice at a cheaper Rate, than we can hope to obtain it for in any future Conjuncture. It can never be admitted, that because Peace is *cheaper* than War, and because it is good to save Money, therefore *any Terms* of Peace are to be gladly received rather than to make war *with any Advantages*: And I shall less admit it *here*, because we have already born an Expence, which, if rightly managed, might have been sufficient to have procured us Victory, and the Fruit of Victory, Peace.

Sir, there is another Way of Reasoning, similar to this, which I foresee, and which beforehand I beg leave to warn you against, That because we ought to have great Apprehensions of the growing Power of FRANCE, if we go on ourfelves as we have done of late, and fuffer *them* to go on to take Advantage of our Conduct, therefore we are to fubmit to all the Injuftice of SPAIN, and give up the Rights we are moft concerned to Support, for fear that FRANCE fhould declare againft us in the War.

I have faid before, it feems highly improbable, *that Court* fhould engage in fuch a Meafure, *at this Time*, from the prefent State of their Government, and the unfettled Condition, which any Change might put it into for fome Years to come. But fuppofing the worft that it is poffible to fuppofe, fuppofing we knew that FRANCE would fide againft us with SPAIN, even in that Cafe I think it is reafoning wrong, it is reafoning with regard to the prefent Day alone, to make *that* an Argument for accepting a Peace upon difadvantageous and difhonourable Terms. For if we are really fallen into fuch a State, that when any Power in EUROPE fhall think fit to infult and injure us, and we take up Arms to defend ourfelves, FRANCE will interpofe, and without any Regard to her Alliance, and the Juftice of our Caufe, *infift on our giving up our Rights*, or elfe declare herfelf *our Enemy*; if this is our Situation, it is *an Extremity*, which we muft *fight ourfelves out of as well*,

and

and *as soon as we can.* For what can we expect by delaying it longer, but to draw on farther Infults, farther Wrongs, farther Contempt; to be treated on all Occafions *as a Province to* FRANCE; to be daily weakened more and more by the Incroachments of all our Neighbours upon every Branch of our Trade; and to be at laft devoured without the Means of Refiftance, when all our Friends *are afhamed of us,* and when a long *State of Dependancy* fhall have funk our Courage, and prepared our Minds, to endure the Infamy of *a foreign Yoke?* But we have the ftrongeft Grounds to think that our Affairs are not fo defperate. FRANCE is no Party concerned in this Difpute with SPAIN, and the prefent Genius of that Court is not to engage without Neceffity, in any Quarrel that muft coft her a War. She may perhaps defire to mediate, and to mediate partially; but it is in the Power of ENGLAND to refufe that Mediation: She may fpeak in an unfriendly, or perhaps an angry Style; but we have profited little by a great deal of Experience, if we have not learnt that there is a wide Diftance *between talking angrily,* and *declaring War.* It feems evident upon the whole, that what we ought to apprehend, is not an immediate, but a future Danger from FRANCE; and the Care of the Legiflature fhould extend to *that,* not

[28]

by approving a Peace, which may deserve to be censured, but by attending to Things, which, either in War or Peace, are of extreme Importance to the Strength of the Kingdom, and therefore demand particularly the Inspection of Parliament.

Such is the State of *our Manufactures*, such is that of *our Colonies*; both should be enquired into, that the Nation may know, whether *the former* can support themselves much longer, under the various Pressures that affect our Manufacturers; and how it is possible that *the latter* should decline, when if it had not been *for a false Report of his Death*, Sir O——o B——n might have *governed one of them*; and so many Gentlemen of *no less Fortune and Character* have been frequently sent *to take Care of the Rest*?

The State of *our Garrisons* abroad too may deserve to be considered, and whether the absolute Power lodged in some of *our Governors there*, has been *discreetly, moderately*, and *humanely* exercised, to the Honour of his Majesty's Commission, and of the English Name.

Sir, what I would farther submit to your Attention is, whether some *new Powers* have not been assumed by the Crown, or old ones
stretcht

stretcht beyond their legal Bounds, by the Construction of Ministers, and the Acquiescence, or perhaps the Authority of the Judges themselves. This is most likely to happen with regard to criminal Prosecutions, and many Instances of it have been complained of formerly, and fallen under the Notice and the Censure of Parliament.

No longer ago than last Year there was a loud Complaint of a Power assumed and exercised by the Secretaries of State against all Law, and particularly against *that most sacred Law* the Habeas Corpus Act; I mean the demanding Security for their good Behaviour, from Persons examined before them on Suspicion of writing, printing, or publishing Libels against the Government.

This having been exercised for the most part upon low and inconsiderable People who had neither Spirit nor Strength enough to support their Right, it had past unquestioned many Years together, till Mr. FRANKLIN was advised not to comply with that Demand, but to insist on giving Bail for his Appearance only. Upon this the Matter was brought by Habeas Corpus before my Lord Chief Justice RAYMOND, who decided it *in his favour*, for he admitted him to Bail without any Security for his good Behaviour.

Notwith-

Notwithstanding which the same Practice continued in the Secretary's Office, and past *sub silentio*, till last Year Mr. AMHURST brought it into publick Discourse.

Though the Circumstances of this Fact are pretty well known, yet as they are of a weighty and a grievous Nature, I will remind you of them by a short Recital of all such Particulars as are come to my Knowledge. Some time after Christmas 1637, Mr. AMHURST hearing that a Warrant from the Duke of NEWCASTLE was out against him, surrendered himself to a Messenger, and was carried before his Grace to be examined. The Crime imputed to him was, that *he was suspected to be Author of a Paper suspected to be a Libel*. As no Proofs were alledged against him, no Witnesses produced, an Examination of this Kind could not last long. As soon as it was over, he was told, that the Crime being bailable, he should be bailed upon finding sufficient Sureties to answer for his Appearance, and his good Behaviour. He offered to take his Trial, and give Bail for his Appearance, but the other Terms imposed upon him he absolutely refused. Upon that Refusal he was remanded back to Custody, and the next Day brought his Habeas Corpus, and was then set at Liberty by Consent, till the twelve Judges
should

should determine the Question, whether he was obliged to give Bail for his good Behaviour, as well as for his Appearance, before he was entitled to his Liberty.

As this Determination would have been the most important to the Liberty of every Man in ENGLAND, that perhaps the Judges ever gave, it was impatiently expected, and desired by the Publick. Several Days were fixed for hearing Council on both Sides; but they were never heard, and the Question remains still undetermined.

A Question of no less Consequence, than whether Ignominy and Punishment (for *such* the being bound to good Behaviour is by the Law supposed to be) shall be inflicted on a Freeman *before any Trial*, and *without his being charged upon Oath*, even of Suspicion of Guilt: A Question of no less Consequence, than whether any Man in the Kingdom, whom the Court are pleased to suspect of writing a Libel, shall by frequent, successive Commitments upon other Suspicions, with no Proof at all, be either constantly imprisoned, from not being able to find Security for his good Behaviour, so often as it is asked, which may be every Week; or be exposed to forfeit many Bails at once, to the Value possibly of ten thousand

thousand Pounds *, for a single Breach of the Peace, which in another Circumstance, he could not be fined ten Shillings for, by any Court in ENGLAND.

A Question of no less Consequence, than whether the Habeas Corpus Act shall be the Rule of Proceedings in all Cases bailable; or whether it shall be in the Power of every Justice of Peace to add *new Terms* to it, and make *new Exceptions* to the Advantages given by that Act to the Subject; that is, whether *they* should do what all the Judges in ENGLAND would deserve to be impeached for if they did, and what the Parliament itself ought no more to do, than to repeal, or alter MAGNA CHARTA.

A Question of no less Consequence, than whether we should lose the entire Benefit of the Liberty of the Press, which secures and strengthens all our other Liberties: Since upon Suspicion only of a Book or Paper being libellous, any Man suspected to be concerned in it, may be put under the Load of finding Security for his good Behaviour, which is such a

* N. B. While a Man is bound to his good Behaviour, if he should chance to commit any common Act of natural Frailty or Passion; get drunk, for instance, or return a Blow, he would be liable to forfeit his Securities.

Vexation

Vexation, and such a Distress, that it is commonly Part, and a heavy Part of the Sentence upon *convicted Criminals*, in all but capital Causes: Since this is in the Power of every Justice of Peace; * and since, by Consequence, no Man can be safe who publishes a Book, how innocent soever it may be, without *as many Licences, as there are Middlesex Justices.*

Why this Question was not decided at that Time, why it remains still undetermined, I cannot tell. If there is no Intention to revive the Practice which occasioned the Dispute, I am surprized and sorry, that the Terror of it is suffered to hang over us still, and that the Opinion of all Mankind concerning it has not yet received the Sanction of a judicial Determination, or the Declaration of Parliament.

From my good Opinion of the present Judges, I hope and believe, that if *they* decide it, we have nothing to fear. They know the Danger and detest the Iniquity, of adding Restrictions of their own to Laws declaratory of Liberty. They know, that Parliaments have often resented such Proceedings; that they have been productive of the greatest Mischiefs, the greatest Disorders, and Con-

---

* The Law knows of no Power in a Secretary of State, in this respect, which is not equally lodg'd in every Justice of Peace.

F   vulsions

vulsions in the State: That the arbitrary Interpretation of our Laws in Westminster-Hall, has been more than once the Cause of Civil War, the Dissolution of our Government, and the Destruction of our Kings. They will therefore decide, not as former Judges have done, who held their Places at the Mercy of the Crown; but as Men, who *deserve* the Places, which, without a Crime, *they cannot lose.*

Yet if this Decision should be longer delayed, it will be highly proper, that the Sense of Parliament be taken upon it, and that we should know to what we may trust. For so long as this is in doubt, so long the noblest Privileges, that Englishmen enjoy, beyond all other Nations, are left in Uncertainty, and may be thought in Danger.

And if the Consideration of this shall come before the Legislature, they will be naturally led at the same Time to consider, if there are not grievous Inconveniences that attend the Trial of criminal Causes by *special Juries*; and whether most of the Provisions made by the Act 3. of GEORGE II. should not be extended *to them*. By the several Regulations in that Act for the return and ballotting of common Juries in civil Causes, the Property tried in small Actions is pretty strongly guarded: But it is very extraordinary, that no Provision

of

of that Kind has been made, where the Question to be tried is of the highest Consequence. It is very well known, that even in civil Causes, few above the Value of a hundred Pounds, are tried without a special Jury, to which this Act does not extend.

Now I can see no Reason for these Regulations with regard to the Property tried by common Juries, which does not hold much stronger for extending the Care of Parliament to the regulating Special Juries also. The small Value of the Causes tried by the former makes it highly improbable, that either of the Parties should attempt to influence the Sheriff to make a partial Return, since the Gain would no way equal the Hazard. The same Reason too will prevent an interested Juryman, supposing such a one was returned, from giving a Verdict contrary to Evidence, and perjuring himself in the Sight of his Country, for so inconsiderable an Advantage to the Party he favours. And that Crimes will be more or less frequent in Proportion to the Temptation to commit them, must be allowed.

In criminal Cases, this is still more dangerous, because the Power of the Crown may be exerted in the Prosecution, and the Question to be tried is the Imprisonment and Punishment of a Freeman. If the Master of the Crown-Office or his Deputy, fhould be ever under any Influence, he may * name twelve of the Defendant's Friends to cover his Purpofe, and thirty fix of thofe who are moft prejudiced againft him upon Reafons of Party, or other Caufes, if he can find fo many in the County; and as the Solicitor for the Crown would ftrike off the former, the Defendant muft be tried from a Jury among the latter. It is true that Officer is *fworn*, but fo is the Sheriff in returning common Juries, and it is juft as likely that the one fhould *name* partially, as the other *return partially*.

But there feems to be lefs Reafon for allowing of Special Juries to be ftruck by the Mafter of the Crown Office, or by any other Officer, upon Informations, or Indictments for Crimes committed in LONDON or WESTMINSTER (which is the Cafe of moft of the Crown Profecutions upon Libels, &c. for very few arife in any other County) becaufe the Sheriffs of LONDON and MIDDLESEX being annual and elective Officers are lefs liable to Sufpicion of Influence, and by Confequence, the moft impartial Officers between the Crown and the Subject.

* The Rule of ftriking Special Juries is, that the Sheriff of the County do attend the Mafter of the Crown Office with the Freeholders Books, out of which he is to name 48 in prefence of each Party, who by their Attornies or Solicitors fhall ftrike off 12 a piece.

The

The usual Argument in support of Special Juries is, that it is sometimes necessary for a Cause to be considered by Persons of a higher Rank and better Education than common Freeholders, and that they are never used in a capital Case.

As to the first, admitting the Reasoning to be right, why may not Special Juries be ballotted for out of a Number of Freeholders, *possest of Estates to such a Value*, and the Lists be made in the same manner as is directed by the Jury-Act with regard to common Juries?

And as to the second Part of the Argument, that special Juries are not used in capital Cases, that, at best, is but to say, that the Practice is *not a bad one*, because *it might be worse*; and that, because the Life of the Subject is safe, therefore his Liberty is not worth Consideration. Sir, I think it is evident, this Practice is such, as requires a new Law, no less than the Abuses and Corruptions, recited in the Preamble to the Jury-Act, required the Regulations thereby made for common Juries; nay, that without they are extended to Special Juries, that Law is of less Utility, than the Parliament, which made it, hoped and designed. It was certainly *well-intended*, and I presume the present Parliament,

liament, when they see the Defects of it, will not have less Zeal for *the Principle* it goes upon, than their Predecessors.

But when this Method of Trial shall be better regulated, I hope it will be also considered by the Legislature whether it be not advisable to *take another quite away*, I mean *Informations* in the King's Bench for *criminal Causes:*

Because, by this Method, the Subject loses one great Benefit, he is by Law entitled to, that of *a Grand Jury:*

Because, though in Cases between Subject and Subject, it is in the Power of the Court to refuse an Information, if the Defendant shew Cause; yet in Crown-Prosecutions, of which the Legislature ought to be most jealous, the Attorney-General, by his own Authority, files an Information, which the Court cannot refuse:

Because, though it comes out to be ever so groundless a Charge, the Crown pays no Costs, and the Defendant may be undone by the Expence:

Because the Act restraining Subjects from this Method of Prosecution, *with regard to each*

each other, without Leave of the Court after hearing both Sides, and some farther Cautions, is a strong Proof that the Parliament thought it a dangerous and oppressive Course, which they ought to discourage: But between Subjects and *the Crown* the Danger surely is much greater, there being more room for Oppression, and the Penalties on Conviction more severe.

Because there is Reason to think, that when the Star Chamber was abolished, the Parliament meant to condemn the Methods of Trial used in that Court, and did not imagine they would rise again in the King's Bench, upon Pretence, that they had been *antiently*, though *very rarely* practised *there*; and that all the Powers the Star Chamber claimed from common Law, did by the Abolition of that Court, devolve on the King's Bench:

Because, in all Cases *purely criminal* the Crown has another Way of proceeding *equally easy to the King*, and much more safe to the Subject, viz. the *Method of Indictment*: And because the retaining *that* which may be made oppressive, when *there is no Occasion for it*, is no Honour to the Crown, and no Advantage *but against the Innocent*.

In answer to all this, it will, I know, be said,

said, that this is an antient Power vested by Law in the Crown; that it is invading the Prerogative to attempt to take it away; and that we ought to preserve the Constitution unchanged. To which I reply; that the Antiquity of this Power is no Defence of it, if it be unfit to remain; since, others as antient, have been taken away: That the Prerogative of the King is no more sacred than the Liberty of the Subject: That *this* has been abridged in several Instances of late, particularly the Riot-Act, on a Supposition, that the Restraint was necessary for the publick Good; and the same reasoning will hold with regard to a Power in the Crown, the exercise of which is supposed to be dangerous to the Publick.

As to the Expediency and Duty of preserving the Constitution *unchanged*, it is no doubt in general a right Maxim. But does not every *new Power given* to the Crown *change* the Constitution, as much as an old **Power** *taken away?*

In the Balance of our Government, is the Scale of the Crown to be always *filling*, and that of the People always emptying?

Is there no Danger to the State, but from the *Abuse of Liberty*, which is daily the Argument for coercive Laws, enforced with heavy

heavy Penalties, and unknown to our Ancestors? May there not also be Danger *from the Abuse of Prerogative*, especially in Prosecutions carried on by the Crown, where Passion may mix itself and where Influence may prevail? And is it not as worthy of a Parliament to provide a Remedy against one of these Dangers, as against the other?

We are told by a great Man, by my Lord BACON, in his Life of HENRY VII. that when that Prince had drawn great Sums of Money by Taxes, and other Impositions from his People, he used *to remunerate them* by good and wholesome Laws, beneficial to Liberty, and of a popular Nature, which, as his Lordship observes, *were evermore his Retribution for Treasure*. And the best Retribution it was that could be made, the most effectual for Relief, and the most capable of stopping Complaints and healing Discontents. This Honour indeed did not belong to him alone; part of it ought to be imputed to his Parliaments; though Parliaments in those Days were not so independent, as, I hope, they are now, but were a good deal influenced by the Power of the Crown and the Will of the King in directing their Proceedings. But they both together had this Merit to the Nation, that what they took in Subsidies, they paid again in Laws.

It is the Misfortune, (I would not say the Fault) of the present Times, to have laid most heavy Burdens, such as were even unknown to the Days of HENRY the Seventh, with unintermitting severity, on the People of these Kingdoms. In this Parliaments and Kings have long concurred, not without great Discontent on the Side of those, at whose Expence it was done, and who have not always been so much convinced *of the Necessity*. But as for Retribution, except that Retribution, which consists in *Salaries* and *Pensions* paid by the Crown, to the happy few, who are the Objects of its Favour, I am afraid little of this will be found to have been given, in the Sense the Word is used by my Lord BACON, to make the People amends for the Hardships they sustain. New penal Laws and new Powers to the Crown have for these twenty Years past been almost the only Presents made by the Legislature to us and our Posterity, in return for above a 100 Millions raised upon the Publick, in all the various Shapes from the Land Tax down to Turnpikes.

But it is full Time to think of *other Retributions*: The Nation requires it from your Hands, requires you to strengthen, to enlarge the Basis upon which their Rights are fixed, and if there are any rotten Parts in that great Fabrick, to take them away, lest they endanger the Whole. Much of this was done at the Renovation

Renovation of our Government by the late happy Revolution, but not all. Some Defects were left through Inattention or other Causes, which it may be the Glory of his Majesty's Reign and of this Parliament by their united Wisdom and Goodness to remove. This will conciliate to both the Affections of the People, and do more, much more towards securing the Government, than *an Army could of an hundred thousand Men.* We hear much of Disaffection; this would crush it at once: It would unite the Friends of the Establishment, and confound its Enemies; it would shew the Cause we support to be *the Cause of Liberty.*

Sir, I have now laid before you, with great Plainness and Sincerity, what I believe the Nation asks of its Representatives. I am one unpractised in writing, and that understand no Rhetorick, but what owes its Prevalence to the single Force of Truth: And least of all do I understand the Method of arguing, which Want of Genius in Writers, and Meanness of Spirit in their Pay-masters, have made so common in political Disputes, attacking *private Characters*, and turning a national Question into *personal* Altercations and abusive *Lies*. I am so much unknown, that I believe myself very secure from this Sort of Answer being made me on Account of this Letter. If any other

other suffers in my stead (as these hired *Assassins* are apt to mistake their Object in the dark) I shall recommend to him, what I would practise myself in that Case, *Silence* and *Contempt*. As to the Facts and Reasonings laid down here, if they are controverted, I am ready to support them against any Attack which comes from a better Hand than ordinary, and has common Sense in it. I am quite a Stranger to the Persons of our Ministers, I know them only by the Effects of their Conduct, and neither *they* nor *their Successors* can please or offend me, but as my Country gains or suffers by their Power. And I pity those, if there are any such, who think *the removing an ill Minister* is a Point of Consequence, if with him *the Maxims* and *the Measures* of his Government, how strongly soever established, are not also *expelled*.

I shall only add to what I have said, that, unless something be done by *this Parliament*, to give new Vigour to our Liberties, stop the Torrent of Corruption, and revive the Principles, and the Spirit of our Fathers, we have less to hope, than to apprehend from *those to come*. The Time, I doubt, is not far off, when by the encrease of Influence, there may be such Difficulties upon Country Gentlemen to oppose the Court in Elections, and such a Despondency, such a Dispiritedness on the Minds of of all, except the Favourites of Power, that no Struggle could be expected, no Opposition at all to the Nomination of the Crown. A Kind of *Congé d'Elire* might be sent down into the Country, and directed *to our Trusty and Welbeloved Officers of the Customs, Excise, and Army*, in all the Towns and Boroughs of ENGLAND, SCOTLAND, WALES, and the *Dutchy of* CORNWAL. Suitable Returns would be made, but, Sir, *this would not be a Parliament*.

May that Providence, which has saved us so often, when we could not, or would not save ourselves, preserve us now. May his Majesty's *gracious Dispositions* operate in our Favour, and remove the Clouds that have been spread so thick about him, to prevent his seeing both our Interest, and *his own*.

May an Alteration of Measures be the Aim, the Effect, and *the Reward* of Opposition: May the publick Good be the Object, the Bound, and the Security of Power: May *the Royal Family*, may all Parties, may the Nation unite in Affection, and be divided no more: May all who obstruct this Union for vile Ends of their own, be *the Victims of it*, and suffer what they deserve: May all who desire it, *understand, assist* and *strengthen one another*.   I am, Sir, &c.

For the Proof of what is advanced in the first Part of this Letter, it may not be improper to recite some Articles of our Treaties with SPAIN and FRANCE, that regard AMERICA.

I^{mo}.

The Treaty of 1667 between ENGLAND and SPAIN.

ART. VIII.

——And for what may concern both the INDIES, and any other Parts whatsoever, the King of SPAIN doth grant to the King of GREAT BRITAIN and his Subjects, all that is granted to the United States of the LOW COUNTRIES and their Subjects, in their Treaty of MUNSTER 1648 Point for Point, in as full and ample a Manner as if the same were herein particularly inserted, the same Rules being to be observed whereunto the Subjects of the said United States are obliged, and mutual Offices of Friendship to be performed from one Side to the other.

The

[47]

The Articles referred to are

ART. V.

La Navigation et Trafique des Indes Orientales et Occidentales sera maintenuë selon et en conformité des Octroys sur ce donnés, ou a donner ci-aprés ; pour seureté de quoy servira le present Traité et la Ratification d'iceluy, qui de part et d'autre en sera procurée ; et seront compris soûs le dit Traité tous Potentats, Nations et Peuples, avec lesquels lesdits Seigneurs Estats, ou ceux de la Societé des Indes Orientales et Occidentales en leur nom, entre les limites de leursdits Octroys sont en Amitié et Alliance ; et un chacun, scavoir les susdits Seigneurs Roy et Estats respectivement demeureront en possession et joüiront de telles Seigneuries, Villes, Chasteaux, Forteresses, Commerce et Pays és Indes Orientales & Occidentales, comme aussi au Bresil et sur les costes d'Asie, Afrique et Amerique respectivement, que lesdits Seigneurs Roy et Estats respectivement tiennent et possedent, en ce compris specialement les Lieux et Places que les Portugais depuis l'an Mil Six cent quarante et un, ont pris et occupé sur lesdits Seigneurs Estats ; compris aussi les Lieux et Places qu'iceux Seigneurs Estats cy-aprés, sans infraction du present Traicté, viendront à conquerir et posseder ; et les Directeurs de la Societé

cieté des Indes tant Orientales que Occidentales des Provinces-Unies, comme auſſi les Miniſtres, Officiers hauts & bas, Soldats et Matelots, eſtans en ſervice actuel de l'une ou de l'autre deſdites Compagnies, ou ayans eſté en leur ſervice, comme auſſi ceux qui hors leur ſervice reſpectivement, tant en ce Pays, qu'au Diſtrict deſdites deux Compagnies, continüent encore, ou pourront cy-après eſtre employés, ſeront et demeureront libres et ſans eſtre moleſtez en tous les Pays eſtans ſoûs l'obeïſſance dudit Seigneur Roy en l'Europe, pourront voyager, trafiquer et frequenter, comme tous autres Habitans des Pays deſdits Seigneurs Eſtats. En ouſtre a eſté conditionné et ſtipulé, que les Eſpagnols retiendront leur Navigation en telle maniere, qu'ils la tiennent pour le preſent és Indes Orientales, ſans ſe pouvoir eſtendre plus avant, comme auſſi les Habitans de ce Pays-Bas ſ'abſtiendront de la frequentation des Places que les Caſtillans ont és Indes Orientales.

ART. VI.

Et quant aux Indes Occidentales, les Sujets et Habitants des Royaumes, Provinces et Terres deſdits Seigneurs Roy et Eſtats reſpectivement ſ'abſtiendront de naviger et trafiquer en tous les Havres, Lieux et Places garnies de Forts, Loges, ou Chaſteaux, et toutes autres poſſedées par l'une ou l'autre Partie; ſcavoir,
que

que les Sujets dudit Seigneur Roy ne navigeront et trafiqueront en celles tenuës par lesdits Seigneurs Eſtats, ny les Sujets deſdits Seigneurs Eſtats en celles tenuës par ledit Seigneur Roy, et entre les places tenuës par leſdits Seigneurs Eſtats feront compriſes les Places que les Portugais, depuis l'an Mil ſix cent quarante et un ont occupé dans le Braſil ſur leſdits Seigneurs Eſtats, comme auſſi toutes autres Places qu'ils poſſedent à preſent tandis qu'elles demeureront auxdits Portugais ; ſans que le precedent Article puiſſe deroger au contenû du preſent.

II^{do}.

The Treaty of 1670 between ENGLAND and SPAIN, commonly called the American Treaty *.

ART. III.

Item uti in futurum omnes inimicitiæ, hoſtilitates et diſcordiæ inter prædictos Dominos Reges, eorumque Subditos, et Incolas ceſſent, et aboleantur : Et utraque pars ab omni direptione, deprædatione, læſione, injuriiſque ac infeſtatione qualicunque tam Terra quam Mari, et Aquis dulcibus ubivis gentium temperet prorſus, et abſtineat.

* This Treaty confirms by its firſt Article that of 1667, and both are particularly confirmed by the Treaty of UTRECHT.

ART. VII.

——Conventum præterea eſt quod Sereniſsimus Magnæ Britanniæ Rex, Heredes et Succeſſores ejus cum plenario jure Summi Imperii, Proprietatis et Poſſeſſionis, Terras omnes, Regiones, Inſulas, Colonias ac Dominia in Occidentali India aut quavis parte Americæ ſita habebunt, tenebunt et poſſidebunt in perpetuum, quæcunque dictus Magnæ Britanniæ Rex, et Subditi ejus impræſentiarum tenent, ac poſſident, ita ut eo nomine, aut quacunque ſub prætenſione nihil unquam amplius urgeri, nihilque controverſiarum in poſterum moveri poſſit, aut debeat.

ART. VIII.

Subditi, et Incolæ, Mercatores, Navarchæ, Naucleri, Nautæ, Regnorum, Provinciarum, Terrarumque utriuſque Regis reſpectivè abſtinebunt, cavebuntque ſibi à Commerciis, et Navigatione in Portus, ac Loca Fortalitiis, ſtabulis Mercimoniorum, vel Caſtellis inſtructa, aliaque omnia quæ ab una, vel ab altera parte occupantur in Occidentali India: Nimirum Regis Magnæ Britanniæ Subditi Negotiationem non dirigent, Navigationem non inſtituent, Mercaturam non facient in Portubus, Locifvè, quæ Rex Catholicus in dicta India tenet, neque viciſſim Regis Hiſpaniarum Subditi in ea loca Navigationes inſtituent, aut Commercia exercebunt, quæ ibidem à Rege Magnæ Britanniæ poſſidentur.

ART.

ART. IX.

Si vero tractu temporis visum fuerit alterutri Regum licentiam aliquam generalem, vel specialem, aut Privilegia concedere alterius Subditis Navigationem inftituendi, et Commercium habendi in quibufvis locis fuae Ditionis, qui dictas Licentias, et Privilegia concefferit, dicta Navigatio, et Commercium exercebuntur et manu tenebuntur juxta et fecundum formam, tenorem, et effectum Permiffionum, aut Privilegiorum, quae indulgeri poterint, quorum fecuritati praefens Tractatus, ejufdemque Ratihabitio inferviet.

ART. X.

Item concordatum eft, quod fi alterutrius Confoederatorum Subditi, et Incolae cum Navibus fuis, five bellicae fint, et publicae; five onerariae ac privatae, procellis abrepti fuerint, vel perfequentibus Pyratis inimicis ac hoftibus, aut alio quovis incommodo cogantur fe ad Portum quaerendum in alterius Foederati Flumina, Sinus, Aeftuaria, ac Stationes recipere, vel ad Littora quaecunque in America appellere, benigne, omnique humanitate ibidem excipiantur, amica gaudeant protectione & benevolentia tractentur. Nullo autem modo impediantur, quo minus integrum omnino habeant reficere fe, victualia etiam & omne genus commeatum, five vitae fuftinendae, five Navibus reparandis, & itineri faciendo neceffarium, aequo & confueto pretio comparare. Nulla quoque ratione prohibeantur ex Portu, & statione viciſſim ſolvere, ac egredi, quin ipſis licitum ſit, pro libito migrare loco, libereque diſcedere quandocunque, & quocunque viſum fuerit, abſque ulla moleſtatione, aut impedimento.

ART. XI.

Pari ratione ſi Naves alterutrius Confœderati, ejuſdemque ſubditorum, ac Incolarum ad oras, aut in Ditionibus quibuſcunque alterius impegerint, jactum fecerint, vel (quod Deus avertat) naufragium, aut damnum quodcunque paſſæ fuerint, ejectos, aut detrimenta paſſos, in vincula, aut ſervitutem abducere nefas eſto, quin periclitantibus, aut naufragis benevolè, ac amiciſſimè ſubveniatur, atque auxilium feratur, Litteræque illis Salvi Conductus exhibeantur, quibus inde tutò, & abſque moleſtia exire, & ad ſuam quiſque Patriam redire valeat.

ART. XII.

Quando autem alterutrius Naves (uti ſupradictum eſt) Maris periculo, aliavé cogente ratione compulſæ, in alterius Portus adigantur, ſi tres, quatuorve fuerint, juſtamque ſuſpicionis occaſionem præbere poterint adventus iſtiuſmodi cauſa, Gubernatori, vel primario loci Magiſtratui, ſtatim exponetur, nec diutius ibi mora trahetur, quam quæ illis à dicto Gubernatore aut Præfecto permiſſa, & victui comparando, Navibuſque tum reſarciendis, tum inſtruendis commoda, atque æqua fuerit,

cautum

cautum vero semper erit, ut onus non distrahant, neque Mercium aut Sarcinarum aliquid è Navibus efferant, & venum exponant, nec etiam Mercimonia ab altera parte in Naves receperint, aut quicquam egerint contra hoc Fœdus.

ART. XV.

Præsens Tractatus nihil derogabit præeminentiæ, Juri ac Dominio cuicunque alterutrius Confœderatorum in Maribus Americanis, Fretis, atque Aquis quibuscunque, sed habeant, retineantque sibi eadem pari amplitudine, quæ illis Jure competit; intellectum autem semper esto libertatem navigandi neutiquam interrumpi debere, modo nihil adversus genuinum horum Articulorum sensum committatur, vel peccetur.

IIIe.

The Treaty of 1686 between ENGLAND and FRANCE.

ART. V.

Et que pour cet effet les Sujets et Habitans, Marchands, Capitaines de Vaisseaux, Pilotes et Matelots de Royaumes, Provinces et Terres de chacun desdits Roys respectivement, ne feront aucun Commerce ni Pesche dans tous les Lieux dont l'on est, ou l'on sera en possession de part et d'autre dans l'Amerique. C'est à sçavoir, que les Sujets de Sa Majesté Tres-Chrê-

Chrêtienne ne fe mefleront d'aucun Trafic, ne feront aucun Commerce, et ne pefcheront point dans les Ports, Rivieres, Bayes, embouchures de Rivieres, Rades, Coftes, ou autres Lieux qui font ou feront ci-aprés poffedez par Sa Majefté Britannique en Amerique : Et reciproquement les Sujets de Sa Majefté Britannique ne fe mefleront d'aucun Trafic, ne feront aucun Commerce, et ne pefcheront point dans les Ports, Rivieres, Bayes, embouchures de Rivieres, Rades, Coftes ou autres Lieux qui font ou feront ci-aprés poffedez par Sa Majefté Trés-Chrêtienne en Amerique. Et au cas qu'aucun Vaiffeau, ou Barque foit furpris faifant Trafic, ou pefchant, contre ce qui eft porté par le prefent Traité, ledit Vaiffeau, ou Barque avec fa charge, fera confifqué, après que la Preuve de la Contravention aura efté legitimement faite. Il fera néanmoins permis à la Partie qui fe fentira gravée par la Sentence de confifcation, de fe pourvoir au Confeil d'Eftat du Roy, dont les Gouverneurs ou Juges auront rendû ladite Sentence de confifcation, et d'y porter fa plainte, fans que pour cela l'execution de la Sentence foit empefchée : Bien entendû néanmoins que la liberté de la Navigation ne doit eftre nullement empefchée, pourveu qu'il ne commette rien contre le veritable fens du prefent Traité.

ART.

ART. VI.

De plus, il à esté accordé, que si les Sujets et Habitans de l'un ou de l'autre desdits Roys, et leurs Vaisseaux, soit de Guerre et publics, soit Marchands et particuliers, sont emportez par les tempestes, ou estant poursuivis par les Pirates ou par les ennemis, ou pressez par quelque autre necessité, sont contraints pour se mettre en seureté, de se retirer dans les Ports, Rivieres, Bayes, embouchures de Rivieres, Rades et Costes quelconques appartenantes à l'autre Roy dans l'Amerique, ils y seront bien et amiablement reçûs, protegez et favorablement traitez : Qu'ils pourront, sans qu'on les empêche en quelque maniere que ce soit, s'y rafraichir, et même acheter au prix ordinaire et raisonable, des vivres, et toutes sortes de Provisions necessaires, ou pour la vie, ou pour radouber les Vaisseaux, et pour continuer leur route : Qu'on ne les empêchera non plus en aucune maniere de sortir des Ports et Rades, mais qu'il leur sera permis de partir, et s'en aller en toute liberté quand et où il leur plairra, sans être molestez ou empêchez : Qu'on ne les obligera point à se defare de leur charge, ou à decharger et exposer en vente leurs Marchandises, ou Balots : Qu'aussi de leur part ils ne recevront dans leurs Vaisseaux aucunes Marchandises, et ne feront point de Pesche, soûs peine de confiscation desdits Vaisseaux et Marchandises, conformement à ce qui a esté convenû dans l'Article precedent. De plus à esté accordè, accordé, que toutes et quantes fois que les Sujets de l'un ou de l'autre desdits Roys seront contraints, comme il a esté dit ci-dessus, d'entrer avec leurs Vaisseaux dans les Ports de l'autre Roy, ils seront obligez, en entrant, d'arborer la Banniere, ou marque de leur Nation, et d'avertir de leur arrivée par trois coups de Mousquet : à faute de quoi faire, et d'envoyer une Chaloupe à Terre, ils pourront être confisquez.

ART. VII.

Pareillement si les Vaisseaux de l'un ou de l'autre desdits Roys, & de leurs Sujets et Habitans viennent à échouër, jetter en Mer leurs Marchandises, ou, ce qu'à Dieu ne plaise, faire Naufrage, ou qu'il leur arrive quelqu'autre Malheur que ce soit, on donnera aide et secours avec bonté et charité à ceux qui seront en danger, ou auront fait naufrage : il leur sera delivré des Saufs conduits, ou Passeports, pour pouvoir se retirer dans leur Pays en seureté, et sans être molestez.

ART. VIII.

Que si les Vaisseaux de l'un ou de l'autre Roy, qui seront contraints par quelque avanture ou cause que ce soit, comme il a été dit, de se retirer dans les Ports de l'autre Roy, se trouvent au nombre de Trois ou de Quatre, & peuvent donner quelque juste cause de soupçon, ils feront aussi-tôt connoître au Gouver-
neur

neur ou principal Magiſtrat du lieu, la cauſe de leur arrivée ; et ne demeureront qu'autant de tems, qu'ils en auront permiſſion du dit Gouverneur ou Commandant, & ce qu'il ſera juſte et raiſonable, pour ſe pourvoir de vivres, et pour radouber et equiper leurs Vaiſſeaux.

That it may appear what was the Senſe both Houſes of Parliament had of theſe Treaties, I have here adjoined the Reſolutions, and Addreſſes of the Lords, and Commons, upon the Petition of the Merchants laſt Year, and his Majeſty's moſt gracious Anſwers.

Jovis 30 *Die Martii* 1738.

Reſolved,

That it is the Opinion of this Committee, that it is the natural and undoubted Right of the *Britiſh* Subjects to ſail with their Ships on any Part of the Seas of *America*, to and from any Part of his Majeſty's Dominions; and that the Freedom of Navigation and Commerce, which the Subjects of *Great-Britain* have an undoubted Right to by the Law of Nations, and by Virtue of the Treaties ſubſiſting between the two Crowns of *Great-Britain* and *Spain*, has been greatly interrupted by the *Spaniards* under Pretences altogether groundleſs and unwarrantable; that before and ſince the

Execu-

Execution of the Treaty of *Seville*, and the Declaration made by the Crown of *Spain* pursuant thereunto, for the Satisfaction and Security of the Commerce of *Great-Britain*, many unjust Seizures and Captures have been made, and great Depredations committed by the *Spaniards*, attended with many Instances of unheard of Cruelty and Barbarity; that the frequent Applications made to the Court of *Spain* for procuring Justice and Satisfaction to his Majesty's injured Subjects, for bringing the Offenders to condign Punishment, and for preventing the like Abuses for the future, have proved vain and ineffectual, and the several Orders or Cedulas, granted by the King of *Spain* for Restitution and Reparation of great Losses sustained by the unlawful and unjustifiable Seizures and Captures made by the *Spaniards*, have been disobeyed by the *Spanish* Governors, or totally evaded and eluded; all which Violences and Depredations have been carried on to the great Loss and Damage of the Subjects of *Great-Britain* trading to *America*, and in direct Violation of the Treaties subsisting between the two Crowns.

A Motion was made, and the Question being put, that the said Resolution be recommitted;

It passed in the Negative.

Then

Then the said Resolution, being read a second Time, was agreed to by the House.

Mr. Alderman *Perry* also acquainted the House, that he was directed by the Committee to move the House, that an humble Address be presented to his Majesty, humbly beseeching his Majesty, to use his Royal Endeavours with his Catholick Majesty, to obtain effectual Relief for his injured Subjects, and to convince the Court of *Spain*, that, how desirous soever his Majesty may be to preserve a good Correspondence and Amity betwixt the two Crowns (which can only subsist, by a strict Observance of their mutual Treaties, and a just Regard to the Rights and Privileges belonging to each other) his Majesty can no longer suffer such constant and repeated Insults and Injuries to be carried on, to the Dishonour of his Crown, and to the Ruin of his trading Subjects; and to assure his Majesty, that in case his Royal and Friendly Instances, for procuring Justice, and *for the future Security of that Navigation and Commerce*, which his People have an undoubted Right to by Treaties and the Law of Nations, shall not be able to procure, from the Equity and Friendship of the King of *Spain*, such Satisfaction, as his Majesty may reasonably expect from a good and faithful Ally, this House will effectually support his Majesty in taking such Measures, as

Honour and Juſtice ſhall make it neceſſary for his Majeſty to purſue.

And Mr. Alderman *Perry* moved the Houſe accordingly.

Reſolved,
That an humble Addreſs be preſented to his Majeſty, humbly beſeeching his Majeſty, to uſe his Royal Endeavours with his Catholick Majeſty, to obtain effectual Relief for his injured Subjects, and to convince the Court of *Spain*, that, how deſirous ſoever his Majeſty may be to preſerve a good Correſpondence and Amity betwixt the two Crowns (which can only ſubſiſt, by a ſtrict Obſervance of their mutual Treaties, and a juſt Regard to the Rights and Privileges belonging to each other) his Majeſty can no longer ſuffer ſuch conſtant and repeated Inſults and Injuries to be carried on, to the Diſhonour of his Crown, and to the Ruin of his trading Subjects; and to aſſure his Majeſty, that, in caſe his Royal and Friendly Inſtances, for procuring Juſtice, and *for the future Security of that Navigation and Commerce*, which his People have an undoubted Right to by Treaties and the Law of Nations, ſhall not be able to procure, from the Equity and Friendſhip of the King of *Spain*, ſuch Satisfaction, as his Majeſty may reaſonably expect from a good and faithful Ally, this Houſe
will

will effectually support his Majesty in taking such Measures, as Honour and Justice shall make it necessary for his Majesty to pursue.

Veneris 7 *Die Aprilis* 1738.

Mr. *Speaker* reported that the House attended his Majesty with their Resolution and Address of the 30th day of *March* last, to which his Majesty was pleased to give this most gracious Answer, *viz.*

Gentlemen,

I AM fully sensible of the many and unwarrantable Depredations committed by the *Spaniards*; and you may be assured, I will make Use of the most proper and effectual Means, that are in my Power, to procure Justice and Satisfaction to my injured Subjects, and *for the future Security of their Trade and Navigation.* I can make no Doubt, but you will support me, with Chearfulness, in all such Measures, as, in Pursuance of your Advice, I may be necessitated to take, for the Honour of my Crown and Kingdoms, and the Rights of my People.

The

The Humble ADDRESS of the Right Honourable the Lords Spiritual and Temporal in Parliament assembled.

Die Martis, 2 Maii, 1738.

Most Gracious Sovereign,

WE your Majesty's most dutiful and loyal Subjects, the Lords Spiritual and Temporal in Parliament assembled, having taken into our serious Consideration the many unjust Violences and Depredations committed by the *Spaniards,* upon the Persons, Ships, and Effects of divers of your Majesty's Subjects in *America,* have come to the following Resolutions, which we beg Leave in the humblest Manner to lay before your Majesty, for your Royal Consideration, *viz.*

I. Resolved, That the Subjects of the Crown of *Great-Britain* have a clear and undoubted Right to navigate in the *American* Seas, to and from any Part of his Majesty's Dominions; and for carrying on such Trade and Commerce as they are justly intitled unto in *America*; and also to carry all Sorts of Goods and Merchandizes, or Effects, from one Part of his Majesty's Dominions to any other Part thereof; and that no Goods, being so carried, are by any Treaty subsisting between

the

the Crowns of *Great-Britain* and *Spain*, to be deemed or taken as contraband or prohibited Goods, and that the searching of such Ships on the open Seas, under Pretence of their carrying contraband or prohibited Goods, is a Violation and Infraction of the Treaties subsisting between the two Crowns.

II. Resolved, That it appears to this House, that as well before, as since the Execution of the Treaty of *Seville*, on the Part of *Great-Britain*, divers Ships and Vessels, with their Cargoes, belonging to *British* Subjects, have been violently seized and confiscated by the *Spaniards*, upon Pretences altogether unjust and groundless; and that many of the Sailors on Board such Ships have been injuriously and barbarously imprisoned and ill-treated; and that thereby the Liberty of Navigation and Commerce belonging to his Majesty's Subjects, by the Law of Nations, and by virtue of the Treaties subsisting between the Crowns of *Great-Britain* and *Spain*, hath been unwarrantably infringed and interrupted, to the great Loss and Damage of our Merchants, and in direct Violation of the said Treaties.

III. Resolved, That it appears to this House, that frequent Applications have been made, on the Part of his Majesty, to the Court of *Spain*, in a manner the most agreeable to Treaties,

ties, and to the Peace and Friendship subsisting between the two Crowns, for redressing the notorious Abuses and Grievances beforementioned, and preventing the like for the future, and for obtaining adequate Satisfaction to his injured Subjects; which, in the Event, have proved entirely fruitless, and of no Effect.

We think it our Duty, on this important Occasion, humbly to represent to your Majesty, That we are most sensibly affected with the many and grievous Injuries and Losses sustained by your Majesty's trading Subjects, by Means of these unwarrantable Depredations and Seizures; and to give your Majesty the strongest and most sincere Assurances, That in case your friendly and powerful Instances for procuring Restitution and Reparation to your injured Subjects, and *for the future Security of their Trade and Navigation*, shall fail of having their due Effect and Influence on the Court of *Spain*, and shall not be able to obtain that real Satisfaction and Security, which your Majesty may in Justice expect; we will zealously and chearfully concur in all such Measures as shall become necessary for the Support of your Majesty's Honour, the Preservation of our Navigation and Commerce, and the common Good of these Kingdoms.

His

His MAJESTY's most Gracious ANSWER.

My Lords,

I AM sensibly touched with the many Hardships and Injuries sustained by my Trading Subjects in *America* from the Cruelties and unjust Depredations of the *Spaniards*. You may be assured of my Care to procure Satisfaction and Reparation for the Losses they have already suffered, *and Security for the Freedom of Navigation for the future*; and to maintain to my People the full Enjoyment of all the Rights to which they are intitled by Treaty and the Law of Nations.

I doubt not but I shall have your Concurrence for the Support of such Measures as may be necessary for that Purpose.

POSTSCRIPT.

SINCE I wrote my Letter News is come into the Country that two or three of our Ships have been very lately taken by the SPANIARDS, one of them by a Spanish Man of War, with the King's Commission, on the High Seas, the Captain of which is now imprisoned at CADIZ; and that two Sloops belonging to the South-Sea Company are detained, and a Guard is set upon our Factory at the HAVANNAH. If *these* are the *First-Fruits* of our Peace, *what will the Harvest be?*

But after all, Sir, have we any Peace at all? Have we any Thing granted us that will even bear that Name? Or have we been only amused by the SPANIARDS, till they could *get their Money home*, (which we hear is hourly expected in two richly-laden Ships) and till the Season should be past for us to act with Advantage?

I would also beg leave to ask one Question more. We were told some time ago that one of our Men of War in the WEST-INDIES had taken the Spanish Register Ship, but that, by Orders of Commodore BROWN, it was immediately afterwards carried back to the Latitude, in which it was taken, and restored again. Did the Captain who took it act *without*, or *against Orders*? If he had Orders *to cruise*, why was his Capture *restored?* Were those Orders

POSTSCRIPT.

Orders only given *for Show*, to *amuse the Merchants*, and *to look like Action*? Would it not have been right and prudent to have kept the Money, that was aboard this Ship, *as a Pledge in our Hands*, in Case that Peace should be refused us upon proper Terms? We might have kept it justly, *as a Security for the Repayment of our Losses*; whereas the Act of the SPANIARDS in detaining our Effects at the HAVANNAH, is in Reality adding *a new Robbery* to the past. Let me however observe, that, though *Reparation to our Merchants* is highly fit, and necessary, and what we ought to demand, *it is by far the Point of least Importance to the Nation.* We are interested no doubt for them upon many Accounts, but both we and they have a much greater Interest *in the future Security of Commerce being firmly established. This* is the national Concern, *this* both Houses of Parliament have strongly insisted on, *this* his Majesty has promised to procure for us. If *this* be neglected, any *present Gratification* will be of little Advantage, and *should be thought of with Scorn.*

The END.

Erratum. Page 30. Line 10. read 1737.

A LETTER TO THE TORIES.

[Price Six-Pence.]

A LETTER TO THE TORIES.

*We do believe thee, and beshrew my Soul
But I do Love the Favour and the Form
Of this most fair Occasion, by the which
We will untread the Steps of damn'd Revolt;
And, like a bated and retired Flood,
Leaving our Rankness and irregular Course,
Stoop low within those Bounds we have o'erlook'd,
And calmly run on in Obedience
Ev'n to our Ocean, to our Great King* JOHN.

Shakespear.

LONDON:
Printed for E. SAY in *Ave-Mary-Lane*; and
sold at the Pamphlet-Shops at the *Royal-Exchange*, *Temple-Bar*, and *Charing-Cross*.

MDCCXLVII.

A LETTER TO THE TORIES.

GENTLEMEN,

I Have a few things to say to you which I think concern you much, and I will endeavour to say them in a few words. It has been matter of wonder to many how it should come to pass that a body of men so considerable, mustering at least two thirds of the gentry and nine in ten of the clergy of this kingdom, should be so long kept under the hatches by a faction, despicable and detestable in its origin; naturally disagreeable to all princes; never popular, except perhaps in the unthinking seasons of sedition and confusion; superior to you in nothing laudable; and equally inferior in numbers, wealth and virtue.] What should be the reason that King *William*, tho' strongly prejudiced in favour of the Whigs, was contented to employ and trust us, and Queen *Anne*, whose inclinations were always quite contrary, suffered herself to be perfuaded to fill her armies, fleets, council, houfhold, and even her bedchamber, with Whigs; and yet the princes of this houfe could never be brought to think of changing hands, and trying what we could do for them, in any of the various diftreffes of their affairs? Is this to be imputed to a natural flexibility in thofe princes, and the contrary temper in thefe? No. King *William* is well known to have been a man by nature fteady, and even obftinate and felf-willed, to a great degree; and the good Queen inherited from her father a conftancy very uncommon, and upon feveral occafions gave convincing and heroical proofs of it. The true reafon is that King *William* was fatisfied that the Tories, though difcontented (and many of them even angry, and, to fay the truth, difaffected) had no quarrel with his title, and would at leaft make him good fubjects whilft in power under him, and not betray him only to change a mafter that employ'd them for one that could do no more and perhaps might not do that; and Queen *Anne* knew the fame of the Whigs (fo that neither of them expofed themfelves to diftant dangers merely to get rid of prefent difficulties, which no wife prince will do; but only facrificed their inclinations to what they thought their intereft, which all wife princes have always done and always will do) But with the princes that fuccceded them the cafe was very

different

different. You may be sure, and it is well known, that early in the Queen's reign the blessed Whigs of those times spared no pains to possess the court of Hanover with an assured persuasion that there were but two parties in the nation, Hanoverians and Jacobites; and that Whig and Tory were only two other names for those two parties. What impression this made, I pretend not to say or know. It is certain that immediately after the accession of King *George* I. the Whigs found themselves in a most triumphant situation. It is as certain, and truth obliges us to own, that those Tories who had distinguish'd themselves in opposing, jointly with the Whigs, such of the late measures as were thought unfavourable to the protestant succession, were also, in the beginning of that reign, employed and rewarded as well as the Whigs. But whatever the King's intentions might be (who in truth was a worthy and well-meaning prince) his Whig ministers, instead of labouring to establish their master's throne upon the only solid basis of an English throne, made it their principal business to supplant their Tory associates, and (contrary, as I have been informed, to the Earl of Halifax's scheme) treated the whole party as if their only view was to drive them to despair and rebellion in order to verify their own calumnies. This design, if it was their design, succeeded, not perfectly indeed (the Tories had too much wit in their anger and too much virtue for that) but far better than such wicked policy deserved. And our resentments (which stopt not at the ministry, as in all reason, and by the principles of the lowest Toryism, they ought to have done) the breaking out of the rebellion (the first the world had seen without a Whig in it) the ill conduct that many of us fell into upon that occasion, the actual revolt of some, though but few, the declared affections of others, the sullen tranquillity and seeming indifference of many, and above all things (as that touch'd the whole party without exception) our strict connection and union with known and professed Jacobites, especially in parliament and parliamentary elections, gave such confirmation to the suspicions before had of us both in court and country, both at home and abroad, that it became an established and almost universal opinion that the whole mass and body of the Tories was corrupted, and that there could be no safety in trusting them; which opinion continues to this day.

The consequence is that we are kept out of all publick employments of power and profit, and live like aliens and pilgrims in the land of our nativity; that no quality, no fortune, no eloquence, no learning, no wisdom, no probity is of any use to any man of our unfortunate denomination, ecclesiastick or layman, lawyer or soldier, peer or commoner, for obtaining the most deserved advancement in his profession, or any favour

vour from the crown; whilst, to our additional and infupportable vexation, the bare merit of hating us, and every thing we love and hold facred, daily advances dunces in the law and church, cowards in our fleets and armies, republicans in the King's houfe and idiots every where. And, what is worfe than all this, and indeed the worft thing that can happen to men of honour and honefty, we lie under the reproach, all the world over, of the moft horrid and impious of all crimes, wilful and perpetual perjury.

To recover our character, and put ourfelves in a condition to pretend to the favours of the crown, there is a plain and eafy way open, and there is but one, and this it is; to *untread the steps* of perverfe and peevifh oppofition, to wipe our hands at once of the Jacobites and their ruin'd and ruinous caufe, *to do our firft works* as well as profefs our old principles, to let the world fee (by our reverence to the perfon of the King, by fupporting his government, by difcountenancing the faucy democratical fpirit of fedition and by a religious obfervance of the laws according to the obligation of our oaths and allegiance) that we are true Tories, and not difguifed and perjured Jacobites. For while we call ourfelves Tories and practife to the King none of thofe principles which Tories have always profefs'd, but on the contrary oppofe and revile him and affift and patronize his avowed enemies, we muft not hope that it
will

will be believed that in our hearts we acknowledge him for our King, that he to whom we behave so undutifully can be the King we mean when we talk of passive obedience and non-resistance. The world will do us the honour to believe us consistent with ourselves; which the supposition of Jacobitism makes us, and nothing else can. But if we shew ourselves honestly consistent by making our actions agree with the principles we profess and with our oaths, there is nothing which we may not expect from the favour of the crown. Convince the King (by making and openly avowing this salutary separation from his enemies) that you are loyal and good subjects, and he will not want to be told that you are his best subjects. That will then be self-evident. Convince him that he may employ you with safety, and he will see of himself that he can employ no others so safely, nor with so much ease to himself or advantage to his affairs. He is fond of the love of his people, and knows the plague and inconveniences of governing the greater number by the less: And no King that can have the Affection and support of the gentlemen of England and the established church will ever put his trust in a puny antimonarchical faction.

It has been said by a false brother that we are too few to do any thing without the Jacobites, that if we forsake them they will forsake us, and then the Whigs will outnumber us; and therefore we we had better keep as we are, and make the beft of a bad market. I deny every thing, both premifes and conclufion. 1. With them you can do nothing. You have tried long, and found it fo. And if you could do nothing with them formerly, you cannot expect to do any thing now, when the proteftant eftablifhment has taken deep root, and daily gains ftrength by their declining and otherwife.

Non tali auxilio, nec defenforibus iftis,
Tempus eget.

Since then you can do nothing with them, what fhould hinder you from trying at leaft what you can do without them? 2. The Jacobites will ftill affift you with their votes, the only affiftance they can give you which will not be more hurtful than helpful. They want you infinitely more than you can ever want them, unlefs you fhould carry your complaifance for them fo far as to bring about a reftoration for them; and then indeed you will ftand in great need of a return of kindnefs from them; but if you expect any other than the Prefbyterians found from the Cavaliers, you have loft the ufe of reafon. They will never forget the hand you had in the revolution, and will not be fo fimple as to leave it in your power to make another as foon as you feel the folly of your Royal Exchange, which probably will be pretty foon. But this by the by. I fay the Jacobites will ftill vote for you. Do you think, if the Whigs fhould
refolve

resolve never to chuse a Dissenter member of parliament, that the Dissenters in their anger would resolve never to vote for a Whig, but rather give their votes to one of us or to a Jacobite? No. The Dissenters will always vote for the Whigs, and the Jacobites for the Tories, whether voted for again or no. All Jacobites are Tories, tho' all Tories be not Jacobites; as every Dissenter is a Whig, though every Whig is not a Dissenter. A Jacobite is a Tory and something more, as a Dissenter is a Whig and something more, All Jacobites have more principles besides Jacobitism, and if they cannot find a man to vote for, that believes all the articles of their creed, they will vote for him that believes the most, for a Whig that is a churchman before a Dissenter, and for the same reason for a Tory that is no Jacobite before any Whig. There is no reason therefore to fear but they will give you their votes and interest (whatever you do in this matter) unless there be Jacobite candidates, in which case you cannot have 'em now. 3. I deny that you have that want of their assistance which is pretended. Their numbers are too great, it must be owned; but nothing nigh so great as their magniloquence and self-deception (in both which they excel mankind) and the malignity of the true-blue Whigs (who are very unwilling to allow any difference betwixt Toryism and Jacobitism) have concurred in representing

'em

'em. Believe them not. Believe not your enemies. Believe your friends. Believe yourselves. It is odds, Sir, but you, who are now reading this letter, have yourself some time or other been unjustly thought or suspected to be a Jacobite and perhaps can name the silly cause and occasion of it. Now if you know that you have been misunderstood and misrepresented, doubt not but the same has happen'd to many others. As I myself have known the same imputation cast upon men that to my certain knowledge were as good subjects as any the King has, and as ready to approve themselves so with their swords in their Hands; upon some only for maintaining the old doctrine of the duty of passive obedience (so evidently due either to all established governments or to none) upon some for ridiculing unreasonable and unseasonable panicks, upon others for calling in question (not very gratefully I confess, but certainly not disloyally) the heroism of King *William*'s intentions towards *England* at the Revolution, and many other such frivolous reasons. I would also advise you not to be so hasty, as some have been, to make this conclusion from premises much stronger than these. Suspicion and caution I commend and recommend. But wisdom is as slow to conclude as quick to suspect. Many most unjustifiable actions I have chose to impute, contrary to the general opinion, to unthinking disaffection

disaffection and the petulance our young men learnt of the Whig patriots during the late coalition of parties, rather to any fix'd and determin'd disloyalty; and have often found myself not mistaken. And for the few protestants (for comparatively they are not many) that really and certainly are Jacobites, as the greater part of 'em became what they are without examination or discourse of reason, by a blind sequacity, they scarce know how themselves and before they were aware, possibly this separation, this lay excommunication and cutting 'em off from the body of the Tories may prove to them a wholesome discipline; and, as the spiritual excommunications of antient times are said to have done to the most harden'd sinners, make 'em examine and bethink themselves and repent and amend.

Besides multitudes are got amongst the Whigs that properly belong to your *corps*; and all these, if you once set up the standard of true Toryism, unquarter'd with Jacobitism, will naturally join it, being in no other sense Whigs than zealous friends to the present establishment. It was not their choice to be called Whigs, but resolving to hold no communion with Jacobites when you were of another mind, they had no other resort. And when this wall of partition is taken away, their union must necessarily be with you, who never differ'd from 'em but in one point, and not with the Whigs, who never agreed with 'em but in one.

Others

Others have been cast into their arms by the accident of education, by nature never design'd for Whigs, and much too good for the company they keep. You must all of you have met with many of this kind, and have said, at least in your hearts (what I have heard several moderate Whigs say of moderate Tories) " If all " the rest were like these, the difference betwixt the " two parties would be more nominal than real." And there can be no doubt but this sort of Whigs (who have too long done the party an honour in many respects undeserved) for the sake of the great advantages that will follow to the common cause of Anti-jacobitism (and consequently to the whole nation and to all Christendom,) and to make one party of all that wish well to the constitution and protestant establishment (a thing long and ardently desired by all true patriots of both denominations) will gladly strengthen this alliance by their ready and unanimous accession. And that in this comprehension no rigid, narrow terms of communion will be exacted, but on the contrary the right hand of fellowship frankly given you, that all this may be accomplish'd without your departing from the practice or profession of any one Tory principle, that you will be met at least half way, and receiv'd with open arms, that there will be no looking backwards, but all forwards, is too evident to admit of dispute or doubt. Those of the Clergy, who are now called Whigs, will lead the way, and will be followed by all of their laity that wish well to the Church and Monarchy, and all that are weary of the licentiousness and anarchy of these times, and desire to see subordination, and reverence of law and magistracy, restored amongst us; and the party, deserted thus by their best men, will soon be reduced to dissenters and commonwealths-men and a few peevish stubborn fellows, in love with their own sourness or the charming sound of their old name; and will not be able to look you in the face either in court or parliament.

This is the only coalition of parties that can do England any good, or indeed subsist for any time. Wretches that know not publick regards, are in perpetual competition for private advantages; and nothing can unite them but the poor illaudable principle that just in the very article of extreme common danger sends every man to the city-wall (for no other reason but because his house will be better defended there with many than singly by himself at his own door) and divides them again as soon as the storm is over. But the union of worthy and good men is built upon the firm and sure foundation of virtue and the love of their country, and lasts and operates accordingly. This will set to rights every thing that is amiss amongst us, except what the degeneracy of the age has made unamendable; as the want of it has been the principal cause of all our misfortunes,

and

and of almost all our other faults, for many years. All the Tories who wish well to this establishment and all the Whigs who love the constitution, united in the administration and defense of the government, would form a body too strong, too homogeneous, and too well compacted and cemented to have any thing to fear from twice the force of all the rest of the nation. A ministry so supported would despise and laugh at the opposition of Jacobites and the few Whigs that would join with them in it, and might apply their whole attention to the great affairs of the nation and of all Europe (which at this time require no less) without any anxiety about parliamentary squabbles. They might, without any danger, exert with spirit and vigour the full power of legal government, check and even suppress the infamous licence of the press (unknown to all other ages and nations, and destructive of all civil society) whet the blunted sword of justice, and make all disloyal subjects feel or fear the edge of it. There would then be no cause why every evil doer should not be brought to that punishment which the law warrants, mercy permits, and good order requires. There would then be no room to say

At such a time as this it is not meet
That every nice offence do bear its comment.

Ministers would then have it in their power to reward modest and unfriended merit notwithstanding

ing the boldeſt demands in favour of undeſervers; and courage, ſkill, probity, underſtanding, learning would be the ways to preferment:

Ἐν δὲ διχοςασίῃ κ' Ἀνδρουλείδης πολεμαρχεῖ.

Then the church will be favour'd and rever'd, the King honoured and obey'd, his miniſters reſpected, and the nation happy; the Diſſenters, Papiſts and Proteſtants, will be as happy as they will pleaſe to deſerve to be, Jacobites and Republicans happier than they deſerve, or, in their great wiſdom, deſire to be, and all the reſt of the kingdom ſo happy, that it will not be in their power not to ſee it.

Having proved that it is your intereſt, I ſhall now endeavour to ſhew you that it is alſo your Duty, utterly to break off all union and alliance with the Jacobites, as I have advis'd you to do, and as I have determined to do myſelf, and many more beſides me, and of much greater conſequence, indeed of the greateſt, and of the higheſt rank; whom I hope you will as chearfully and unanimouſly follow in the right way, as you have formerly done in the wrong.

1. I take it to be the duty of every elector to vote for none but honeſt men, and he cannot be an honeſt man that, to get into a prince's council, and there betray and ruin him, promiſes upon his honour to be true and faithful to him. Obſerve that I ſay *promiſes*. Now if that Word ſtrikes more than if I had ſaid *ſwears*, and con-

veys

veys a stronger idea of the wickedness of this treachery, to what a pass has the frequency of perjury brought us!

2. I think it a clear rule of conscience to chuse such as are most likely to vote as we should think ourselves bound to do, especially in matters of great importance. How then can a loyal subject put his vote in the mouth of a traitor? Can a Jacobite be the likeliest man to vote as I would do who am no Jacobite?

3. I conceive it to be the duty of a subject by the bonds of allegiance (leaving oaths out of the question) not to support the King's enemies: And to comfort, aid and assist such, to put power of any kind into their hands, which may enable 'em to accomplish their wicked ends, I take to be in conscience, whatever it may be in law, no less than high-treason. Now it is certain that a vote in the house of commons may do the King more harm than a troop or a regiment of Rebels with the voter at the head of 'em. And it is as certain that the Jacobite candidate that asks my assistance does it with an intention to vote in that manner if opportunity offers. Silly and impious as they are, we cannot think that they spend their money and *endanger their Souls gratis*, with no view at all: And what else can be the view of a Jacobite?

4: Our duty to God obliges us to keep our oaths, and our oaths bind us to defend the King and the protestant succession *to the utmost of our power against*

against all attempts whatsoever; and he that sends such a man to parliament is clearly as much a traitor *in foro conscientiæ*, and as much forsworn, as if he sent his servants and tenants into a rebellion.

5. He is accessary not only to his treason but to his perjury.

6. Our duty to God obliges us to support true religion: And is that done by chusing parliament men that will do all they can to overturn the protestant establishment? Are we bound to maintain and defend the protestant religion ourselves, and at liberty to vote for such as seek to get into parliament for no other end than to place a bigotted papist upon the throne?

7. Our duty to our country absolutely requires us to change our conduct in this respect. That obliges us to chuse such parliament-men as we think will in all things consult and promote the welfare and true interest of the country: Now you and I do not think the interest of the pretender to be consistent with the interest of the country: How then can we vote for a Jacobite, who either thinks them to be perfectly the same, or cares not whether they be or no? If we love our country, we can vote only for such as desire to see *France* humbled, which the Jacobites dread as much as the *French*; such as while we have war abroad will endeavour to preserve peace at home, which is not the way to bring in *their* master; such as will carry on the war vigorously

in order to procure a speedy and permanent peace, both which things the Jacobites detest and deprecate, and must oppose. The *French* are their countrymen, not we. At their successes they rejoice and hold up their heads; at ours they droop and are dejected; and our peace is their ruin.

It will be said perhaps, Do you advise us then to vote for Whigs? I answer, By no means, if you have the opportunity of voting, with probability of success, for gentlemen nearer your own way of thinking: but if the contest lies between Jacobites and Whigs, my answer must be, without the least hesitation, for Whigs, for any body, rather than Jacobites. I will go farther with you. I think that in the case last put you not only may with a safe conscience vote for Whigs, but ought, and are not at liberty to stand neuter; for that very neutrality may bring in a Jacobite, and then to avoid voting for a Whig, because he differs from you in opinion, you have brought in one who differs with you ten times more, and (what clinches the matter, and compleats the inconsistency of your scrupulous casuistry) one that you have swore not only not to assist but to oppose.

But you do not like to be called turncoats. Away with such childishness! The thing is either your duty or it is not. If you think it is not, say so, and there's an end. But to say (explicitly

plicitly or implicitly) I muſt own it is in ſtrictneſs my duty, but I cannot bear diſgrace.

'Αιδέομαι Τρῶας κ̓ Τρωάδας ἑλκεσιπέπλυς,—

it is not the voice of a man, much leſs of a Chriſtian. And who, I pray, are they from whom you apprehend this dreadful appellation, and upon what ground? A turncoat is the angry name for a convert, but you are no converts; how then can you be turncoats? You are not Jacobites 'tis true, but you were not Jacobites before; how then turncoats? You were Tories before, you are Tories ſtill; how then turncoats? I am not writing to Jacobites. I am not endeavouring to perſuade them to turn loyal, but loyal Tories not to ſupport their cauſe. My aim is to incite you, not to change your principles, but to adhere ſtedfaſtly to them. And if that brings upon you a reproach which can only belong to change, I do not ſee how you can avoid it but by deſerving it.

But ſuppoſe you were Jacobites, and I was endeavouring to convert you from Jacobitiſm, would the fear of this imputation be a good anſwer to me? If you had been bred Jacobites (by the by a ſtrange education for a man to give his children that he does not deſign ſhould be nonjurors) and had been fully ſatisfied of your error, muſt you have continued the profeſſion of Jacobitiſm and acted accordingly, againſt the conviction of your own minds? Muſt you have ſupported and encou-

raged

raged rebellion and treason against your lawful King, acknowledg'd and recogniz'd by your own consciences, *daring damnation,* and *giving both the worlds to negligence,* and all this only for fear of an idle, mobbish, black-guard word? If a man is in such a situation that of necessity he must either suffer the reproach of men or of his own conscience; if he deliberates a moment, he is neither a wise nor an honest man.

Therefore let those of you (the glory of our nation) who have held fast your integrity in the great corruption of these times, who have gone on in the good old way of loyalty and obedience without turning either to the right hand or to the left, either to the treason of the Jacobites or the seditious practices of republicans, let all such give thanks to God (as they have great cause) for his preventing grace, and rejoice and persevere in their innocence and virtue. And as for such as either thro' heat of youth, extremity of opposition, contagion of company, reverence of imaginary wisdom, bad education, false notions of honour, misrepresentations of persons or things, resentment, personal affection, or any other delusion, have been misled more or less, and done those things which they ought not to have done; they must mend, and not persist in sin to avoid the shame of repentance, remembring that it is the glory of a man to conquer prejudices and submit to truth.

Many

Many other things might be said, well deserving your most serious consideration: But time presses; and perhaps it is no matter. If you fear God and love your country, what has been said is more than sufficient; if not, more would be of no use; you are undone and there is no help for it.

Neque jam Salus servare, si volt, vos potest.

But I will hope better things. Your country, engaged in a war with two great nations and torn with civil dissensions, threaten'd with invasions from abroad and new rebellions at home, calls upon you to assist and save her, and that only by doing what your duty to God and your own private interest jointly demand of you; to sacrifice to her peace and preservation, not your lives or fortunes, but hurtful animosities and unreasonable prejudices. Let her not make such a request in vain.

I am, GENTLEMEN,

Your sincere Well-Wisher,

And humble Servant,

June 9, 1747.

J. H.

F I N I S.

A MODEST

APOLOGY

FOR MY

OWN CONDUCT.

When I was a Child I conceiv'd as a Child, I reason'd as a Child: But when I became a Man, I put away Childish Things.
    St. *Paul's* Epistle to the *Corinthians*, Chap. xiii. Ver. 11.

Duplices tendens ad sydera Palmas, Talia voce refert,
                    VIRG.

LONDON:

Printed for *M. Cooper* in *Paternoster Row*,
M.D.CCXLVIII.

A
Modest Apology, &c.

THEY who judge of Men, their Morals or Steddiness, either by their own narrow Principles, Pique or Prejudices; or by this or that distinct Action, Speech, or Manner of Conduct, will always subject themselves to the Hazard of being deceived. Times, Seasons, Circumstances of Affairs, and Difference of Age and Experience, in the Course and Reason of Things, naturally and justly create Variety of Opinion; else were we at first infallible, and in the Order of our Lives incapable of further Improvement. This, seriously consider'd, will produce Matter sufficient to vindicate a Man from Immorality, or Unsteadiness, who with Time, and the Change of Events, alters his Scheme of Thinking and Acting, and thereby happens to vary essentially from the Many, whose Thoughts previously coincided

coincided with his own. There are Abundance of Points in Government-Affairs, as in Religious Matters, which have not any determinate Standard, that can fix us to any tolerable Degree of Certainty: And in regard to them, Steaddiness is only another Name, or Term, for Political Bigotry. He must therefore not have a very moderate Share of Pride and Presumption, who assumes to himself a Right of determining arbitrarily in Points purely Political; how this or that Man shall always act, what Party or Set of Men he shall co-operate with, or how he shall in particular conduct himself; as the confin'd Circle of our Reason but too often evinces, in the Rotation of a few Hours, how easily we are mistaken: And it is hence wise Men conclude, that those who assert positively, generally argue falsly. A settled Imagination and sound Judgment, contribute greatly to form our Conceptions of Men, Manners and Things: These, aided by Experience, raise the Mind to the utmost Extent of its known moral Capacity. The first owes its Existence, in a great Measure, to a good State of Health, an easy Fortune, and a calm and deliberate Habit of Thinking.

The

The last is the natural Effect of the former, corrected and ripened by Experience. In order therefore to judge of the Rectitude of this or that Man's Conduct, it is necessary at least that our Imagination be clear and disengaged from all Bias, and that we have a perfect Knowlege of the present State of Affairs, as well as a thorough Acquaintance with the Transactions of the past; and consider in both, what the Wisest, and most Experienc'd have done, and are now every Day doing.

When our Judgment is once rectified by Observation and Reflections of this Nature, a new Light breaks in upon us, and we then come to see very plainly how far human Opinion is from being infallible. There is nothing more easy, than to say rude and indecent Things, or to endeavour to brand each other with Marks of Infamy and Reproach; but to take all Things together, and thence prove by fair Argument, that the varying from our former Sentiments, and from those with whom we associated, must necessarily be wrong, is, I fancy, much too difficult a Matter for those to effect, whose warm Imaginations never suffered them to consider more than one Side of the Question, and, in general, not even that, with due Care and Circumspection. Men entertaining superstitious Prejudices, in Political Matters, which they either imbibed with their Milk, or have acquired by conversing too narrowly, forget how much they decry the same Turn of Thinking in Religious Affairs. Yet, if it be an Error, it is equally so in both Cases, as neither can be brought to a Point, nor so well ascertain'd, as to conclude all Men by it. If the Opinions of Men are, and necessarily must be various, as to the Practice of Religion, so they must be as to Government; and he must be Master of a very uncommon Presumption, who would, on so unbounded a Subject, make his Opinion the Standard of every Man's. In particular Circumstances, there are such Things as evident Right and Wrong; as Blasphemy in Religion, Immorality in common Life, Cowardice in War, and the Betraying ones Country to an Enemy: But no Man that reasons freely, will presume to determine whether I shall pray kneeling or standing. Yet the Priest, whose Interest it is that you should do as he bids you, will reflect severely, if that is not done which he and his Colleagues prescribe.

There

There are Priests in Politics as well as in Religion; and while it is the Interest of this or that Man that I should be of his Party, I naturally expect to be hardly used, when I find Reason to alter my Opinion. But every honest Man will think at the same Time, that I have full as much Right to judge for myself as he or they can pretend to, at least hope, that a little Modesty may teach him or them to give the Public some fair Reasons, why I should not have varied my Sentiments; and not imagine that I am to be talked out of my Freedom of judging for myself, by such Peculiarities of Thinking as are the Result of Self-interest or Political Superstition. I conceiv'd it proper to premise thus much, in order to fix the Attention of the Reader to my future Reasoning; and as I am now entering on obvious Facts, to unbiass him from all Party Prejudice until I have finish'd my Defence, when, let him be of whart Party he may, I hope he will do me the Justice to own that I have treated the Argument fairly.

The Antiministerial Party who acted in Opposition to the Power of Sir *Robert Walpole*, are allowed, by all, to have been Men of the greatest Genius and Abilities,

bilities, and, in all their Actions and Pursuits, carried the evident Marks of *Englishmen* and Patriots. I was then, as were most of the Gentlemen now reflected on, in the Vigour of my Youth, had a warm Imagination, little Experience in Men, and less in Public Affairs, but the Interest of my Country then, as now, sincerely at Heart; but instead of presuming at those Years to examine too curiously into the general State of Things, I had the Modesty to submit my own Judgment to the Conduct of Those who seemed to have the Interest of their Country solicitously in View. I could not possibly then see that the Antiministerial Party were compos'd of Men who only sought their own Interest, of Men who blindly followed them, and of profest *Jacobites*, blended together in one common Union. 'Tis Evident now to all Mankind that this was the Case, and that when the Leaders of the Party had fully matured their Scheme, by long Labour, great Art, and infinite Assiduity, the Farce concluded very differently from the sanguine Expectations of most People. The *Jacobites* were generally dropt; the blind Followers of the great Leaders were held dexterously

rously in Suspence; a kind of Coalition was framed between the Court and Anti-court-Chiefs; and all the Minister's Crimes and Errors, as we were before taught to call them, on a sudden buried in Oblivion. It may readily be believ'd that I was by this Time somewhat more experienc'd than at first; and so were several other Gentlemen, then, and now, my Friends, Companions, and Colleagues; and as this remarkable Event contributed to open our Eyes, we naturally clubb'd Understandings, in order to concert, the best in our Powers, what Measures were most right for us to take. We saw ourselves imposed on by the Appearance of Patriotism; and while we all had the Subject warm at Heart, and nothing but our Country's Welfare in View, and saw the Effect very widely from what we always proposed, we enter'd into a strict League and Amity; and having out of Three Families formed a very considerable Alliance, we resolved thenceforth to be our own Leaders. Mr. *P------as*, a Person of the steadiest Countenance, and best Eloquence, was indeed elected into the Chair, but had not the Power of Leading more than the rest of the Confederacy. Our
first

first Enquiry center'd in examining why Men, whom we always thought our Superiors in Judgment, whose Candour none before questioned, and whose Experience could hardly be equall'd by any set of Politicians in the Kingdom, after having carried their Point, as it seemed to us, should quit all their former Principles, and the Credit of leading so formidable a Party, for what was evidently little better than a Dream. Upon a thorough Inquisition into the Matter, we found the Case to stand thus: Our Capital Chief had all along acted on the Principle of Resentment, and his Adversary, whose Ruin he had sworn, being now displaced, and himself advanced in Dignity equal to him, the Contention, as to them, ended; and the General being by this Means bought off, and the most Eminent of his Colleagues provided for, all who immediately followed them went to the Court; and the Combination being thus broken, the rest were left to make the best Use in their Power of those Principles, which they had so steadfastly maintain'd, against a Majority which their old Leaders had now establish'd. The Effect of this Change is rather to be remark'd on, than related.

If

If one of the Secretaryships was better filled up than before, a Counterbalance to the Party was preserv'd, by continuing the other in its former State. A new Chancellor of the Exchequer, who tho' a Man of Understanding in other Respects, yet being a Stranger to Business, in no Sense counterpois'd the first Lord of the Treasury. And as to the Privy Seal, Admiralty, &c. it matter'd little who were there, because their Fate wholly depended on that of their Friends in the more ruling Stations. I can't avoid a short Digression here, on a single Circumstance that struck our little Party very sensibly. It had been made a Point by our Grand Confederacy to get Mr. *Vernon* employ'd, in order to break the then Minister's peaceable Schemes, by convincing the World what a *British* Navy was capable of effecting, when a Man of Skill and Courage commanded. Mr. *Vernon*'s high Worth and consummate Experience, gave him a great Advantage over the Minister's Ignorance in Maritime Affairs; and Mr. *Vernon* being in the House of Commons, when the Minister was using all his Eloquence to shew the Impracticability of harming the *Spaniards* in the

West

West Indies, he stood up, and told the House, That though it was made an Argument that Mr. *Hosier*'s great Fleet could not take *Porto Bello*, the Fact he knew to be false; and to prove it so, would undertake it with Five Ships *only*. The Minister taking this for a meer Bravado, consented to his being employ'd: He was so, and executed what he undertook, and much more afterwards. This Success rais'd at once both the Spirits and Credit of the Anti-Courtiers, and gave them that Majority at the next general Election, which threw out the Minister. I have only left to remark what so affected us: This same Mr. *Vernon*, whom our Leaders so much rever'd, as appears by his Letters since publish'd, and who indeed gave them Being, if I may so express myself; these Leaders were no sooner in Power, but they immediately discarded their Father and Benefactor, took great Pains to lessen the Glory of his Conduct, and treated him with the greatest Contempt and Insolence imaginable; putting a Land-Admiral and a Gamester in the Station that ought only to have been Mr. *Vernon*'s, and who, with the first Party of the Band

of

of Honourable *Coalizers*, soon made his Exit.

It was principally under the Being of this famous Confederacy that I acquir'd my political Education, and with the Aid of their Hints, made the first rude Sketches of my *Perfian Letters*, since more rudely quoted against me. I thought then, as perhaps every Man of my Age would have thought, with such seeming great and noble Precedents before me. The Event, my Mind could not be supposed to reach at that Time; but as that happened, and Experience taught me another Lesson, the whole Circle of my Thoughts gradually took a new Colouring, Images differently cloath'd planted themselves on the Surface of my Imagination, and my Ideas glowed with fresh Warmth and Vigour, on a nearer View of some agreeable Prospects which now began to open to me. It was now agreed in our little Circle, that Patriotism had been only made the Dupe of Ambition; that those who had not enter'd on the first Coalition, were preparing to enter, and to push their Power so warmly, as that many Mischiefs would result from their being refused Preferment. On the other Side, it seemed too dangerous to trust them all in together; as on the Apprehension of it, the Friends of the late Ministry, who had now recover'd again in some Measure their wonted Power and Influence, began to mutiny, as foreseeing in it their own Ruin, or what they esteem'd so, the inevitable Loss of their Pensions and Places, which the long Enjoyment of, had made them forget by what Means to subsist on their own private Fortunes. Their warm Addresses quickned the Minister's Spirits, and so effectually alarm'd all about him, that it was determined at last to make their utmost Efforts to rid themselves of the first intruding Patriots, to make Room for the Second Band. But even this their old Friends objected to, and desir'd that the whole Course of the Stream might be turned into its former Channel, and none of these pretended Patriots admitted among them, since they had a Right by long Prescription to divide all the Wealth of the Nation. But they were wisely answer'd, That it was only proposed to take them in, in order to expose to the People the Nonsense of Patriotism; after which they should be properly

perly difpos'd of, without the leaſt future Danger either to the Miniſter or his Party: Thenceforth the Name of Patriot would become a Jeſt, and they might reſt ſecure from any further Attempts of the like Nature. As this Conference came preſently to our Knowlege, it diverted us very pleaſantly for the preſent; and on comparing Notes, we found ourſelves in a Humour to form a Scheme for the overreaching of the Miniſter in his own Way. The Hint was no ſooner given, but unanimouſly aſſented to; and as we fancied ourſelves old enough to effect what we reſolved on, ſo we inſtantly reſolved on what to effect; reſerving in our Breaſts all the old true Public Spirit, we determined to ſeem Apoſtates, and follow our Leaders in Appearance, in order to ſerve our Country in Reality. We were ſenſible enough how acceptable ſo conſiderable a Body as we were muſt be to the Miniſter, and conſequently that we ſhould be readily received, and when received, at once revenge ourſelves of thoſe who had left us, by turning them out; and being once in, play the ſame Game upon the Miniſter and his Party, we found they had played with the pretended Patriots.

triots. There lay but one Stumbling-Block in our Way, which was, that it had come more than once to our S----n's Ear what Company we had formerly kept, what Parties made againſt his Intereſt, and what Healths drank that were highly reſented. We canvaſs'd this Point in every Light, and at Length came to a Concluſion to ſtop at no Condeſcenſions that might be required, ſo they contributed in the leaſt to the great End aimed at. There was indeed another Obſtacle, but of ſuch a Nature, as it ſeemed we ſhould not find much Difficulty in removing. This was a Perſon not only of higher Rank, but of much better Abilities, and more experienc'd in Public Affairs, and in the World, than either of us ſeperately conſider'd, and perhaps, without a perfect good Underſtanding among ourſelves, ſuperior to us alltogether. In order to carry our Point, it was firſt neceſſary to get him out of the Way, diſpos'd into an honourable and profitable Exile, which we ſoon found Means to effect, but which had but Part of the deſir'd Iſſue; for he grew ſo great a Favourite with the People over whom he govern'd, as alarm'd the Miniſtry,

and

and occasion'd their hurrying of him
Back again; and to prevent his being
irritated at this sudden Recall, they very
wisely confer'd on him one of the first
Dignities of the State. Before we apprehended the true Cause of this Change,
it did not a little startle us; but when
we had studied and found out the Bottom
of this Affair, it appeared to us clear
as Light, that he would not continue
long in his new Post; and that the real
View of his Removal, was purely to
discard him in the Event with a better
Grace.

Here I can't help reflecting to what
numerous Inconveniencies, not to say
Mischiefs, a Nation is subject, where
the very Nature and Necessity of the
Public Affairs, or of those who direct
them, makes it absolutely necessary to exclude the greatest, the wisest, and the
best Men. This noble Lord was certainly the best formed for the Government
of a Free People, taking all Things together, that the Nation ever produced;
if unequal to some in Depth and general
Knowlege, his Wit and Politeness exceed all; in fine Learning not excelled
by any; his Steadiness, Judgment and
Honesty,

Honesty, superior to most Men, infinitely above *Chicane*, and all the little Arts of narrow-minded Statesmen; he loves his Country, and pursues its Welfare on the best moral Principles; smiles at the Mention of Party, and considers Men only as they are good or bad, wise or weak; disdains every Thing that is merely notional; and while he loves his Country, for his own Sake as well as of his Sovereign and People, he is determined on one plain Point, which is, either to serve his Country as he ought, with his best Reason and Understanding, or totally to decline interfering with that Kind of Government, which can only bring Disgrace to himself, and Ruin on his Fellow-Subjects.

Such a Character, and the endeavouring to keep him out of the Public Service, may seem at first Sight not the fairest Manner of Dealing among Men professing that they have the Interest and Welfare of their Country alone in View. But as I before observ'd, such are the Inconveniencies to which a Free State is liable. This Noble Person would either not have joined with us, or if he had, must have been the sole Manager; which

in

in it felf we fhould not have difliked, provided he would have ftood the fame Tefts we were refolved to do, and not boggled at any feeming Apoftacy, by which only the old Courtiers might in the End have been entirely thrown out, and a new Set of Men eftablifh'd in their Places, refolute in purfuing the great End of Religion, Virtue, and good Government. The laft he would readily have concurred in, but fo very refin'd, nice, and delicate in his Principles, that he would not even imitate that great Apoftle St. *Paul, In being every Thing to all Men.* And therefore when we confider'd how impracticable it was to gain him, and compared that with the fundamental Principles of our own Scheme, and the determin'd Refolution we were all in, to facrifice every Appearance to the great End of preferving our Country, common Prudence, added to the Nature and Neceffity of Things, caufed us very readily to conclude, that it was much better to have this great Man quite out of the Way, than that our Defign fhould perifh.

We were, during a Variety of Changes and Counter-Changes, enabled to put

D   the

the firſt Part of our Scheme in Execution; That is to ſay, we made a bold Puſh, and got into Play. And it is very difficult to determine whether we, or the Miniſter and his Party, were the beſt pleas'd, as they had, or fancied they had, gain'd over a Body of the moſt ſhining Orators, as well as uſeful Men, from the Service of the People; and we enter'd ſuccefsfully on the firſt Part of our Project. Our little Cabal were no ſooner got into Power, than we began making ourſelves uſeful to the Miniſtry; we found the Teſt of our being what we pretended, muſt be not only ſpeaking, but voting as ſpecially directed; we made a Jeſt of that, becauſe we were not only determined to do ſo ourſelves, but to make every one of the old Patriots, ſtill remaining in Power, do the ſame; and even carried this Point farther than the Miniſter expected, every now and then giving him a Hint, that the Patriots were very far from being his Friends; on the contrary, were contriving how to joſtle him out, with his old Friends, and to bring an entire new Set of Men in. This at once piqu'd his Pride, alarmed his Jealouſy, and confirmed us in his Confidence; yet,

after

after all, we had a very difficult Point to manage; for as he was extremely diffident of himself, not a little afraid to increase the Number of his potent Enemies, and at a Loss what Reason to give his Master, for being every Day turning out of his Service, Men of Weight, Virtue, and Significance; so we were drove to the pushing him on to the last Test, *viz.* that of making them fully declare themselves in Public, in such a Manner, as either to give them no Room to retreat, or to do it immediately. He seem'd very well satisfied with this Thought, and, of himself, took preparatory Measures, by acquainting his Master of what he had learned concerning the Purposes of those People; and that a Nobleman of the First Rank was a Principal in the Design, and one of the capital Scribes his Co-adjutor; and, in short, that all those who were formerly called Patriots, had formed a Design to force a new Ministry upon him, except the Three Families, meaning us, who came over the last to the present Measures The K---- immediately took Fire, told the Minister that he might displace them at his Pleasure; but soon after cooling again, and reflecting on the

Confequence of fuffering any Thing of this Kind to be done rafhly, as he had much more at Stake than his Minifter, he commanded him to take his Steps very cautioufly, and to contrive it fo, that while he was difgracing them on the one Side, he muft find Means to oblige them fome other Way; and, at all Events, not be too precipitate, but to let them walk off one after another gradually. This was not only wife Advice, but a Command that muft neceffarily be obey'd. So that now it only remain'd to bring the Matter to a fair Iffue, by founding them thoroughly: How to effect this, ftagger'd him for a Time; but our Chairman being now one of his Council, and refolved not to let fo fine an Opportunity flip, whifper'd him in the Ear, that he and all his Colleagues fhould lead the Way below Stairs, if the Minifter would contrive fome Means above to fecond him; which was no fooner mentioned, than affented to.

About this Time I receiv'd a Letter from a certain noble Perfon, and inclofed the following Spectator, No. 162; it is one of Mr. *Addifon*'s, and which he thought particularly reach'd me, but did
not

not consider, at the same Time, how much nearer it touch'd himself. But when Men aim at Power only, they naturally consider every Man in the Wrong, who does, or seems, to interfere, with what they vainly imagine alone their Right. And as this was the Case here, and the said noble Person quite a Stranger to our Views or Designs, and for many Reasons we resolved should be so, it was no Wonder to find him piqued at our seeming Apostacy, when by it he must evidently lose some of the best Aids to lift him up to that Power he aim'd at, and had been, in some Measure, for a Time possessed of. I shall wave here giving his own Epistle, as the Style is too well known among us, and because the Reader will see his Thoughts in a finer Light and better digested, than from his own Words.

The SPECTATOR.

——————— *Servetur ad imum*
Qualis ab incæpto processerit & sibi constet.
HOR.

NOTHING, That is not a real Crime, makes a Man appear so contemptible in the

the Eyes of the World as Inconstancy; especially when it regards Religion, or Party; in either of these Cases, tho' a Man perhaps does but his Duty in changing his Side, he not only makes himself hated by those he left, but is seldom heartily esteem'd by those he comes over to.

In these great Articles of Life, therefore, a Man's Conviction ought to be very Strong, and, if possible, so well timed, that worldly Advantage may seem to have no Share in it; or Mankind will be ill natur'd enough to think he does not change Sides out of Principle, but either out of Levity of Temper, or Prospects of Interest. Converts, and Renegadoes of all Kinds, shou'd take particular Care to let the World see they act upon honourable Motives; or whatever Approbations they may receive from themselves, or Applauses from those they converse with, they may be very well assured, that they are the Scorn of all good Men, and the public Marks of Infamy and Derision.

Irresolution on the Schemes of Life, which offer themselves to our Choice, and Inconstancy in pursuing them, are the greatest and most universal Causes of

all

all our Disquiet and Unhappiness. When Ambition pulls one Way, Interest another, Inclination a third, and, perhaps, Reason contrary to all, a Man is likely to pass his Time but ill who has so many different Parties to please. When the Mind hovers among such a Variety of Allurements, one had better settle on a Way of Life that is not the very best we might have chosen, than grow old without determining our Choice, and go out of the World, as the greatest Part of Mankind do, before we have resolved how to live in it. There is but one Method of setting ourselves at Rest in this Particular; and that is, by adhering steadfastly to one great End, as the chief ultimate Aim of all our Pursuits. If we are firmly resolved to live up to the Dictates of Reason, without any Regard to Wealth, Reputation, or the like Considerations, any more than as they fall in with our principal Design, we may go thro' Life with Steadiness and Pleasure; but if we act by several broken Views, and will not only be Virtuous, but Wealthy, Popular, and every Thing that has a Value set upon it by the World, we shall live and die in Misery and Repentance.

One

One wou'd take more than ordinary Care to guard one's self againſt this particular Imperfection, becauſe it is that which our Nature very ſtrongly inclines to; for if we examine ourſelves thoroughly, we ſhall find, that we are the moſt changeable Beings in the Univerſe; in Reſpect to our Underſtandings we often embrace and reject the very ſame Opinions; whereas Beings above and beneath us, have probably no Opinions at all; or, at leaſt, no Waverings and Uncertainties in thoſe they have. Our Superiors are guided by Intuition, and our Inferiors by Inſtinct; in Reſpect to our Wills, we fall into Crimes, and recover out of them; are amiable, or odious, in the Eyes of our great Judge; and paſs our whole Life in offending and aſking Pardon. On the contrary, the Beings underneath us are not capable of Sinning, nor thoſe above us of Repenting. The one is out of the Poſſibilities of Duty, and the others fix'd in an eternal Courſe of Sin, or an eternal Courſe of Virtue.

There is ſcarce a State of Life, or Stage in it, which does not produce Changes and Revolutions in the Mind of Man; our Schemes of Thought, in Infancy, are
loſt

lost in those of Youth; these too take a different Turn in Manhood, till old Age often leads us back into our former Infancy; a new Title, or unexpected Success, throws us out of ourselves, and, in a manner, destroys our Identity. A cloudy Day, or a little Sunshine, have as great an Influence on many Constitutions, as the most real Blessings or Misfortunes. A Dream varies our Being, and Changes our Condition while it lasts; and every Passion, not to mention Health and Sickness, and the greater Alterations in Body and Mind, makes us appear almost different Creatures. If a Man is so distinguish'd among other Beings by this Infirmity, what can we think of such as make themselves remarkable for it, even among their own Species? It is a very trifling Character, to be one of the most variable Beings of the most variable Kind; especially if we consider, that he who is the great Standard of Perfection, has in him no Shadow of Change, but is the same Yesterday, to Day, and for Ever. As this Mutability of Temper and Inconsistency with ourselves is the greatest Weakness of human Nature, so it makes the Person who is remarkable for it, in a very particular Manner, more ridiculous than any other Infirmity whatsoever; as it sets him in a greater Variety of foolish Lights, and distinguishes him from himself by an Opposition of Party-colour'd Characters. The most humourous Character in *Horace* is founded upon this Unevenefs of Temper, and Irregularity of Conduct.

>―――― ―――― *Sardus habebat*
>*Ille Tigellius hoc. Cæsar, qui cogere possets,*
>*Si peteret per Amicitiam patris, atque suam, non*
>*Quidquam proficeret: Si collibuisset, ab ova*
>*Usque ad mala citaret. Io Bacche, modo summâ*
>*Voce modo hâc, resonat quæ chordis quatuor ima,*
>*Nil æquale homini fuit illi: Sæpe velut qui*
>*Currebat fugiens hostem: Persæpe velut qui*
>*Junonis sacra ferret. Habebat sæpe ducentos,*
>*Sæpe*

*Sæpe decem servos. Modo reges atque
  tetrarchas,
Omnia magna loquens. Modò sit mihi
  Mensa tripes
Et concha salis puri, & toga, quæ defen-
  dere frigus,
Quamvis crassa, queat. Decies centena
  dedisses
Huic parco paucis contento: Quinque
  diebus
Nil erat in loculis. Noctes Vigilabat
  ad ipsum
Mane: Diem totum stertebat, Nil fuit
  unquam
Sic impar sibi.* ————
HOR. SAT. 3. Lib. 1.

Instead of translating this Passage in *Horace*, I shall entertain my *English* Reader with the Description of a parallel Character, that is wonderfully well finished by Mr. *Dryden*, upon the same Foundation.

In the first Rank of these did *Zimri*
  stand:
A Man so various, that he seem'd
  to be
Not one but all Mankind's Epitome.

Stiff in Opinions, always in the Wrong;
Was every Thing by Starts, and no-
 thing long;
But in the Course of one revolving
 Moon,
Was Chymist, Fidler, Statesman, and
 Buffoon:
Then all for Women, Painting, Rhim-
 ing, Drinking,
Besides ten thousand Freaks that dy'd
 in thinking:
Blest Madman, who cou'd every Hour
 employ,
With something new to wish, or to
 enjoy!

If our own particular Interests had been the Rule of our Conduct, and a View of advancing ourselves the sole Motives of our Actions, the Contents of the above recited *Spectator* had operated against us in its full Force and Efficacy. But as what has been previously said, and what hereafter will be shewn, amply evinces the contrary, I shall only beg leave to make a few short Observations on the Nature of this little labour'd Piece. It was wrote at a Time when

Parties

Parties and Factions ran high, and when, as of late it has happened, a War was in Hand, a Peace in Agitation, and a total Change of Men and Measures in Prospect, if not attain'd. And Mr. *Addison*'s Friendships and Interests being fixt to the declining Party, it is no Wonder that he for once digressed from his usual Course of Amusements, and, on so critical an Occasion, turn'd Politician. And as it is evident his Motives, and those of the noble Lord above, were precisely the same, so, as far as the Strength of Reasoning therein extends, it equally well served both their Purposes. But to me, who see Things in quite another Light, I conceive that Man only honest, who attaches himself to no Party, but acts simply, as induced by the Nature and Reason of Things, and as led by a disinterested Judgment.

We had now work'd into some Kind of Shape and Perfection, out of its Embrio State, that Brilliant Scheme which we intend, when fully matured, shall be as a Light to direct the Footsteps of the *British* People to Peace and Harmony at Home, and to Fame and Glory Abroad.

The same noble Person, whose Character is faintly drawn in the early Part of this Defence, had an Intimation given him, that it would be for the public Service if he would, for some Time, quit the honourable Station he held, as thereby the bringing of a Set of Men together into the Council, as would chearfully and unanimously concur to the getting out of the War with Honour, might be effected; which could not be, while so many perturb'd and contradictory Spirits interfer'd in, and disorder'd that sweet and happy Concord, so essentially necessary to be preserved amongst them. His Lordship took some Time to consider of it, and while Matters were concerting above, our Chairman acted his Part below to the utmost Perfection. He said, he had hitherto consider'd himself as in a puerile State, but now was at Leisure to inspect his Heart, in the Character of a Man, who had digested his Thoughts and Reflections as became every reasonable Person to do, who intended himself to be of any important Service to the Common-wealth. That a Kind of new Light had thereupon broke in on his Mind, whereby the Transactions

actions of Times paſt appeared to him very differently to what had heretofore met his Obſervation; and only wonder'd how Prejudice could ſo blind him, as not to ſee Things in the ſame Light long before. But he eſteem'd that as much owing to his Youth and Inattention, as to thoſe fatal Party-Principles early imbib'd into him by bad Examples; and that as the ſeeing an Error, and rectifying it, was an Acquiſition to his Wiſdom, he hoped that every Perſon who had formerly thought with him, and now ſaw Reaſon, as he did, by accepting Places, to vary their former Manner of Thinking, would be as candid as he was; and by publickly acknowleging their firſt Miſtake, convince the World that they were grown wiſer, and eſtabliſh'd in a new Set of Thoughts. Otherwiſe he could not help thinking, that thoſe who had formerly, in a Kind of Joke, chriſten'd themſelves Patriots, held ſtill their old Tenets; and only accepted Places, to make a Property of the Miniſter, and to impoſe upon and deceive the People.

This was fair Warning to all the Patriots, to prepare themselves for a close and steady Attachment to those Measures which they had always affected to abhor; or to make their Exit, and retire from that Power they were as yet but slenderly possess'd of. The first we were sensible many of them would not submit to, as the Change was too sudden, and fresh in every Man's Memory on what Principles they had attracted the Affections of the People. It was yet too soon to throw off the Virgin Blush and Coyness of the innocent, undebauch'd, Maiden Patriot: And Pride and Fear, operating at the same Time with Reason, Judgment, and the remaining Taint of Native Modesty, gave Bashfulness the Ascendant, and banish'd the quite abandon'd Prostitute from their Bosoms. So that they chose, as we expected they would, to stand their Ground on their old Terms as long as possible, and, at last, quit all, rather than go the Lengths so arbitrarily prescribed them. The noble Person, last mentioned, had too penetrating an Eye not to see, tho' but through a dark Medium, what we
were

aiming at, and having a Hint given him that some Removes were necessary to get rid, by Degrees, of these odd Kind of wavering minded Men, unripe for absolute Prostitution, and that himself or Relations should have any handsome Returns, in the Power of the Ministry to oblige them with, he very readily seiz'd Time by the Forelock, quitted the honourable Station which himself almost could only hold with Honour, and was succeeded by the first Patriot, in Rank, tho' perhaps the last or least in Judgment, or Experience, among them all. My Lord *Clarendon* has somewhere drawn his Character, before he was born, when he speaks of a Secretary of State that cou'd not write. This Noble Person indeed could write, but not in Lord *Clarendon*'s Sense, which is, that he cou'd not write any Thing to the Purpose.

He was now in the leading Way down Hill, having quitted a Higher Post for a Lower, at least for one more Unstable and Impermanent, which within the Compass of seven Years had been occupied

cupied by a Variety of Operators, and sometimes the same over again, and was now so placed, as to render his future Removal easy. For his prime Counsellor, and who first put him into the Head of Intermedling with public Affairs, and much his Superior in Abilities, now following him close, possess'd the Post he quitted, and was ready to enter upon that, he could not refuse to leave, if so worthy a Person, and so establish'd a Friend, had the Honour to succeed him in it.

There happened, soon after this, an Affair which was near destroying all those happy Measures, so finely calculated for giving the Nation Peace and Prosperity, by fixing a steady unchangeable Ministry, on the old genuine Whig Principles. One of the Gentlemen of the Family Triumvirate, took it into his Head to go a Step farther than our Leader had done, or any of us ever intended; and this in an Affair that would make a great Noise, without answering any essential Purpose: A Point that had nothing to justify it, but meer Pique and Resentment;

ment; but the Minister was very humorous, and must be gratify'd in this seeming Trifle at our Expence. This was to set on Foot a Law, which was to be a Precedent, for taking away at Pleasure the old Rights and Customs of judicial Officers, and making them do their Business for the Future in Places peremptorily appointed, however inconvenient to them or grievous to the Parties interested: And this only because one of these Officers had not been quite so complaisant to the Minister, as he thought he had Reason to expect, tho' at other Times, and on various Occasions, he had gone very great Lengths in the same Interest. But this, that one would have thought, should have been a Reason for not prosecuting him too violently, or rashly, and in a Matter too, that could neither injure him, nor benefit the Nation, nor in fact hardly pleasure any Body, was the very Reason for doing it; as the Appearance of Apostacy from the old Measures, was the greatest Incitement imaginable, to Minds ireful and vindictive, to express their Resentment on the most trivial Occasion.

The very Nature and Neceffity of our Situation, obliged us to run Headlong into this whimfical Piece of Conduct; and to concur in every Meafure neceffary to accomplifh the important End fo ardantly aim'd at, which all together amounting to little or nothing, put us a good deal out of Countenance; as it naturally induced People to believe that our Wantonnefs had no Bounds; and that when we had really nothing fignificant in Motion, to exprefs our unfeigned Attachment to our new Engagements by, we muft then employ ourfelves in doing all the Mifchief in our Power to thofe, who did not concur in every Particular with us. But this I muft beg leave to clear my Friends and Affociates from. That we did it is true, and that we were oblig'd to do it is as true. And the Misfortune was, that we either muft do it, or the minifterial Confidence in us had, after all the Lengths we had gone, now ceafed entirely; the Effect whereof would have been the utter Diffolution of our Scheme, and confequently all thofe glorious Views,

which

which the Good of the Nation required we ſhould ſteadily purſue, had vaniſh'd into Smoke.

To make this more clear to the Underſtanding of the Reader, and to perfect this my Work of Juſtification, it is neceſſary to ſet in a true Light, the univerſal, political Situation, of Public Affairs. It has been obvious enough to the Senſe of all Mankind, how many vain Attempts have been made, by the greateſt Geniuſes of the Age, to give a new Turn to the old Political Syſtem, founded on Corruption, and ſupported by Bribery and Venality. The Men who attempted this, however wiſe in other Reſpects, miſtook the Road. They judged perhaps from their own Hearts, and from what had been writ or ſaid on the Subject, that the Nation was deſirous of ſuch a happy Change, which no doubt was very true: But the Means to attain it was evidently miſtaken. The old miniſterial Train, their Agents, Relations and Dependents, were infinitely too numerous, for thoſe who had more Inclination than Abilities to retrieve the

Domeſtic

Domestic Honour of the Nation. By Abilities here, I don't mean Sense and Judgment, but Numbers and Votes. To change the old System, was in Effect to take from these Numbers the Right they had to live on the Plunder of the People. They were possess'd of this Right, as of a Kind of legal Inheritance, which they would no more part with willingly, than they would with the Church Lands: Nor consequently would let any Man, however great in other Respects, establish himself in the Ministry, who had an Eye to the Overturning this System, because that would have been turning them out of their Bread; which no Man who reason'd judiciously, could have suspected them of assenting to: And as they were too powerful to be forced, such End could not possibly be attained. The Anti-System Men made indeed a great Shew at first, as they were attended to by a third Party, who in fact were for entirely overthrowing the Constitution; and as some of the old System Men had Hopes of being continued, they did not immediately join in the Opposition to new Measures. But one fatal Error

in

in the Conductors of the Anti-System Scheme, soon destroyed all their Views. They were observed to be in a great hurry to provide for their Relations, and very particular Friends, without the least Regard, to the Interest or Recommendation of the old System Men, many of whom still held their Station. This Manner of Acting taking Place of the more necessary Attention to the main End, and those who could do most good or harm being entirely neglected, the Scene naturally changed again, and returned once more into its former Channel. Now all Parties, except a very few Men, who did not see the Error of such Proceedings, began to consider the Necessity of having some Man at the Head of the Ministry, who was rather versed in, and Master of the old System, than a very deep Politician, whose Brains was playing Tricks with foreign Potentates, instead of attending to the Management of domestic Policy, the Basis whereon alone, any great Designs were capable of being constructed. They soon fixed their Eyes on a Man of Significance, one who was always consider'd as the

most

moſt proper to ſucceed the former Miniſter on the old ſyſtem Principle. Not that they had any Shadow of Reaſon to expect the ſame eaſy Advantages under his Conduct, as they enjoyed under that of his Predeceſſor; but as he was at once the beſt they could think of, and not a little in the Favour of his Maſter, they ſoon concluded on him, and as ſoon gave Birth to that Power he is now poſſeſſed of.

This plainly enough evinces, that the great Men above mentioned were very far from being in the right Way of eſtabliſhing a new Siſtem; and which ſeriouſly reflecting on, naturally induced us to purſue another Courſe, with the ſame Views. We were all of us moſt deeply affected with a Senſe of the Neceſſity of bringing, by ſome Means or other, the new Syſtem into play, and as ſenſible how much the People panted for, and deſired it. On the old Syſtem reviving, it appeared evident enough to the Miniſter, what a ſtrong Party had been formed againſt it, which only meer Negligence, or if you pleaſe, too great a Contempt of little Things, in their Leaders.

Leaders, prevented from taking Place, and consequently was convinced of the Necessity of purchasing in, with Honours, or by other Means, the most Important of them. As we had not at first finish'd our Scheme, we all agreed to hold back, tho' valuable Offers daily presented, and when we saw it the right Time, and were thoroughly determin'd what to do, and what to submit to for the future Good of the People, we all fell readily into the Minister's Measures, and acted from Time to Time as you have either read here, or otherwise heard of.

A very little Reflection will shew, that our Sentiments of Men or Measures, did not vary in the least from our former Conceptions of them, or that our Minds co-operated with the seeming Change; but as we found this the only possible Method of getting into Power, and thereby of effectually serving our Country, no reasonable Man will condemn us for using Art, for the Attainment of so important an End. Nor does it signify what either our Leader or any of us have said, or may be obliged to say hereafter in Public; since when a Point is to be gained, the necessary Means leading thereto must be pursued. The first *Brutus* was not the more an Ideot for seeming so, untill all Things were duly prepared for the Banishment of *Tarquin*; nor, by a Parity of Reasoning, are we less the Friends of the Constitution, because the World cannot suddenly perceive our Drift. While the Plot of *Brutus* was forming, and *Lucretia* instructing how to conduct herself in the Character of a ravish'd Matron; while the Friends to Liberty and the Constitution of *Rome*, were contriving how to make the younger *Tarquin* the Dupe of their Designs, it signified little to those in the Secret, what the Run of Mankind thought about the Matter: It was sufficient that all turn'd out Right at last; that the Power of the King thenceforth ceased, and the Constitution became thereby, and by the refin'd Conduct of the Conspirators, changed and re-establish'd on a firm, happy, and permanent Basis.

We

We need not indeed carry our Retrospect, in Regard to Things of this Nature, so far back, nor be under any Necessity of justifying our present Conduct, from Instances recorded in the *Roman* History, as many of a similar Nature, and more recent, present from our own. Any Man who either has or will take the Pains to read my Lord *Clarendon*'s History of the Rebellion, will plainly see, That Sir *Harry Vane* did more Service to the Views of those who then intended to purge the Common-wealth and secure our Liberties, by being in with the Ministry, than all the rest that were out of Place, would have been capable of effecting together. Those that appeared publickly in the Opposition, were carefully guarded against; and from any Thing that appears to the contrary, would have been totally disappointed, nay had, if the same Historian may be depended upon, given up all for lost, and were on the Point of making their retreat to *Holland*, if those who seemed to take Part with the regal Interest, had not come in suddenly to their Aid, and

given

given that surprising Turn to the whole System, as is too well known to need reciting. It is almost needless to add, that the like Conduct in a certain noble Lord, produced a similar Effect in a later Reign, which obliged the Sovereign to abdicate, and the ever memorable and glorious Revolution to take Place, and gave Being to that Spirit of Liberty, which, I hope, will continue to the End of Time.

In a Word, the changing of Ministries, being a Matter not so easily effected as Men generally dream, in the Manner they now act, and on the Footing they are constituted, which is better known, than proper to be explain'd; it will evidently follow, that it is not the Great, the Wise, or the Judicious, who publickly declare themselves to that Purpose, who are capable of removing Men, which every Way answer the great End of their Constitution, but one. It is therefore become absolutely necessary, that such Men of Parts, Genius and Ability, as are determin'd on using their utmost Efforts, to serve the Nation with their

their best Powers, must not hesitate at such Kind of Condescensions, which may in any Manner contribute to carry them dexterously to the intended Point. The S-------n's Ear must be gain'd by Degrees, it requires Time to be fixed in his Confidence; and to attain the Friendship and Compliance of a Set of Men, who only can support a Minister, and who are generally too well situated to be fond of Changes, be the Voice of the People ever so vehement, demands all the Skill and Address of a steady, consummate Politician. I have therefore, upon the whole, the best Reason imaginable to hope, that as I pursue no worse Maxims, than such as the wisest Men in all Ages have either acted upon or approved, and as have been happily found successfull, the public Disgust will not be the Result of my ardent Wishes for the People's Welfare; but that they will wait with Patience the Event of Measures, which have been, with the greatest Care, Attention, and Consideration, calculated for the common Welfare; and which I doubt not will be in due Time the Means of reviving,

viving, and establishing the now dormant System, that can alone recover the Nation's Honour, and give Peace, Happiness, and Prosperity to the Community.

FINIS.

Soc
DA
500
L93

DATE DUE